The Elements of Rhythm

Volume I

2^n

**Binary Theory and Creation of
the Fundamental Rhythm Patterns**

David R. Aldridge

Rollinson Publishing Co.

© 2012 Rollinson Publishing Co.

All Rights Reserved

International Copyright Secured

Any unauthorized duplication of this book or its contents is a violation of copyright laws. No parts of this publication may be reproduced, stored in retrieval systems, or transmitted, in any form or by any means, electronic, mechanical, photocopying, recording, or otherwise, without the prior written permission of Rollinson Publishing Co.

Published 2012 by Rollinson Publishing Co., Los Angeles, California

First Edition

First Printing 2012

ISBN 978-0-9852237-0-0

www.RollinsonPublishing.com

Production and Book Design: David R. Aldridge
Layout: David R. Aldridge, Michelle Nati
Proofreading: Betsey Stephens, Yvette Conklin
Cover Photo: Clearview Stock

Cover art inspired by Kaikay Hwang

"It is the function of science to discover the existence of a general reign of order in nature and to find the causes governing this order."

– Dmitri Mendeleev
creator, *The Periodic Table of the Elements*

Table of Contents

Preface — x

Introduction — xi

Prologue — 13

Part I 2^n - Binary Theory of the Fundamental Rhythm Patterns — 15

Part II Applying, Organizing, and Practicing the Patterns — 25

Part III Creation of the Fundamental Patterns — 37

Level 1 - 4 Event Point Patterns — 38
Binary Combination Tables
- 0/1 — 39
- 2/2 - 4/2 — 40
- 2/4 - 4/4 — 41
- 2/8 - 4/8 — 42
- 2/16 - 4/16 — 43
- 2/32 - 4/32 — 44

Level 2 - 4 Event Point Patterns - Music Measure Formats (Beat) — 45
- 2/2 - 4/2 — 47
- 2/4 - 4/4 — 48
- 2/8 - 4/8 — 49
- 2/16 - 4/16 — 50
- 2/32 - 4/32 — 51

Level 5 Event Point Patterns — 52
Level 5 Event Point Patterns - Discussion — 53
Binary Combination Tables
- 0/1 — 58
- 5/2 — 59
- 5/4 — 60
- 5/8 — 61
- 5/16 — 62
- 5/32 — 63

Level 5 Event Point Patterns - Music Measure Formats (Beat) — 64
- 5/2 — 65
- 5/4 — 66
- 5/8 — 67
- 5/16 — 68
- 5/32 — 69

Table of Contents (cont'd)

Level 6 Event Point Patterns	70
Level 6 Event Point Patterns - Discussion	71
Binary Combination Tables	
0/1	72
Level 6 Event Point Patterns - Compound Beat	74
Binary Combination Tables	
6/2	76
6/4	78
6/8	80
6/16	82
6/32	84
Level 6 Event Point Patterns - Music Measure Formats (Compound Beat)	86
6/2	88
6/4	90
6/8	92
6/16	94
6/32	96
Level 6 Event Point Patterns - Simple Beat Division	98
Binary Combination Tables	
3/2	100
3/4	102
3/8	104
3/16	106
3/32	108
Level 6 Event Point Patterns - Music Measure Formats (Simple Beat Division)	110
3/2	112
3/4	114
3/8	116
3/16	118
3/32	120
Level 7 Event Point Patterns	122
Level 7 Event Point Patterns - Discussion	123
Binary Combination Tables	
0/1	126
7/2	130
7/4	134
7/8	138
7/16	142
7/32	146

Table of Contents (cont'd)

Level 7 Event Point Patterns - Music Measure Formats (Beat)	151
7/2	152
7/4	156
7/8	160
7/16	164
7/32	168

Level 8 Event Point Patterns — 172

Level 8 Event Point Patterns - Discussion	173
Binary Combination Tables	
0/1	174
Half Rest/Note	182
Quarter Rest/Note	190
Eighth Rest/Note	198
Sixteenth Rest/Note	206
Thirty-second Rest/Note	214
Level 8 Event Point Patterns - Music Measure Formats (Beat Division)	222
4/2	224
4/4	232
4/8	240
4/16	248
4/32	256
Level 8 Event Point Patterns - Music Measure Formats (Beat Subdivision)	264
2/2	266
2/4	274
2/8	282
2/16	290

Epilogue — 298

Appendices — 299

Appendix A	301
Appendix B	302
Appendix C	303
Appendix D	304
Appendix E	306

Acknowledgments

Many people over many years helped me complete this long journey. **Professor George Moore**, formerly of the University of Southern California's Biomedical Engineering Department (Los Angeles, CA), provided great encouragement during the early stages when I had little idea of where the project might lead. **Professor Emeritus Kay Roskam**, of Chapman University's Music Therapy Department (Orange, CA), believed in my ideas and inspired me to aim broadly.

The staff in the computer lab at **Cabrillo College** (Capitola, CA) were my programming salvation, and more than a few hours were spent in the **University of California, Santa Cruz** library, with grateful help from their staff. The very accommodating associates at the **Library of Congress** (Washington, DC) were wonderful in their endless retrieval of materials, and the **University of California, Los Angeles** Music Library staff were equally helpful in handling my simple requests on many occasions. I am also indebted to Henry Cowell's late wife, **Sidney Cowell**, for granting me permission to read her late husband's works in the New York City Library's Special Collections.

Andy Doershuck gave me the opportunity to learn the craft of music journalism under his editorial direction for *DRUM!* magazine. **Keith R. Ball**, former Editorial Director of Paisano Publications, taught me how to do the impossible with ink. **John Tharnstrom** introduced me to the wonders of software programming back in the day and ignited the binary fires. **Marie Tran** is an I.T. goddess without whom this book surely would have never seen digital completion.

Betsey Stephens interviewed me for her blog **(www.oddtimeobsessed.com)** and really got me energized and back into the game when I was about ready to fold. She also dove in fearlessly to proofread this beast. **Yvette Conklin** helped with a pass at the proofreading as well, reminding me that it's a true friend who will sit with you and stay focused for hours.

Deep appreciation goes to **Lori Baron**, a very tasteful drummer who was there in the beginning and who made life possible during the hand-written stages of creating the patterns. Thirty years later, she understands better than anyone how difficult it was for me to push the writing rock to the top of the hill. **Vance Burberry (www.milktfilms.com)** provided the most important last-minute save of all, one that would have otherwise brought the entire project to a screeching halt.

Two fellow Texans offered cherished friendship and support over many years. **Tommy Robertson**, owner of Tommy's Drum Shop **(www.tommysdrumshop.com)**, let me spend many hours pounding away on his percussive stock to unwind and is a man who appreciates the entertainment value of processed sugar. **Dirk Price**, studio guitarist and dedicated teacher **(www.dickgrove.com)**, provided excellent music instruction suggestions that often kept me going when my energy was low.

To the late **Adam Ward Seligman**, my writing mentor, I owe thanks that cannot be repaid. Adam reminded me that writing, drumming and any other talents we are blessed with are *never* to be taken for granted. He also showed me how to overcome obstacles that seemed insurmountable, a notion that has taken a lifetime to integrate and apply.

Lastly, I am indebted to **the world of drumming**, which has been my musical family for over four decades. While this book is designed for all musicians and music-related researchers, whatever comes of it will ultimately be related to every drummer who ever picked up a pair of sticks and asked themselves, "I wonder what I should practice today?"

Special Thanks

Charles Aldridge, my brother, who deftly threw lifelines;

Matt Aldridge, my fearless nephew, who inspired;

Hank Levy, composer, who urged exploration far beyond 4/4;

Peter Erskine, drummer, who planted a powerful seed;

Terry Bozzio, drummer, who revealed pieces of the temporal puzzle;

John Tharnstrom, drummer, who provided binary guidance;

Lou Harrison, composer, who offered wisdom and encouragement;

and *Kaikay Hwang,* artist, for her tremendous support, love and understanding.

Dedicated to the memory of my parents

Elden and Lolita Aldridge

Preface

The Elements of Rhythm Volume I is a comprehensive rhythm pattern resource, based on the notion of there being a finite number of fundamental rhythmic "elements" that make up all the larger possible combinations. Our text's two primary objectives are to provide you with that collection of elements and to make them the foundation of your rhythm vocabulary.

Designed for all musicians and for researchers in music-related fields, our text offers a unifying theory of rhythm pattern development based on simple binary principles. This work is preceded by several publications with varying approaches to fundamental rhythm pattern theory:

- Peter Randall - *Rhythm in Action* (Belwin-Mills Publishing Corp., 1981)
- Chuck Braman - *Drumming Patterns* (Drumstroke Publications, 1988)
- Mike Mangini - *Mike Mangini's Rhythm Knowledge Vol. I & II* (Rhythm Knowledge, 1997-1998)
- Joseph Schillinger - *Encyclopedia of Rhythms* (Clock & Rose Press, 2003)
- Mick Goodrick and Mitch Haupers - *Factorial Rhythm for All Instruments, 2nd Edition* (Mr. Goodchord Publications, 2008)
- Johnny Rabb - *The Official Freehand Technique* (Hudson Music, 2008)
- Benny Greb - *The Language of Drumming* (Hudson Music, 2009)
- Thom Hannum - *A Percussionist's Guide to Check Patterns* (Alfred Publishing, 2009)
- John Favicchia - *Elements* (Alfred Publishing, 2010)

Musicians and academic authors who have explored math and binary logic include:

- Lou Harrison - *Music Primer* (C. F. Peters Corp., 1971)
- Andranik Tangian - "A Binary System for Classification of Rhythm Patterns" (*Computing in Musicology* 8 1992, pp. 75-81)
- Mike Mangini - *Mike Mangini's Rhythm Knowledge Vol. I & II* (Rhythm Knowledge, 1997-1998)
- Daniel LaBerge - Rhythm Explained (www.daniellaberge.com/music/rhythm/rhythm1.htm) (2002)
- Godfried T. Toussaint - "The Euclidean Algorithm Generates Traditional Musical Rhythms" (Proceedings of BRIDGES: Mathematical Connections in Art, Music, and Science, Banff, Alberta, Canada, July 31 to August 3, 2005, pp. 47-56)
- Vi Hart - "Using Binary Numbers in Music" (Proceedings of the 11th Annual BRIDGES Conference: Mathematics, Music, Art, Architecture, Culture (BRIDGES 8), Leeuwarden, Netherlands, July 2008)
- Bernhard Wagner - Rhythmic Patterns As Binary Numbers (www.bernhardwagner.net/musings/RPABN.html) (2009)

Our text furthers the exploration of fundamental rhythm pattern theory by expanding on binary logic, applying a systematic pattern combination method, and introducing a unique categorizing system. Applicable to many areas of music study and related research, *The Elements of Rhythm Volume I* provides readers interested in rhythm with the essential building blocks of their art and the primary colors of their temporal palette.

Introduction

This book owes its initial inception to drummers Peter Erskine and Terry Bozzio, and its completion to drummer John Tharnstrom and American music composer Lou Harrison. The journey began in 1976, when I attended a summer jazz camp where Peter Erskine was the drummer-in-residence. One night during the camp, Erskine had to sight-read some challenging sheet music for an evening faculty performance. The next day in our master class, Erskine mentioned how glad he was to have seen some "familiar friends" on the charts.

Five years later, I had the opportunity to study with Terry Bozzio, who introduced me to the math concept of permutations (order possibilities) as they applied to quarter and eighth rests and notes in a measure of 2/4. Bozzio told me that if I could master the sixteen basic possibilities, I would have seen and played many of the patterns from which larger, more complex combinations in simple meter were constructed.

I recalled Erskine's comment about "familiar friends" and wondered if it would be possible to systematically combine the sixteen basic patterns into a larger, more comprehensive list. My initial thought was to create a "vocabulary of rhythm patterns" for drummers, because the value was immediately obvious: If you knew all the basic possible patterns, you could practice reading and thinking about them, then play them to further develop your overall rhythmic abilities.

In 1982, after spending months hand-writing hundreds of these patterns in a variety of time signature and note value contexts, I met John Tharnstrom, a drummer and college student in Austin, Texas. John helped me greatly by writing a software program on a mainframe that would generate as large a list of rhythm patterns as I wanted, using 0's and 1's. Seeing them in this context served as the impetus to create a binary theory of rhythm pattern development.

In 1986, while living in Santa Cruz, California, I had the honor of meeting Lou Harrison, the esteemed American music composer. I'd recently discovered Harrison's *Music Primer*, in which he presented the math expression 2^n and the possible applications it held for creating the fundamental rhythm patterns. This simple binary tool, first shown to Harrison by composer Henry Cowell, serves as the core of our approach to rhythm pattern theory.

Harrison invited me to his home for an amazing afternoon of conversation, and I'll never forget the bemused look on his face when I showed him the hundreds of handwritten patterns I'd generated using essentially the same binary approach he had explored. His nod of approval meant a great deal, but completing what you are now reading was initially overwhelming. I was young and ill-prepared, and many times over the following decades, I wanted to abandon this project. Humble thanks are owed to Lou Harrison that afternoon for his kind words of encouragement; they were ones I fell back on often to recharge, regroup and move forward.

Still, it took many years and *many* revisions to arrive at a point where what needed to be said (and to whom) was reasonably resolved. In the end, the idea of this text as a **rhythm pattern resource** covers the most bases, with an emphasis on drumming, teaching, musical performance, and suggestions for academic applications. Certain needs for all groups may not have been met, but if this broad effort generates on-going research and idea exchanges between the arts and sciences, the highest hopes will have been realized.

David R. Aldridge
Los Angeles, California 2012

* / / *

Prologue

Imagine traveling on a road to someone's house and reaching a cul-de-sac. Taking either circular path would ultimately lead you to the house on the far end, but if possible, the most direct route would of course be to go straight.

In the journey to discover the fundamental building block rhythm patterns, the objective could possibly be arrived at through years of improvisation or composition. With our approach, we use basic math and proceed **directly** to the source of these patterns.

Once we get there, you'll know that you possess the absolute and complete list of what is fundamentally possible. What could have taken you years to discover is accomplished in a fraction of the time, leaving you with much *more* time to explore, play, and grow as a musician.

That said, let's begin our journey by first ignoring the proverbial fork in the road...

> "[Those] who wish to know about the world must learn about it in its particular details."
>
> – *Heraclitus*

Part I

2^n - *BINARY THEORY OF THE FUNDAMENTAL RHYTHM PATTERNS*

In this section, we will:

- discuss an overview of our approach to rhythm pattern theory

- present a model of the underlying structure of rhythm pattern development with 0's and 1's used to express silence and sound

- introduce new vocabulary terms

- explain how the 2^n math expression is applied to create the fundamental building block rhythm patterns

- conclude by systematically pairing 0's and 1's in binary combination tables to produce a model for generating the fundamental patterns

Our Premise and Approach

There exists a finite number of building block rhythm patterns from which all larger and more complex patterns are comprised. Our book presents these building blocks, generated and organized using a simple math expression based on binary logic.

We first calculate the number of basic rhythm pattern possibilities, and then we substitute 0 for silence and 1 for sound to create this list of patterns, with help from a series of binary combination tables. Next, we re-write these patterns within the combination tables using traditional music notation. Finally, we present the patterns in single-staff music measure formats.

Our method lets us systematically build larger rhythm patterns out of smaller ones, leaving no possible combination overlooked or excluded. This is significant, because while fundamental music tones can be found on a keyboard or on a guitar fret board, fundamental rhythm patterns have no such a presentation format. With our method, we can actually see where and how **any** possible rhythm pattern combination originates.

Discovering The Fundamental Rhythm Patterns

For most musicians, the traditional music theory approach to studying rhythm has consisted primarily of learning the fundamentals of music notation division (**Figure 1**), and then seeing how these notes can occur in measured time (**Figure 2**).

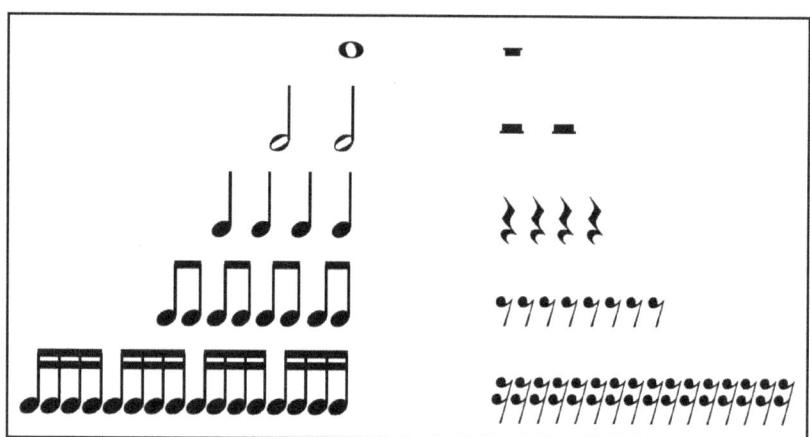

Figure 1. *Whole Note/Rest Division Structure*

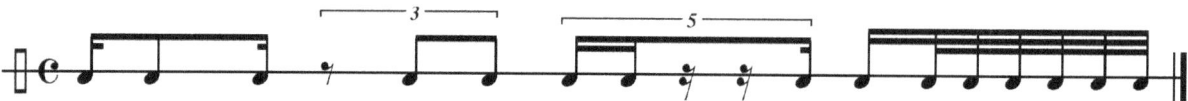

Figure 2. *4/4 Measure with Simple and Complex Rhythm Patterns*

Figure 2 contains a sample of rhythm patterns, but suppose we wanted to see all the possible triplet groupings, or all the possible five-note groupings. Where would we go to *find* them?

The answers are in the binary combination tables we'll be creating. But first, we need to address some issues concerning the relative nature of music notation.

There are many ways to write a rhythm pattern and its possible variations (e.g., ties, dotted notes). Additionally, a rhythm pattern may occur in varying beat note contexts. **Figure 3** illustrates this complexity, which only compounds the challenge of finding a pattern's point of origin:

Figure 3. *Beat Subdivision Pattern Expressed Using Three Different Beat Note Values*

Figure 3 also generates two distinctly important questions:

1. What is it that these rhythm patterns share in common?
2. What are they versions of in terms of core sounds?

The answers to these questions largely define the scope and approach of our text:

1. The initial silence and sound events occur at the **same** points in measured time.
2. They're all relative versions of the **same** absolute sound shape.

What we need now is a way to **create** that absolute sound shape.

Figure 4 (limited here to eight levels) shows that a beat in measured time can be divided into any number of levels containing "points," where one of two events, **silence or sound**, can occur.

```
1   /
2   * *
3   * * *
4   * * * *
5   * * * * *
6   * * * * * *
7   * * * * * * *
8   * * * * * * * *
```

Figure 4. *Event Point Level Table*

The following three new terms are useful for further explaining our theory:

- **EVENT POINTS** - Points in measured time where silence/sound occur
- **EVENT POINT PATTERNS** - Combinations of silence/sound
- **EVENT POINT LEVELS** - Beat and division levels where silence/sound occur

Now we'll modify our table, using 0 for silence and 1 for sound of basic duration (e.g., tapping a surface). Doing this lets us depict any pattern's "absolute sound shape" without using notation.

```
1   0
2   0 1
3   0 1 0
4   1 1 1 0
5   1 1 0 1 1
6   1 0 1 0 0 1
7   0 1 1 0 0 0 1
8   1 0 1 1 0 1 1 1
```

```
1   0
2   0 1
3   0 1 1
4   1 1 0 1
5   1 1 0 0 1
6   1 1 1 0 0 1
7   1 1 1 0 0 0 1
8   1 0 1 1 1 1 1 1
```

Figure 5. *Binary Rhythm Patterns, Level 4*   **Figure 6.** *Binary Rhythm Patterns, Levels 3, 4, 5, 8*

The 0/1 combination at Level 4 in **Figure 5** is the absolute sound shape of the rhythm pattern in **Figure 3**. The 0/1 combinations at Levels 3, 4, 5 and 8 in **Figure 6** are the absolute sound shapes of the rhythm patterns presented in **Figure 2**.

Our binary model is not intended to replace music notation, but when combined with the use of a simple math expression, it offers a powerful platform for our exploration of the fundamental building block rhythm patterns.

2^n

In *Music Primer* (C. F. Peters Corp., 1971), American music composer Lou Harrison discussed 2^n as a tool for creating the basic rhythm patterns. Progressive rock drummer Mike Mangini significantly explored the 2^n concept and its applications with similar emphasis in *Mike Mangini's Rhythm Knowledge, Volumes I & II* (Rhythm Knowledge, 1997-1998).

Building on our model of measured time, we can use 2^n as well, to calculate the **exact** number of 0/1 patterns that are possible for **any** event point level. In basic terms, "2" represents a specific number of objects, and "n" represents how many times those objects are combined with (multiplied by) themselves.

For example, $2^1 = 2 \times 1$, $2^2 = 2 \times 2$, $2^3 = 2 \times 2 \times 2$, $2^4 = 2 \times 2 \times 2 \times 2$, etc.

In **Figure 7**, we use 2^n to calculate the exact number of 0/1 combination possibilities for up to eight divisions of the beat. Here, "2" is replaced with either 0 or 1, and "n" is replaced with 1 through 8 event points:

```
1   *                $2^1$    2 x 1 = 2
2   * *              $2^2$    2 x 2 = 4
3   * * *            $2^3$    2 x 2 x 2 = 8
4   * * * *          $2^4$    2 x 2 x 2 x 2 = 16
5   * * * * *        $2^5$    2 x 2 x 2 x 2 x 2 = 32
6   * * * * * *      $2^6$    2 x 2 x 2 x 2 x 2 x 2 = 64
7   * * * * * * *    $2^7$    2 x 2 x 2 x 2 x 2 x 2 x 2 = 128
8   * * * * * * * *  $2^8$    2 x 2 x 2 x 2 x 2 x 2 x 2 x 2 = 256
```

Figure 7. *Finite Number of Event Point Possibilities per Event Point Level*

Our next objective is to **produce** these event point possibilities, using an ordering method that is equally logical and thorough. Our goal is to develop a way to see the fundamental building block rhythm patterns, similar to how we can see fundamental tones on a piano keyboard or a guitar fret board.

To accomplish this, we'll be systematically pairing up 0's and 1's in a progressive series of binary combination tables. While there are other methods for producing combinations of rests and notes (see ***Preface***), our approach starts by generating the absolute sound shapes and then creating the music notation versions.

When we're done, we'll have a unique and elegant means of discovering and exploring the elements of rhythm.

The Binary Combination Tables

A Tool for Creating the Absolute Sound Shapes of the Fundamental Rhythm Patterns

The following sample binary combination tables (binary because they use two primary variables) generate some of the event point possibilities we calculated in **Figure 7** with our modified Event Point Level Table. We're using Event Point Levels 2 - 4 as examples, substituting 0/1 for silence and sound. These patterns are then re-written in notation combination tables, replaced with quarter rests and quarter notes.

This process shows not only how 0's and 1's can be systematically combined, but also further illustrates the relativity of notation. We can interchange any rest/note values in these tables, and the resulting absolute sound shapes remain unchanged. As we add a 0 and a 1 to each initial combination, the larger and more complex combinations are formed.

Before we begin, we must mention an important note: Our binary combination tables were developed using the order of 0/1 to place emphasis on silence as a valid musical event and because 0 precedes 1 in the standard number line. However, the tables could have just as easily been constructed with identical resulting combinations in a **different** order by using 1/0. Various other orders are also possible (reference any of the authors' works listed in **Preface** who have explored binary logic, particularly Mike Mangini).

Regardless, be assured that the binary combination tables we'll be presenting clearly let us "see" **where** and **how** rhythm patterns originate, starting with creation of their 0/1 absolute sound shapes.

Table A pairs the individual 0's and 1's of a single event point to create the **four** 0/1 combination possibilities for two event points. These results are identical, regardless of whether we are combining two beats or dividing a single beat into two equal parts by using event point levels.

Two beats: | / / | or   One beat, **two** equal parts: $2^2 = 4$

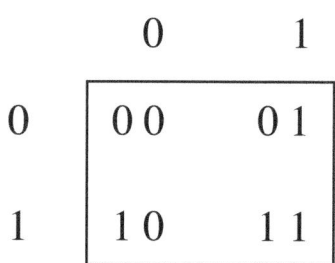

Table A
*Level 2 Event Point Patterns
Created Using 0's and 1's*

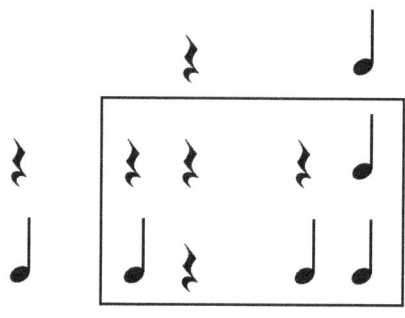

Table B
*Level 2 Event Point Patterns
Created Using Quarter Rests/Notes*

Table C builds on the patterns from **Table A** to create the **eight** 0/1 combination possibilities for three event points. These results are identical, regardless of whether we are combining three beats or dividing a single beat into three equal parts by using event point levels.

Three beats: | / / / | or   One beat, **three** equal parts:
```
/
* *
* * *
```
$2^3 = 8$

	0	1
0 0	0 0 0	0 0 1
0 1	0 1 0	0 1 1
1 0	1 0 0	1 0 1
1 1	1 1 0	1 1 1

Table C
Level 3 Event Point Patterns
Created Using 0's and 1's

Table D replaces **Table C's** 0's and 1's with quarter rests and quarter notes:

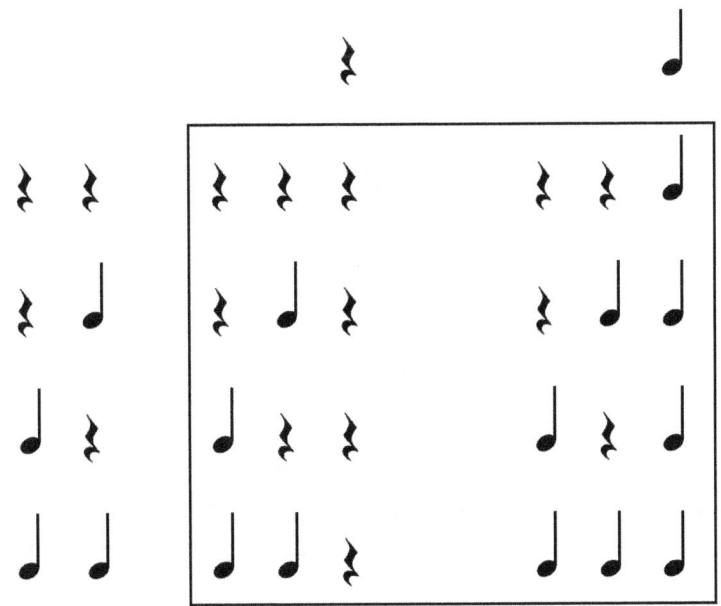

Table D
Level 3 Event Point Patterns
Created Using Quarter Rests/Notes

Table E builds on the patterns from **Table C** to create the **sixteen** 0/1 combination possibilities for four event points. These results are identical, regardless of whether we are combining four beats or dividing a single beat into four equal parts by using event point levels.

Four beats: | / / / / | or   One beat, **four** equal parts:

```
 /
 * *
 * * *
 * * * *
```

$2^4 = 16$

	0	1
0 0 0	0 0 0 0	0 0 0 1
0 0 1	0 0 1 0	0 0 1 1
0 1 0	0 1 0 0	0 1 0 1
0 1 1	0 1 1 0	0 1 1 1
1 0 0	1 0 0 0	1 0 0 1
1 0 1	1 0 1 0	1 0 1 1
1 1 0	1 1 0 0	1 1 0 1
1 1 1	1 1 1 0	1 1 1 1

Table E
Level 4 Event Point Patterns
Created Using 0's and 1's

For the sake of brevity, we could stop after completion of the Level 4 Event Point Table, since all the larger patterns we'll encounter will be combinations of these basic elements. However, it is very beneficial to see the 5-note quintuplets and 7-note septuplets for polyrhythm practice.

It is equally beneficial to see the compound beat and simple division beat versions of the 6-note sextuplets. The real payoff are the octuplets, the 8-note beat divisions in 4/4 and the 8-note beat subdivisions in 2/4, that occur in two of the most commonly used time signatures.

Continuing, **Table F** replaces **Table E**'s 0's and 1's with quarter rests and quarter notes:

Table F
*Level 4 Event Point Patterns
Created Using Quarter Rests/Notes*

Before moving on to *Part II*, important comments are required regarding beamed notes, dotted rests/notes, and ties. Our premise is that we must look past notation and its many possible variations in order to find the fundamental rhythm patterns. We demonstrated this by using 0's and 1's to produce absolute sound shapes, but as we progress, certain notation conventions are needed to improve the patterns' readability for practice purposes.

The 0/1 patterns' rest/note substitutions use appropriate note beaming to emphasize beat division and subdivision groupings. Dotted notes are included to emphasize compound beat division and to reduce excessive rests in both simple and compound meter contexts, as well as beat subdivisions. Ties, however, are omitted entirely, because their use constitutes an additional variable that would greatly increase the number of fundamental patterns far beyond practical application.

"Music is given to us with the sole purpose of establishing an order in things, including, and particularly, the coordination between man and time."

– *Igor Stravinsky*

Part II

APPLYING, ORGANIZING, AND PRACTICING THE PATTERNS

In this section, we will:

- present basic ***Applications*** for musicians and music-related research groups

- introduce ***The Binary Rhythm Pattern Indexing System*** to organize and analyze the patterns

- elaborate on the concept of ***A Rhythm Pattern's Vertical and Lateral Absolute Sound Shape***

- explore three techniques for ***Programming the Fundamental Patterns***

APPLICATIONS

This text presents a binary-based alternative to the traditional study of where and how rhythm patterns originate in measured time. In addition to the following applications, the ***Appendices*** contain college course guidelines for drum set, percussion, and instrumentalists/vocalists.

Guidelines for middle, high school and college students are provided both for dedicated rhythm studies as well as modification of existing music theory classes. Presentation/teaching guidelines are also provided for drum circle facilitators.

Drummers, Instrumentalists and Vocalists: A Self-Study Approach

To make effective progress, start simple. Begin by studying ***Part I: 2^n - Binary Theory of the Fundamental Rhythm Patterns,*** and then proceed to ***Part II: Applying, Organizing, and Practicing the Patterns.*** Place emphasis on comprehending the relative nature of notation and counting syllables, and the concept of absolute sound shapes.

Next, study the Level 2 - 4 Event Point Patterns in ***Part III: Creation of the Fundamental Pattens*** to understand the pattern development and practice applications used throughout this text. From there, you can proceed to any of the other sections in ***Part III*** (Levels 5 - 8) to target desired pattern groups you wish to focus on.

For **drum set players,** finding the origin of the source patterns lets you master the basics and then derive additional benefit from related study materials. For example, you could practice the two-hundred fifty-six 4/4 beat division patterns in Level 8 played against a jazz ride cymbal beat, and then, shift your focus to exploring that newfound mastery with Jim Chapin's *Advanced Techniques for the Modern Drummer, Volume I* (Alfred Publishing, 2002).

For **instrumentalists and vocalists**, reading pages full of patterns all using the same tones will become boring very quickly. Feel free to experiment with and incorporate a wide variety of scales and modes to perform the patterns, remembering that while notation duration is a focal point for performance, mastery of **where** in time the patterns occur is our focus.

For **all musicians, listen to the space between the notes**. As jazz drummer Peter Erskine has mentioned many times in his clinics, silence is a musical event too. Equally important, set up small practice sessions with specific practice goals. For example, suppose you decided to focus on mastering sixteenth note quintuplets. Your initial objective would be to familiarize yourself with the basic quintuplet sound shapes.

To accomplish this, you'd first read through the Level 5 0/1 combination tables, the 5/16 combination tables, and then the 5/16 music measure format. Your goal would be to perform all the patterns in the 5/16 combination tables and the music measure format. You could then apply the quintuplets to polyrhythms, improvisation, composition, etc.

Study of the patterns in all levels may also be used to augment rhythmic ear training segments in computer-based music theory programs. See ***Appendix D***, p. 305, for detailed study guidelines.

Private Music Teachers

This book offers a vast resource of possible rhythm pattern explorations for **private music teachers** of all instruments. Using either the suggested *Self-Study Approach*, or *Appendix C (College Course Teaching/Guidelines for Instrumentalists/Vocalists)* found in the *Appendices*, you can provide students with an overview of rhythm pattern theory and development, and then incorporate the patterns into existing levels of music performance and study. The degree of detail you address will of course depend on the individual skill level of your students.

It's very helpful to break down complicated portions by finding the source patterns within combination groups (i.e., individual Event Point Levels). A difficult-to-read passage in 4/16 may be found first in 4/4 and then be practiced to master the absolute sound shapes. Returning to its 4/16 version will make it easier to perform as a result of having learned and performed it in a simpler reading context.

For example, suppose your middle school guitar student needs work with triplets and sextuplets at the 4/4 level. You can introduce *Part I: 2^n - Binary Theory of the Fundamental Rhythm Patterns* to show that there are eight fundamental triplet possibilities (Level 3 Event Points) and sixty-four sextuplet possibilities (Level 6 Event Points).

Next, you can review the Level 3 0/1 combination tables, the 3/8 beat combination tables, and follow up with the 3/8 beat music measure presentation. Then you can proceed to the Level 6 0/1 combination tables, the 6/16 beat combination tables, and the 6/16 beat music measure presentation.

Additional User Groups

Composers - Any composer in almost any style of music can use the patterns as a definitive list for virtually any type of composition in measured time. They can select from this rhythmic palette to create pieces based on many levels of temporal complexity.

Music Theorists - Students ranging from high school to doctoral candidate can fundamentally analyze a composition's overall rhythmic structure and then categorize a composer's use of primary rhythmic themes and variations for that piece.

Ethnomusicologists - Students of world music can incorporate the patterns to supplement and enhance existing methods of categorizing and assessing a culture's use of rhythm, particularly if that culture utilizes rhythmic modes.

Music Therapists - Clinical practitioners can apply the patterns to construct fundamental rhythm exercises related to movement rehabilitation, social interaction, and personal expression. Simple percussion instruments and hand drums are excellent tools for these types of explorations.

Drum Circle Facilitators - Hand percussion-based facilitators can teach and lead guided performances of the patterns based on simple themes and improvisations. Guidelines for pattern presentation and teaching scenarios are provided in *Appendix E*.

Music Researchers

The potential for application of our fundamental rhythm patterns is unprecedented not only in music studies, but in cross studies of fields such as Neuromusicology, Cognitive Science/Music Perception, Linguistics, and Human Movement/Robotics.

Our comprehensive list of patterns offers music researchers an absolute starting point for the origin of rhythm pattern development, providing a temporal blueprint that can be applied by virtually any discipline exploring rhythm and meter.

The expansion of cross studies and information exchange has created powerful opportunities for rhythm pattern research. It is beyond the scope of this volume to provide an in-depth discussion of the applications in the arts and sciences. However, a few notions are worth suggesting:

- Mapping the brain's perception/execution of the fundamental patterns with respect to *readiness potential* (the pre-execution process of movement), *audiation* (the hearing/creating of music in one's thoughts), and *eupraxia* (the normal ability to perform coordinated movements)

- Comparing basic speech patterns to the basic rhythm patterns in order to determine similarities in processing and execution

- Verbal (music-counting syllables) and motor skill acquisition

- Developing rhythm pattern exercises for neural pathway analysis and motor rehabilitation

- Modifying existing timing research with an analysis of rhythm perception and execution

- Four-way limb coordination applied to the drum set

- Bio-mechanical analysis of drum set performance and its therapeutic aspects

- Bio-mechanical analysis of solo snare drum performance

- Development of polyrhythm performance skills

- Haptic (vibrotactile) technology applied to rhythm pattern instruction

- Brain-computer musical interface technology applied to rhythm pattern instruction

[*Author's note: At the time I was writing this page, I typed "rhythm pattern research" into a search engine and received exactly* one *listing. When I typed in "music theory research", there were over 900,000 listings. Significant exploration potential for the former is most evident.*]

A Special Note for Drummers

These words of respect and admiration are meant for the community of which this author has been a lifelong member. Our instrument holds room-shaking potential when played with the fullest release of energy. It can paint a whisper in the hands of a brush master, breezing over the sonic canvas with the lightest touch. At any dynamic level, it makes us the keepers of time.

This text was originally intended solely for drummers, but it diverged along the way and expanded considerably. However, the patterns in this book remain the core of our craft, and mastery of them will allow us to more fully integrate our understanding of odd meters, polyrhythms, and metric modulation. Exploring these concepts will vastly expand whatever rhythmic limits we might presently have and will increase our collective musical knowledge.

As a side note, this text will also hopefully make us consider how we can contribute to furthering the academic study of rhythm, because for far too long, it has been overshadowed by the study of tonal music. There are presently a wide variety of music research-related fields giving rhythm increased attention, and the well-prepared drummer may be able to greatly help advance the studies addressing how musicians conceive, understand and perform musical rhythm.

Getting back to the beat: The rest/note combinations most likely to draw the greatest practical interest are the two-hundred fifty-six patterns found in Event Level 8. They are presented in several contexts, including beat division in 4/4 and beat subdivision in 2/4. The 4/4 section provides a great advantage for players wanting to expand their knowledge of common rhythms found throughout jazz and Latin music, and the 2/4 section will provide equal benefit for rock and funk players. For drummers of all styles, these sections contain essential rhythm concepts.

Equally important is that you not let our math approach dissuade you. It is necessary, as it will save *years* of time expanding your rhythmic potential. Don't let the number of patterns overwhelm you either. Set small practice and reading goals, 15-20 minutes long, and you'll experience steady progress. Following this approach will make your studying very manageable, and you'll more fully appreciate the process of discovering the true structure of rhythm that underlies notation.

As mentioned earlier, the patterns can also be explored using the same methods from snare and drum set practice books you are already familiar with, including studies of accents, hand/foot exercises, polyrhythms, etc. A good instructor will be a valuable ally in helping make this happen and will keep you on track with specifically targeted objectives.

Most importantly, remember that these patterns are the core of your rhythm vocabulary. Become intimately familiar with their shape and sound. Your explorations could produce the next groundbreaking polyrhythm or odd meter trailblazer. The generation that you then go on to inspire will take even further strides. Enjoy this fascinating journey, as a keeper of the temporal flame.

THE BINARY RHYTHM PATTERN INDEXING SYSTEM

We've created a simple and effective way to help catalog our fundamental patterns, derived from two inspirations: Peter Randall's suggested rhythm pattern numbering sequence, found in Appendix II, Table of Rhythms, p. 157, *Rhythm in Action* (Belwin-Mills Publishing Corp. 1981), and Dmitri Mendeleev's classic Periodic Table of the Elements.

In chemistry, each element in the Periodic Table has an atomic number, a unique identifier based on that particular element's total number of protons (e.g., gold - Au, has seventy-nine protons). We use a similar notion to create a **Binary Indexing Number (BIN)** for each of our fundamental rhythm patterns.

As mentioned in ***Preface***, there are several other methods for generating the patterns, each with their own sequence of creation. Therefore, we must again bear in mind that like our binary combination tables which use 0/1 as their order, our Binary Rhythm Pattern Indexing System is a **relative** method for cataloging the absolute sound shapes. That's because we could have just as easily chosen 1/0 as our initial binary combination table order.

For purposes of exploration, the methodology we've selected provides a logical, sequential and complete pairing process, based on the standard notion of 0 preceding 1 in the number line. Each rhythm pattern created at an individual event point level is assigned **two sets** of numbers: The first is the **event point level** at which it occurs, and the second is the **sequence** in which it occurs within that level.

For example, with Event Point Level 2…

$$
\begin{array}{cc}
1 & * \\
2 & * \, *
\end{array}
$$

… we have the following 0/1 combination possibilities:

	0	1
0	$0\,0_{2.1}$	$0\,1_{2.2}$
1	$1\,0_{2.3}$	$1\,1_{2.4}$

0 0 would be the first pattern in Level 2, assigned the following binary code in subscript: $0\,0_{2.1}$

0 1 is the second pattern in Level 2 and would logically be assigned $0\,1_{2.2}$

This sequence would then be followed by $1\,0_{2.3}$ and $1\,1_{2.4}$

We will be applying our indexing system to catagorize up to eight event point levels.

The Binary Rhythm Pattern Indexing System
As a Tool for Rhythm Pattern Analysis

In **Figure 8**, a single measure of 4/4 illustrates how we can analyze basic rhythm patterns to identify their elemental origins. We see a group of patterns with various rest/note values, but we need to remember that their durations and all other variables are stripped away when we examine them in their respective Event Point Pattern tables.

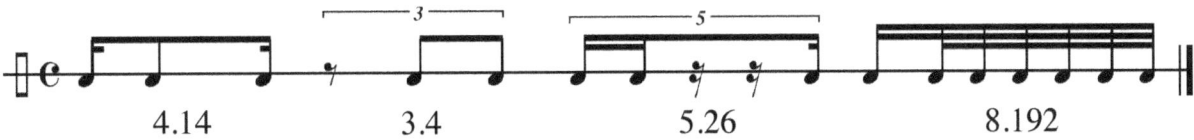

4.14   3.4   5.26   8.192

Figure 8. *Binary Indexing Numbers (BINs) Assigned to Individual Rhythm Patterns*

The first pattern 4.14 comes from the Level 4 Event Point Pattern tables.

	0	1
0 0 0	$0\ 0\ 0\ 0_{4.1}$	$0\ 0\ 0\ 1_{4.2}$
0 0 1	$0\ 0\ 1\ 0_{4.3}$	$0\ 0\ 1\ 1_{4.4}$
0 1 0	$0\ 1\ 0\ 0_{4.5}$	$0\ 1\ 0\ 1_{4.6}$
0 1 1	$0\ 1\ 1\ 0_{4.7}$	$0\ 1\ 1\ 1_{4.8}$
1 0 0	$1\ 0\ 0\ 0_{4.9}$	$1\ 0\ 0\ 1_{4.10}$
1 0 1	$1\ 0\ 1\ 0_{4.11}$	$1\ 0\ 1\ 1_{4.12}$
1 1 0	$1\ 1\ 0\ 0_{4.13}$	$\mathbf{1\ 1\ 0\ 1_{4.14}}$
1 1 1	$1\ 1\ 1\ 0_{4.15}$	$1\ 1\ 1\ 1_{4.16}$

The second pattern 3.4 comes from the Level 3 Event Point Pattern tables.

	0	1
0 0	$0\ 0\ 0_{3.1}$	$0\ 0\ 1_{3.2}$
0 1	$0\ 1\ 0_{3.3}$	$\mathbf{0\ 1\ 1_{3.4}}$
1 0	$1\ 0\ 0_{3.5}$	$1\ 0\ 1_{3.6}$
1 1	$1\ 1\ 0_{3.7}$	$1\ 1\ 1_{3.8}$

The third pattern [musical notation] comes from the Level 5 Event Point Pattern tables.

5.26

	0	1
0 0 0 0	$00000_{5.1}$	$00001_{5.2}$
0 0 0 1	$00010_{5.3}$	$00011_{5.4}$
0 0 1 0	$00100_{5.5}$	$00101_{5.6}$
0 0 1 1	$00110_{5.7}$	$00111_{5.8}$
0 1 0 0	$01000_{5.9}$	$01001_{5.10}$
0 1 0 1	$01010_{5.11}$	$01011_{5.12}$
0 1 1 0	$01100_{5.13}$	$01101_{5.14}$
0 1 1 1	$01110_{5.15}$	$01111_{5.16}$
1 0 0 0	$10000_{5.17}$	$10001_{5.18}$
1 0 0 1	$10010_{5.19}$	$10011_{5.20}$
1 0 1 0	$10100_{5.21}$	$10101_{5.22}$
1 0 1 1	$10110_{5.23}$	$10111_{5.24}$
1 1 0 0	$11000_{5.25}$	$\mathbf{11001}_{5.26}$
1 1 0 1	$11010_{5.27}$	$11011_{5.28}$
1 1 1 0	$11100_{5.29}$	$11101_{5.30}$
1 1 1 1	$11110_{5.31}$	$11111_{5.32}$

The fourth pattern [musical notation] comes from the Level 8 Event Point Pattern tables.

8.192

	0	1
1 0 1 0 0 0 0	$1010000_{8.161}$	$1010001_{8.162}$
1 0 1 0 0 0 1	$1010010_{8.163}$	$1010011_{8.164}$
1 0 1 0 0 1 0	$1010100_{8.165}$	$1010101_{8.166}$
1 0 1 0 0 1 1	$1010110_{8.167}$	$1010111_{8.168}$
1 0 1 0 1 0 0	$1011000_{8.169}$	$1011001_{8.170}$
1 0 1 0 1 0 1	$1011010_{8.171}$	$1011011_{8.172}$
1 0 1 0 1 1 0	$1011100_{8.173}$	$1011101_{8.174}$
1 0 1 0 1 1 1	$1011110_{8.175}$	$1011111_{8.176}$
1 0 1 1 0 0 0	$1100000_{8.177}$	$1100001_{8.178}$
1 0 1 1 0 0 1	$1100010_{8.179}$	$1100011_{8.180}$
1 0 1 1 0 1 0	$1100100_{8.181}$	$1100101_{8.182}$
1 0 1 1 0 1 1	$1100110_{8.183}$	$1100111_{8.184}$
1 0 1 1 1 0 0	$1101000_{8.185}$	$1101001_{8.186}$
1 0 1 1 1 0 1	$1101010_{8.187}$	$1101011_{8.188}$
1 0 1 1 1 1 0	$1101100_{8.189}$	$1101101_{8.190}$
1 0 1 1 1 1 1	$1101110_{8.191}$	$\mathbf{1101111}_{8.192}$

A more thorough and complex analysis would require that existing music theory software programs be modified to include a database of the fundamental binary patterns. The details of such an undertaking are beyond the scope of our text, but it is hoped that such incorporations will be developed and explored for applications across the arts and sciences.

Ethnomusicology, for example, could apply further refinement of their current rhythm pattern classification methods using these binary identifying numbers (BINs). While not all music occurs in precisely measured formats, many world cultures utilize standardized groups of patterns called "rhythmic modes," containing source elements found within the tables we'll be generating. These modes could now be identified with a common numbering scheme.

The cross-study music research fields listed on page 28 (Neuromusicology, Cognitive Science/Music Perception, Linguistics, and Human Movement/Robotics) could likewise benefit by sharing a common numbering scheme to reference the evolution of the fundamental patterns.

For example, haptic technology studies the use of vibration (vibrotactile feedback) to teach skill acquisition. The Haptic drum kit, developed by the e-sense project (www.esenseproject.org), uses sensors attached to the wrists and ankles to teach drummers basic rhythm patterns. Imagine an experiment where the quintuplets in Event Level 5 are presented in various random sequences, where each of the patterns are identified using a BIN.

The same patterns, using the same BINs, could be categorized and integrated into brain music computer interface (BMCI) research, such as the work being done by the Interdisciplinary Centre for Music Research (ICMR), at the University of Plymouth. Their website, www.neurosymphonics.com, discusses how a sensor-modified cap worn on your head allows users to interface with musical instruments and generate electrical signals to play those instruments.

The use of BINs would allow both groups of researchers to identify rhythm patterns with the same numbering scheme, permitting much clearer lines of communication for data exchange.

In whatever context it may be applied, the Binary Rhythm Pattern Indexing System can be used to help further organize the infinite number of rhythm pattern combinations into a finite group of logical and masterable possibilities. Rhythm pattern theory has never really had such an organizing system, and its cataloging potential remains to be realized through the creative explorations of readers seeking a greater understanding of temporal order.

A RHYTHM PATTERN'S VERTICAL AND LATERAL ABSOLUTE SOUND SHAPE

The 0/1 patterns created in our binary combination tables can be re-written with many variations of duration, accents, volume, etc., but their absolute sound shapes remain unchanged. This characteristic occurs both in vertical and lateral contexts.

By **vertical**, we refer to beat and division levels occurring within a single measure. In **Figure 9**, four quarter notes played in a measure of 4/4 create the same absolute sound shape as four sixteenth notes occurring over one beat of 4/4:

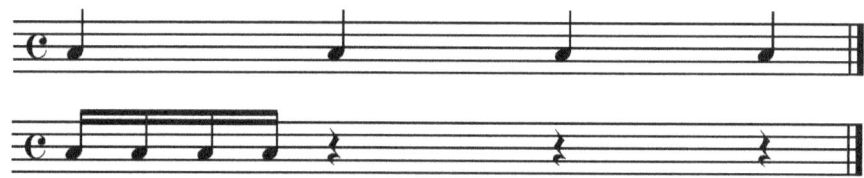

Figure 9. *Identical Vertical Quarter and Sixteenth Rest/Note Sound Shapes*

By **lateral**, we mean that a rhythm pattern's absolute sound shape can be compressed within a single measure or be expanded across multiple measures, as in **Figure 10**:

Figure 10. *Identical Lateral Quarter and Sixteenth Rest/Note Sound Shapes*

We can apply the concept of vertical and lateral absolute sound shapes to help simplify our exploration and integration of polyrhythms. For example, by playing the simple quarter rest/note pattern in a measure of 7/4 **(Figure 11)**...

Figure 11. *Quarter Rest/Note Combinations*

... we are using an easy-to read-method to also learn and **hear** the absolute sound shape of its polyrhythmic counterparts, seen in this measure of 3/4 **(Figure 12)**:

Figure 12. *Eighth and Sixteenth Rest/Note Septuplet Combinations*

PROGRAMMING THE FUNDAMENTAL PATTERNS

Audiation, Mental Rehearsal and Vocalization

Audiation is a term developed by music researcher Edwin E. Gordon to describe the process of hearing music in your mind and actively manipulating it. *Mental rehearsal* incorporates audiation's many levels, such as visualizing music notation and visualizing the movement associated with the performance. *Vocalization* has long been employed as a teaching tool and has been especially refined by Indian tabla drummers, who have used mnemonic syllable systems such as *bol* and *konnakol* for generations to pass on the lessons of ancient rhythms.

Audiation and mental rehearsal formulate and strengthen our performance of the building block rhythm patterns prior to their execution. Vocalization articulates the external performance, and you should work to develop a personal vocabulary of sounds relative to your instrument (e.g., jazz scat singing) to mimic the patterns once you have mastered their counting. Singing rhythms in a manner similar to speaking in a conversation helps greatly with sight reading and improvisation.

We can incorporate all three techniques to create and re-enforce our neural pathways by using the following practice sequence:

- **Read and Play** the patterns
- **Sing** the patterns
- **Audiate** (generate the sound in our minds) and **Visualize** performing the patterns

For drummers, the **Audiate/Visualize** steps are of great benefit for developing individual limb performance and four-way coordination. As an example, try audiating a pattern and visualize performing it with one, two, three and finally all four limbs simultaneously. For a similar approach, read *Inner Drumming* (George Marsh, 1982, www.marshdrum.com), a book well ahead of its time that incorporates visualization and Tai Chi energy movement principles around the drum set.

Audiation may hold even greater potential for practice, based on the results of a fascinating academic study published in 2001 by J. Haueisen and TR Knösche. Their research paper, "Involuntary motor activity in pianists evoked by music perception" (Journal of Cognitive Neuroscience, 13 (6), 786-792), revealed that a group of pianists who listened to piano music registered signs of involuntary muscle movement in their fingers and thumbs.

The implications of this study are profound. If listening to music evokes a neural response, can **intentionally** audiating an instruments' sounds excite and refine the associated performance pathways? Hopefully, music cognition researchers will explore this question further in conjunction with readiness potential (the pre-execution process of movement), as both concepts hold great promise for enhancing a performer's abilities.

Whether you employ the suggested practice methods individually or in combinations, you'll be strengthening the connection between mind and body. Remember, you are creating and re-enforcing neural pathways. Be patient, be precise, and enjoy the growing process.

That said, let's take a look at a bit of ink...

"Will he not be perplexed? Will he not fancy that the shadows which he formerly saw are truer than the objects which are now shown to him?"

– Plato, Allegory of the Cave

Part III

CREATION OF THE FUNDAMENTAL PATTERNS

- **Level 1 Event Points (Beat)**   0 = silence, 1 = sound

- **Level 2 - 4 Event Points (Beat)**   2/2 - 2/32, 3/2 - 3/32
                                            4/2 - 4/32

- **Level 5 Event Points (Beat)**   5/2, 5/4, 5/8, 5/16, 5/32

- **Level 6 Event Points (Compound Beat)** 6/2, 6/4, 6/8, 6/16, 6/32

- **Level 6 Event Points (Simple Beat Division)** 3/2, 3/4, 3/8, 3/16, 3/32

- **Level 7 Event Points (Beat)**   7/2, 7/4, 7/8, 7/16, 7/32

- **Level 8 Event Points (Beat Division)** 4/2, 4/4, 4/8, 4/16, 4/32

- **Level 8 Event Points (Beat Subdivision)** 2/2, 2/4, 2/8, 2/16

Level 1 - 4
Event Point Patterns

In this section, we will:

- introduce the event point possibilities for Level 1, letting 0 = silence and 1 = sound

- create the event point possibilities for Levels 2 - 4 by systematically pairing 0's and 1's in three binary combination tables

- substitute the 0/1 combinations with five beat note values (half, quarter, eighth, sixteenth and thirty-second) in five groups of binary combination tables

- place these re-written patterns in their respective music measure formats for reading/practice in the contexts of 2/2 - 2/32, 3/2 - 3/32, 4/2 - 4/32

There are:

    2   Level 1 Event Point Patterns
    4   Level 2 Event Point Patterns
    8   Level 3 Event Point Patterns
    16 Level 4 Event Point Patterns

```
1 0              1 *              1 *              1 *
2 * *            2 0 1            2 * *            2 * *
3 * * *          3 * * *          3 0 1 0          3 * * *
4 * * * *        4 * * * *        4 * * * *        4 1 0 1 1
5 * * * * *      5 * * * * *      5 * * * * *      5 * * * * *
6 * * * * * *    6 * * * * * *    6 * * * * * *    6 * * * * * *
7 * * * * * * *  7 * * * * * * *  7 * * * * * * *  7 * * * * * * *
8 * * * * * * * *  8 * * * * * * * *  8 * * * * * * * *  8 * * * * * * * *
```

Level 2 - 4 Event Point Patterns
0/1

	0	1
0	$00_{2.1}$	$01_{2.2}$
1	$10_{2.3}$	$11_{2.4}$

	0	1
0 0	$000_{3.1}$	$001_{3.2}$
0 1	$010_{3.3}$	$011_{3.4}$
1 0	$100_{3.5}$	$101_{3.6}$
1 1	$110_{3.7}$	$111_{3.8}$

	0	1
0 0 0	$0000_{4.1}$	$0001_{4.2}$
0 0 1	$0010_{4.3}$	$0011_{4.4}$
0 1 0	$0100_{4.5}$	$0101_{4.6}$
0 1 1	$0110_{4.7}$	$0111_{4.8}$
1 0 0	$1000_{4.9}$	$1001_{4.10}$
1 0 1	$1010_{4.11}$	$1011_{4.12}$
1 1 0	$1100_{4.13}$	$1101_{4.14}$
1 1 1	$1110_{4.15}$	$1111_{4.16}$

Level 2 - 4 Event Point Patterns
Half Rest/Note

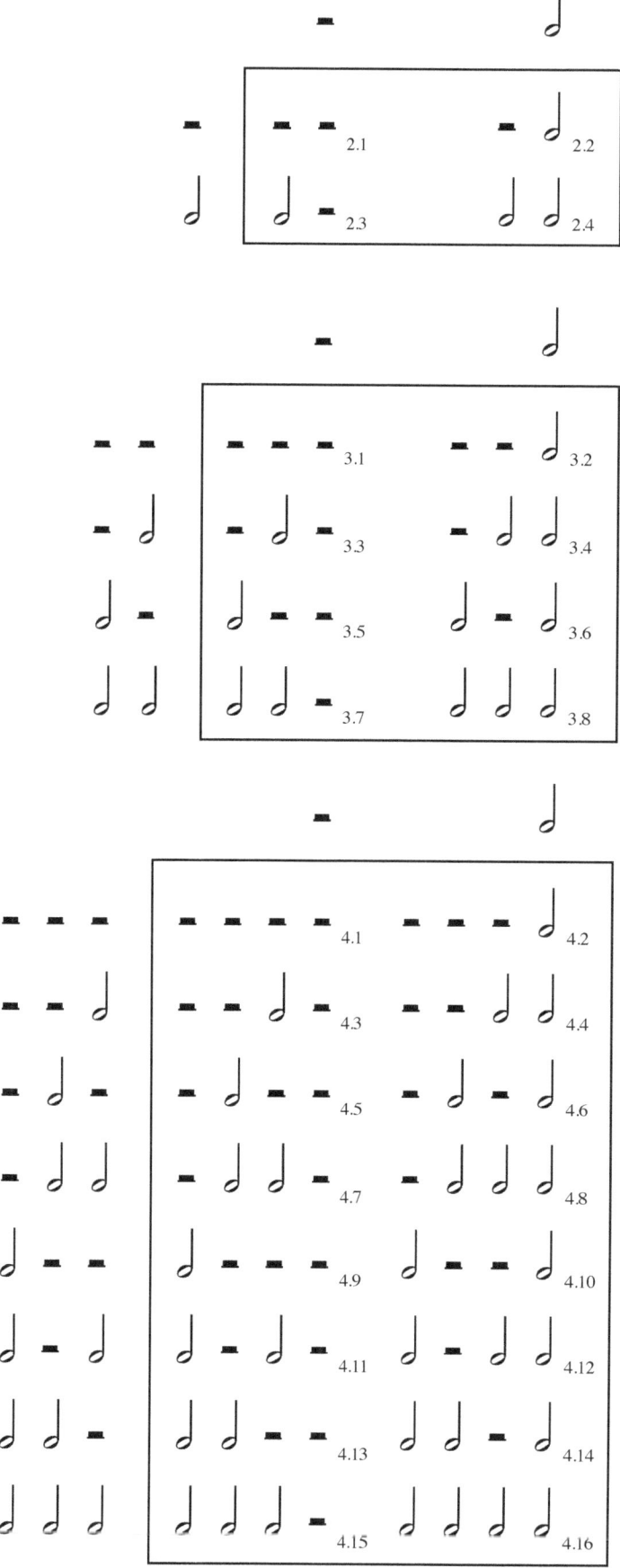

Level 2 - 4 Event Point Patterns
Quarter Rest/Note

Level 2 - 4 Event Point Patterns
Eighth Rest/Note

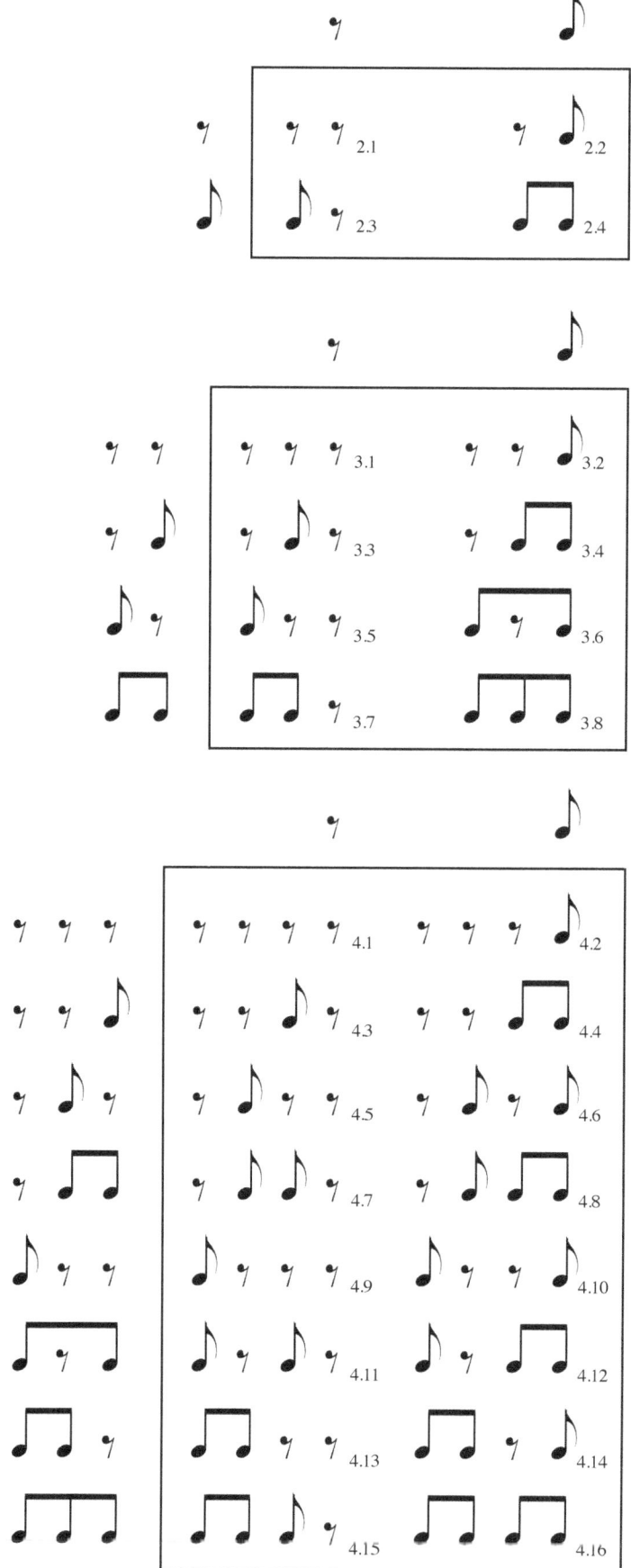

Level 2 - 4 Event Point Patterns
Sixteenth Rest/Note

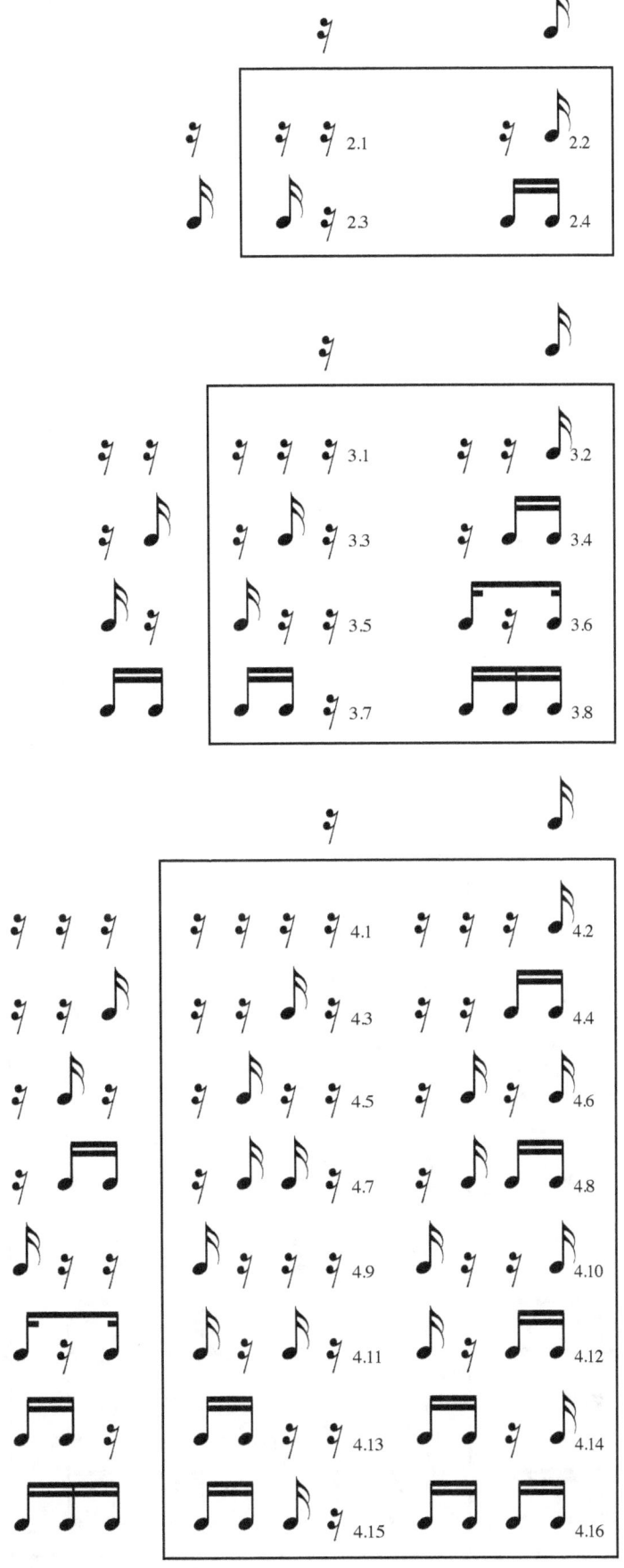

Level 2 - 4 Event Point Patterns
Thirty-second Rest/Note

Music Measure Presentation of the Level 2 - 4 Event Point Patterns as Beat Notes

The following pages contain the re-written rhythm patterns from the preceding binary combination tables for the Level 2 - 4 event point patterns. They are presented in five groups of beat note values:

- 2/2, 3/2, 4/2

- 2/4, 3/4, 4/4

- 2/8, 3/8, 4/8

- 2/16, 3/16, 4/16

- 2/32, 3/32, 4/32

To apply the practice methods discussed on page 35:

- **Read and Play** the patterns

- **Sing** the patterns

- **Audiate** (generate the sound in your mind) and **Visualize** performing the patterns

PRACTICE SUGGESTIONS

Audiation and Mental Notation

The following patterns are relatively easy to read, but they are a good place to start in terms of applying **audiation** as a practice technique. It can be used to expand your inner musical abilities in ways you may have never considered.

For **drummers and percussionists**, audiate different drum, hand percussion and cymbal sounds.

For **instrumentalists**, audiate the sound of your primary instrument and others.

For **vocalists**, audiate your own voice and others.

Another way to apply these patterns is to audiate them and "write" the notation in your mind at the same time. Select any pattern from the 2/4 - 4/4, audiate it, and then mentally transpose the time signature to create the half, eighth, sixteenth and thirty-second beat note versions of these same patterns and measures in your mind.

The greater you refine this ability, the easier it will become to literally hear **and** see the notation in your mind. When you can do this, you open doors to an entirely different and very powerful way of looking at and making music.

This practice method may be applied to any of the Level 2 - 8 Event Point Patterns.

Level 2 - 4 Event Point Patterns
Beat - 2/2, 3/2, 4/2

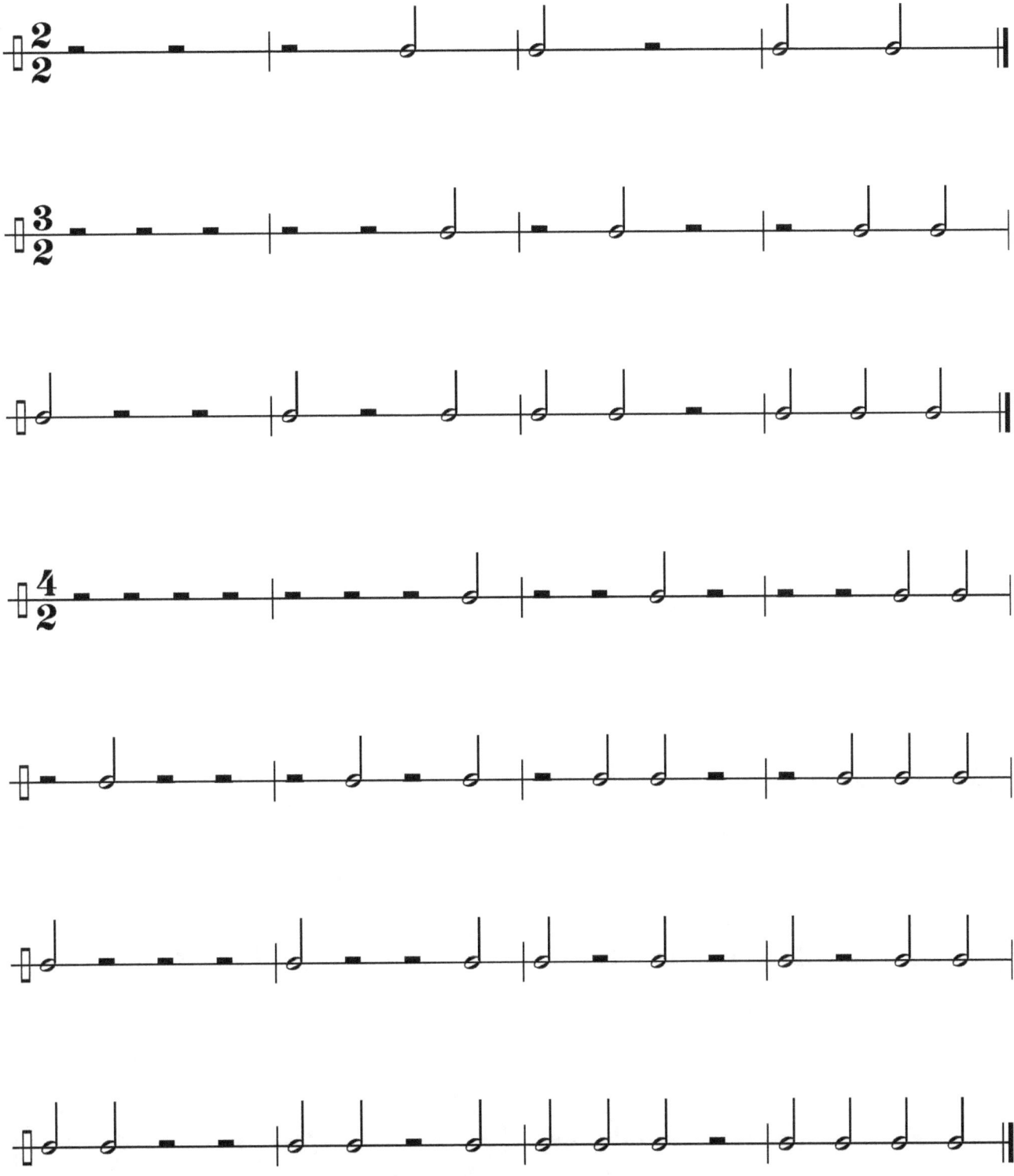

Level 2 - 4 Event Point Patterns
Beat - 2/4, 3/4, 4/4

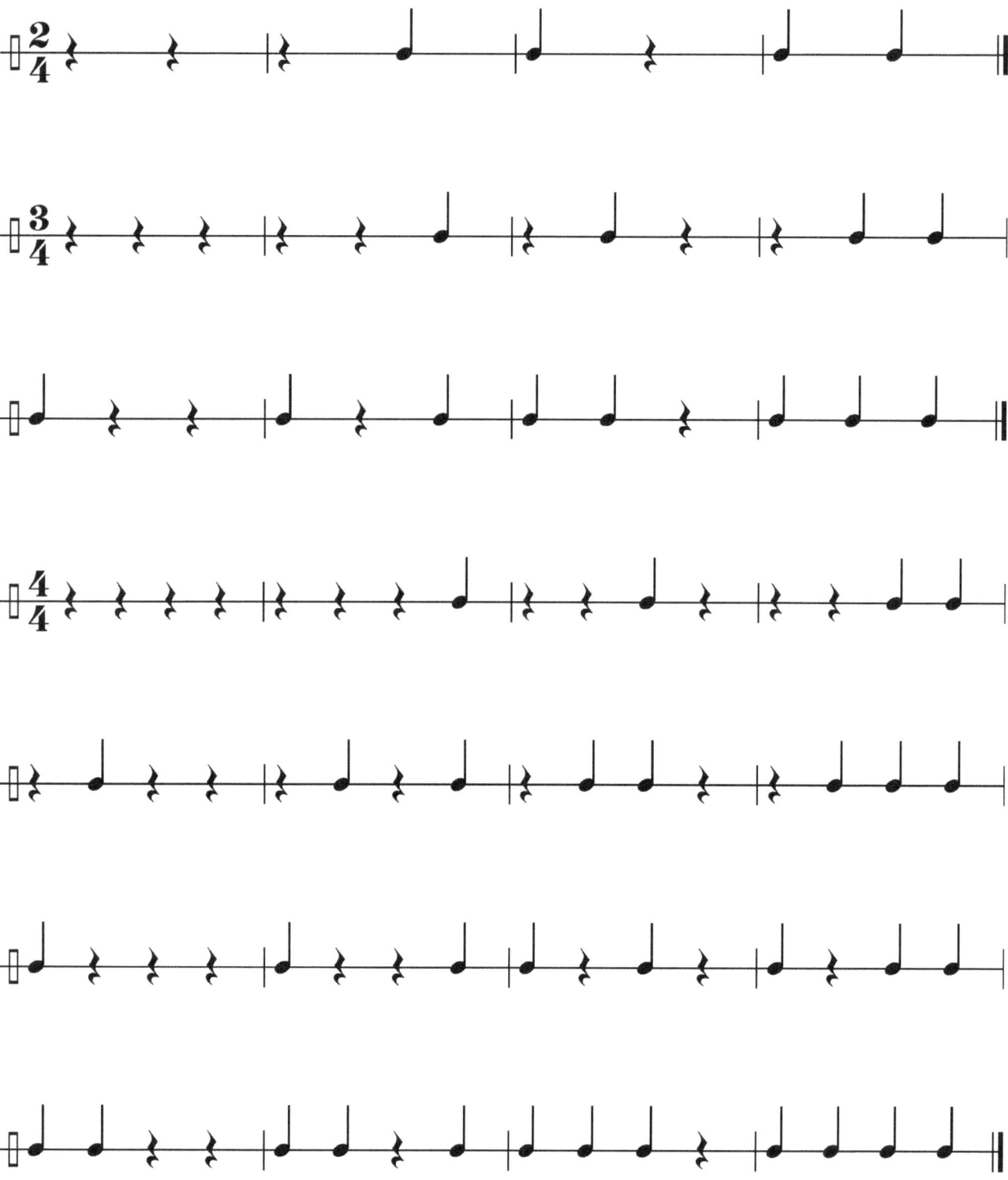

Level 2 - 4 Event Point Patterns
Beat - 2/8, 3/8, 4/8

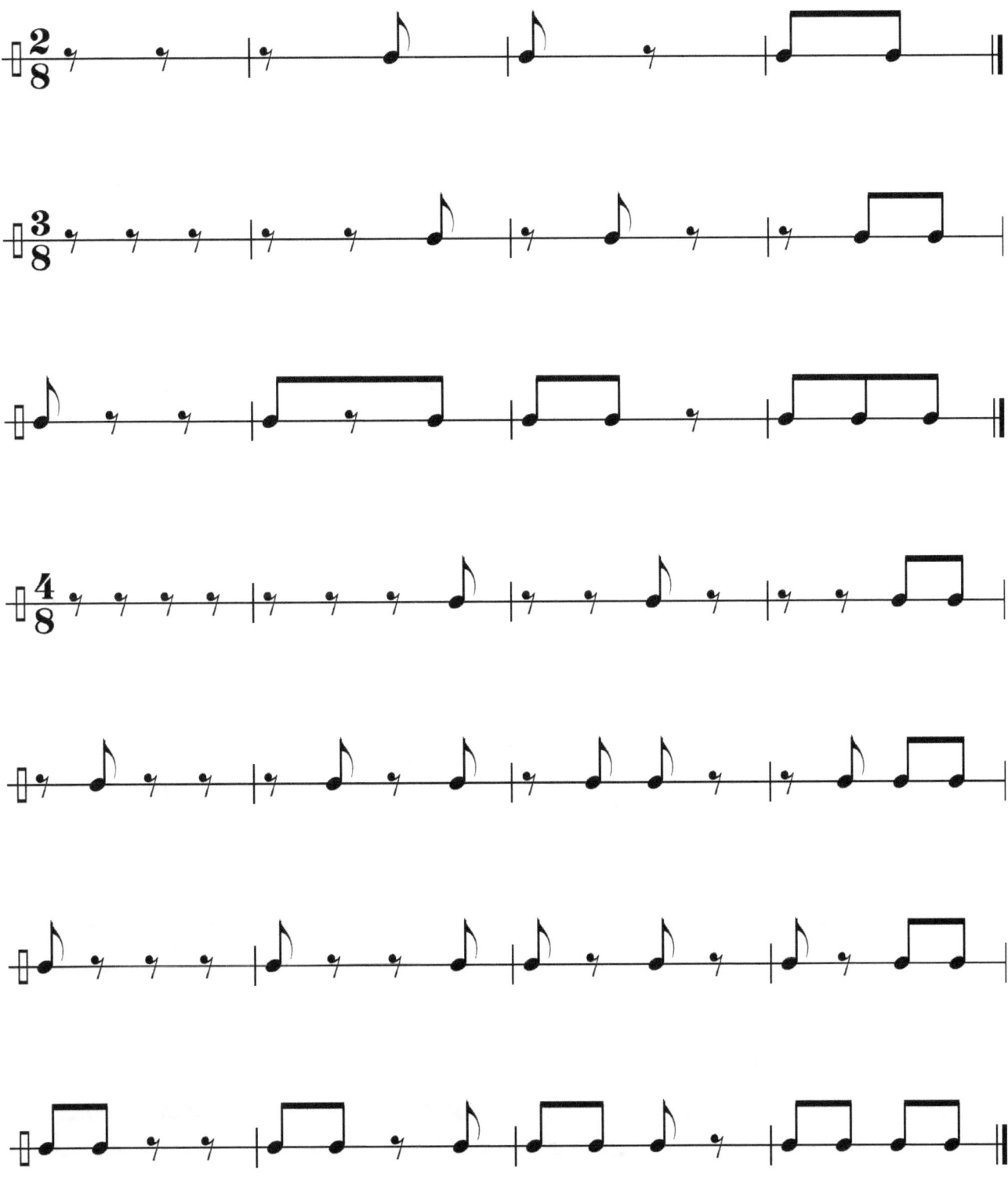

Level 2 - 4 Event Point Patterns
Beat - 2/16, 3/16, 4/16

Level 2 - 4 Event Point Patterns
Beat - 2/32, 3/32, 4/32

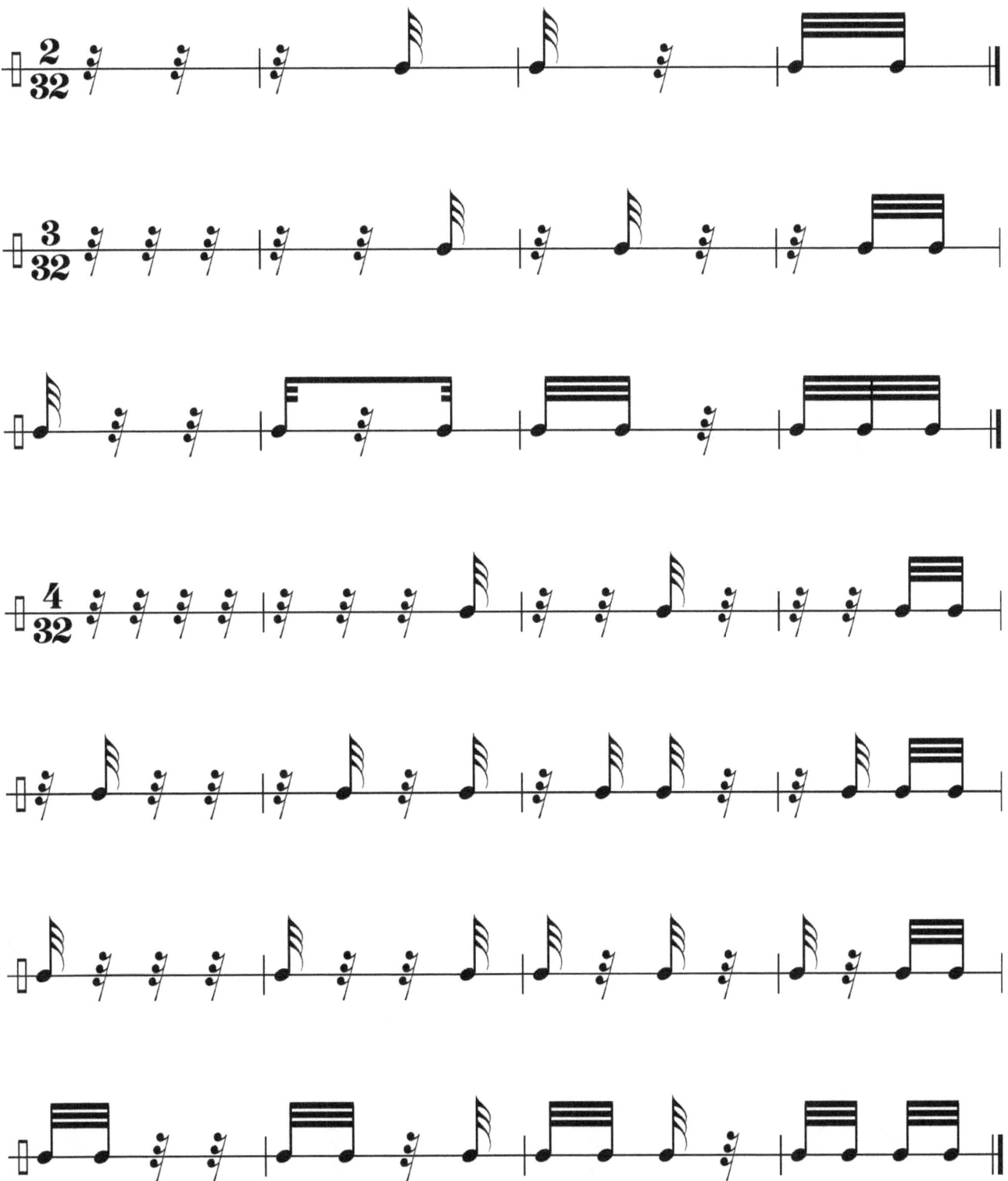

Level 5
Event Point Patterns

In this section, we will:

- create the event point possibilities for Level 5 by systematically pairing 0's and 1's in one binary combination table with the Level 4 possibilities

- substitute the 0/1 combinations with five beat note values (half, quarter, eighth, sixteenth and thirty-second)

- place these re-written patterns in their respective music measure formats for reading/practice in the contexts of 5/2, 5/4, 5/8, 5/16, and 5/32

There are **32** Level 5 Event Point Patterns.

```
1 *
2 * *
3 * * *
4 * * * *
5 0 1 0 0 1
6 * * * * * *
7 * * * * * * *
8 * * * * * * * *
```

Level 5 Event Point Patterns - Discussion

In the course of becoming conditioned to 4/4 as a dominant meter in Western music, there are likely more than a few readers who have not had many opportunities to perform compositions containing a five-sided sound shape.

From a practical standpoint, the Level 5 event point patterns we'll be seeing don't occur only in the beat note context. They can also appear as **quintuplets**, both individually and in the context of larger polyrhythms played over multiple notes. Quintuplets are generally expressed as ratios (e.g., 5:2, 5:3, 5:4), or sometimes simply as 5.

The relative nature of notation can actually be used an effective tool to help master quintuplets and their absolute sound shapes. We do this by first learning how to play the basic patterns in a beat note context. We then play **groups** of these patterns with accents on the first beat. This lets us create the identical sound of a pattern as though it was performed as a polyrhythm.

Exercise #1

Any of the notation groupings on pp. 59-63 can be used in this way, but let's apply sixteenth notes for our initial example:

- Play all the sixteenth rest/note event point patterns on page 62 to become familiar with them

- Repeat each pattern **four** times, accenting them as **1**-2-3-4-5, **2**-2-3-4-5, **3**-2-3-4-5, **4**-2-3-4-5

By mastering the execution of patterns in **Figure 13** using this method...

Figure 13. *Accented Sixteenth Notes as Beat Notes*

... you will have also played identical-sounding quintuplets, now divided over four quarter notes in a measure of 4/4 as in **Figure 14**:

Figure 14. *Accented Sixteenth Notes as Quintuplets*

You can modify this exercise by playing groups of four five-beat measures on pp. 65-69 as though they are polyrhythms, by accenting the first beat of each measure.

If reading in 5/16 presents an initial challenge, try playing the patterns first in the 5/4 context, as seen below in **Figure 15**. From there, reading **Figure 16** can soon follow.

Figure 15. *Five Quarter Rest/Note Measures in 5/4*

Figure 16. *Five Sixteenth Rest/Note Measures in 5/4*

This same group of patterns can then be experienced in the context of polyrhythms (**Figure 17**). While they may look more complicated, the sound is virtually identical. That's because the absolute sound shape **remains unchanged.**

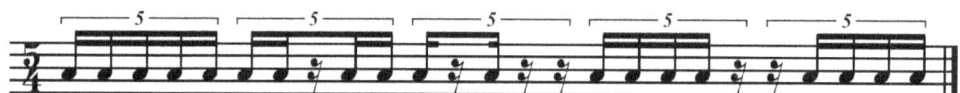

Figure 17. *Five Quarter Notes in 5/4 Subdivided into Quintuplets*

In **Figure 18**, we move on to an even more complex version of these patterns, placing them in the context of five quintuplets performed in the space of three quarter notes.

Reading this example may require some practice, but if you refer back to **Figure 15**, you'll recognize the source of its very simple origins.

Figure 18. *Five Quarter Notes in 3/4 Subdivided into Quintuplets and Played in the Space of Three Quarter Notes*

Clearly, the complexity of the context is relative. This is good to know, because if you can read quarter rests and quarter notes, you can quickly become familiar with virtually any polyrhythmic division of a beat note.

But how do we become familiar with playing polyrhythms over more than one note?

Exercise #2

Figures 19-21 let you play and hear quintuplets as ratios of 5 against 2, 5 against 3, and 5 against 4. The 5/4 measures provide an easy-to-read method of conceptualizing the ratios, followed by groups of quintuplets depicting how the notes in the ratios occur in relation to each other. Tap the top notes of each measure with your right hand and the bottom notes with your left hand. The tempo of the top notes in the 5/4 measures can be used as the tempo of the quintuplet notes in the respective 2/4, 3/4, and 4/4 measures, making both examples sound identical.

[*Author's note: You can hear these three sets of ratios played using Wolfram Winkel's* Polyrhythm *app for your iPod, iPhone or iPad, or by visiting his book site,* www.fiveoverthree.com]

The Sound of 5 against 2

Figure 19. *Quintuplet Sound Played in the Space of 2 Notes*

The Sound of 5 against 3

Figure 20. *Quintuplet Sound Played in the Space of 3 Notes*

The Sound of 5 against 4

Figure 21. *Quintuplet Sound Played in the Space of 4 Notes*

Once you become comfortable with playing the basic quintuplet sound shape, revisit the thirty-two Level 5 event point patterns and master them in the context of these three ratio sets, using the five metric contexts (half, quarter, eighth, sixteenth, thirty-second rest/notes). You can quickly conceptualize the quintuplets in these contexts. After you master the absolute sound shapes, adjusting to the relative notation is not that difficult.

Exercise #3

The next skill we want to master is playing simple quintuplets shifted across the measure. **Figures 22-27** depict polyrhythms using ratios based on note values. In **Figure 22**, the 5:4 ratio literally means, "Five eighth notes played in the space of four eighth notes." However, you could also **hear** it as five eighth notes played in the space of two quarter notes or even eight sixteenth notes. The mathematics of any polyrhythm is relative to the notation used to express it, but its sound shape remains absolute.

For **all musicians:** After you are able to play these note-shift groupings, you can go back and practice playing all of the thirty-two Level 5 event point patterns against them. This may take some time, but it is time well spent. For **drummers:** Start by playing these patterns with your right hand while tapping the beat note with your left foot, on the hi-hat. With practice, you'll be able to feel where the quintuplet falls naturally against the pulse in all the examples.

5 against 2 Beat Notes

Figure 22. *Quintuplet Played Over Beats 1 and 2 in 4/4*

Figure 23. *Quintuplet Played Over Beats 2 and 3 in 4/4*

Figure 24. *Quintuplet Played Over Beats 3 and 4 in 4/4*

5 against 3 Beat Notes

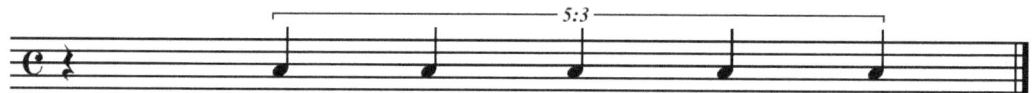

Figure 25. *Quintuplet Played Over Beats 1, 2 and 3 in 4/4*

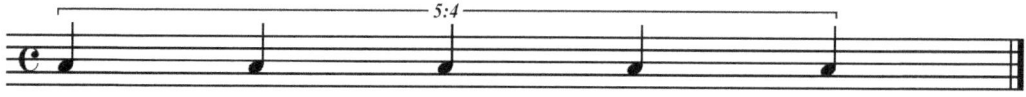

Figure 26. *Quintuplet Played Over Beats 2, 3 and 4 in 4/4*

5 against 4 Beat Notes

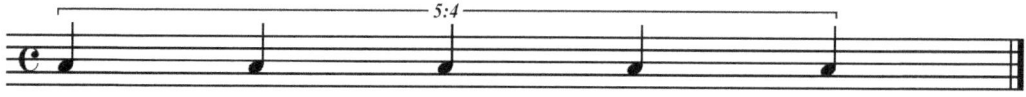

Figure 27. *Quintuplet Played Over Beats 1, 2, 3 and 4 in 4/4*

Exercise #4

This exercise may be applied by **all musicians** to help you hear the **doubling** and **tripling** of quintuplets by tapping on two separate surfaces, but it is especially helpful for **drummers**.

After you become comfortable with performing the 5:2, 5:3 and 5:4 quintuplet ratios on page 56, repeat the 2, 3 and 4 ratio pulses with your right hand on the ride cymbal while playing the quintuplet pattern with your left hand on the snare.

Once you can cleanly execute these three exercises, switch hands. Practice listening to each sound source (snare, ride cymbal) as individual sounds, and count them out loud as you play.

- Start by working on the 5:2 ratio, counting the right hand ride pattern first (1, 2)

- Next, count the left hand snare pattern (1, 2, 3, 4, 5)

- Then, play and hear both hands as **one sound**

Now comes the interesting part...

Play the ride cymbal (1, 2), and now **subdivide** the snare (1, 2, 3, 4, 5), first by **doubling** and then **tripling** the basic pulse.

- To **double** the pulse, count "**1 + 2 + 3 + 4 + 5 +**"

- To **triple** the pulse, count, " **1** + uh **2** + uh **3** + uh **4** + uh **5** + uh"

- After you are able to smoothly play this version of the exercise **ambidextrously**, continue on to the 5:3 and 5:4 ratios, doubling and tripling the quintuplets

From there, you can work this approach into various limb combinations around the drum set. It might sound extremely difficult in theory, but once you master the absolute sound shapes of the ratios using these simple exercises, it becomes fairly easy to hear and play the subdivisions.

This definitely takes some work, and the first time you are able to play this entire series of exercises, it will seem surreal. But that's a very good thing, because it means your mind and body have evolved to a level that will serve as a springboard for even more amazing rhythm explorations.

Level 5 Event Point Patterns
0/1

	0	1
0 0 0 0	$00000_{5.1}$	$00001_{5.2}$
0 0 0 1	$00010_{5.3}$	$00011_{5.4}$
0 0 1 0	$00100_{5.5}$	$00101_{5.6}$
0 0 1 1	$00110_{5.7}$	$00111_{5.8}$
0 1 0 0	$01000_{5.9}$	$01001_{5.10}$
0 1 0 1	$01010_{5.11}$	$01011_{5.12}$
0 1 1 0	$01100_{5.13}$	$01101_{5.14}$
0 1 1 1	$01110_{5.15}$	$01111_{5.16}$
1 0 0 0	$10000_{5.17}$	$10001_{5.18}$
1 0 0 1	$10010_{5.19}$	$10011_{5.20}$
1 0 1 0	$10100_{5.21}$	$10101_{5.22}$
1 0 1 1	$10110_{5.23}$	$10111_{5.24}$
1 1 0 0	$11000_{5.25}$	$11001_{5.26}$
1 1 0 1	$11010_{5.27}$	$11011_{5.28}$
1 1 1 0	$11100_{5.29}$	$11101_{5.30}$
1 1 1 1	$11110_{5.31}$	$11111_{5.32}$

Level 5 Event Point Patterns
Half Rest/Note

Level 5 Event Point Patterns
Quarter Rest/Note

Level 5 Event Point Patterns
Eighth Rest/Note

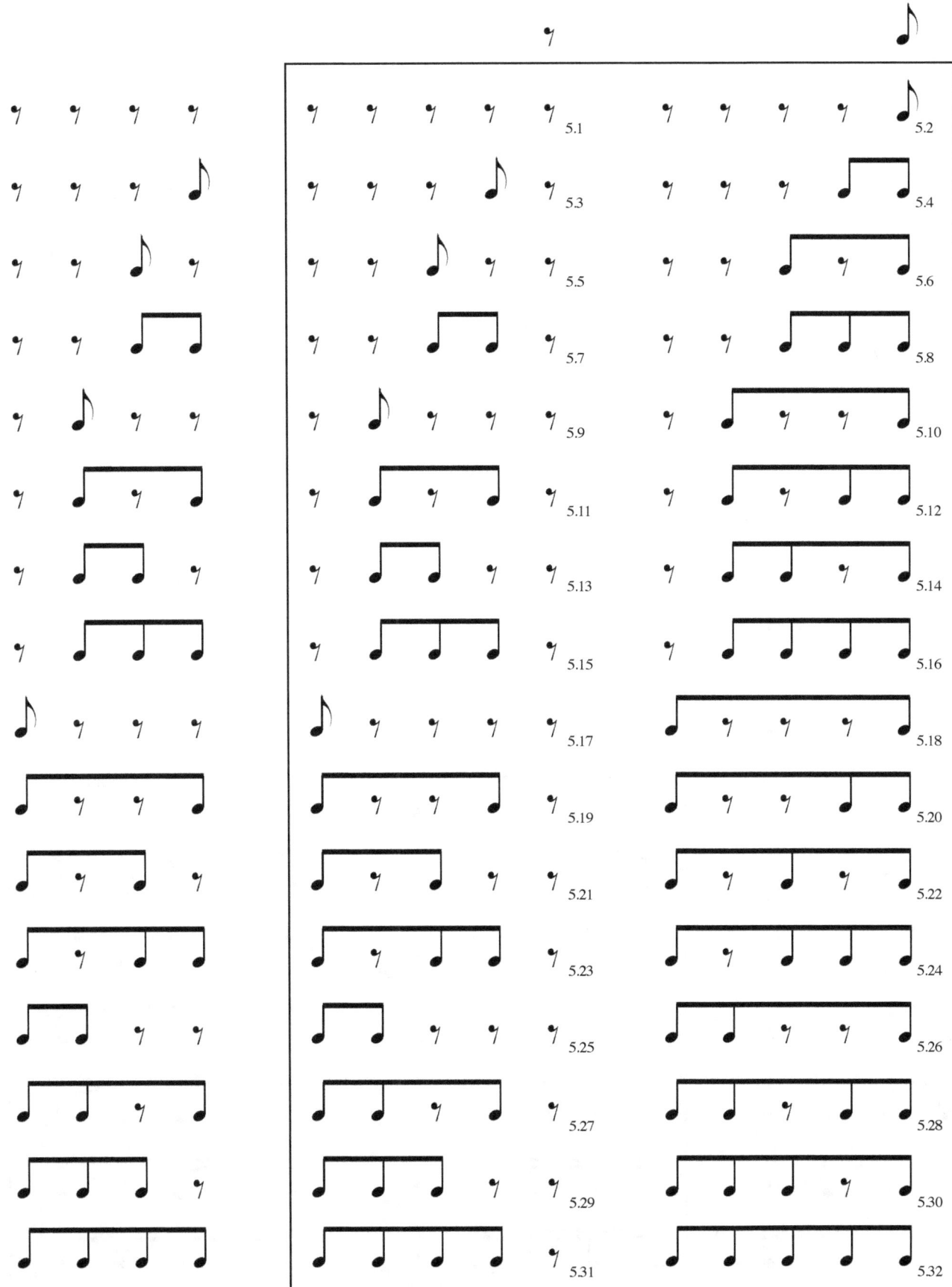

Level 5 Event Point Patterns
Sixteenth Rest/Note

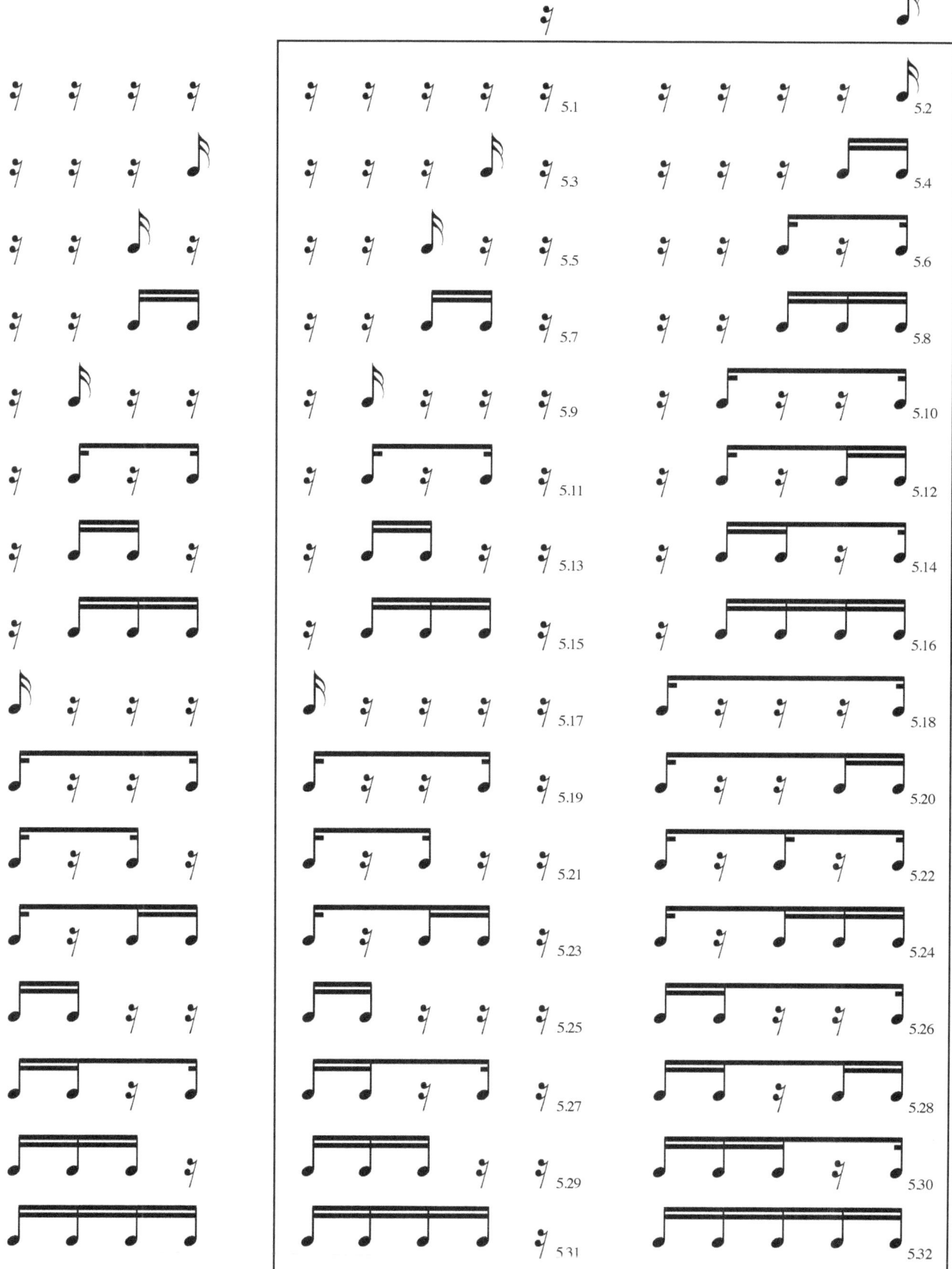

Level 5 Event Point Patterns
Thirty-second Rest/Note

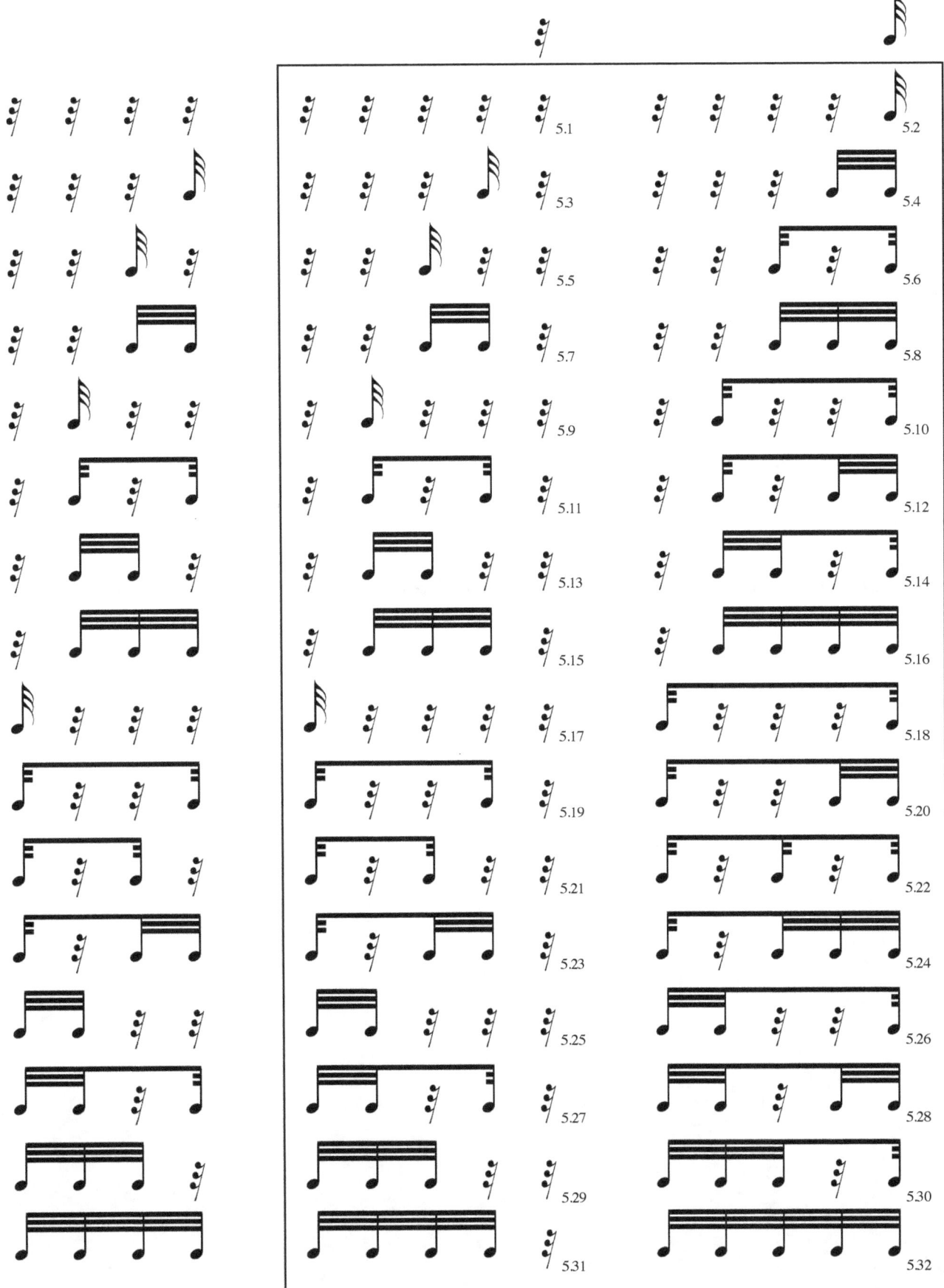

Music Measure Presentation of the Level 5 Event Point Patterns as Beat Notes

The patterns are presented in the beat contexts of 5/2, 5/4, 5/8, 5/16 and 5/32.

The rests have been consolidated to make reading the patterns easier. They have been grouped into the largest rest values where possible, with dotted rests included as well.

Note values remain at the beat note level, where they have been beamed to improve their readability. Their durations are not altered from the binary combination tables.

To apply the practice methods discussed on page 35:

- **Read and Play** the patterns

- **Sing** the patterns

- **Audiate** (generate the sound in your mind) and **Visualize** performing the patterns

Level 5 Event Point Patterns
Beat - 5/2

Level 5 Event Point Patterns
Beat - 5/4

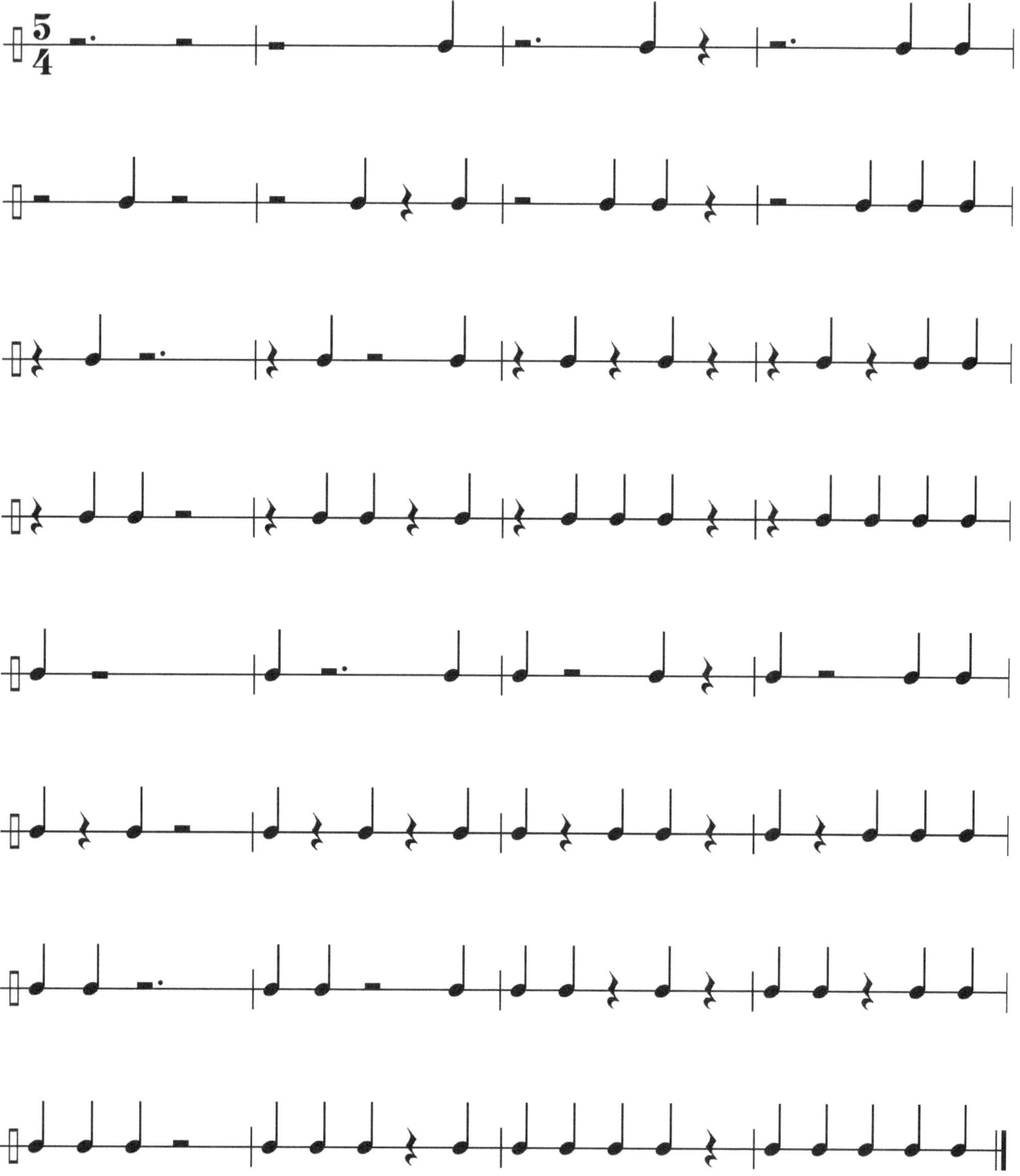

Level 5 Event Point Patterns
Beat - 5/8

Level 5 Event Point Patterns
Beat - 5/16

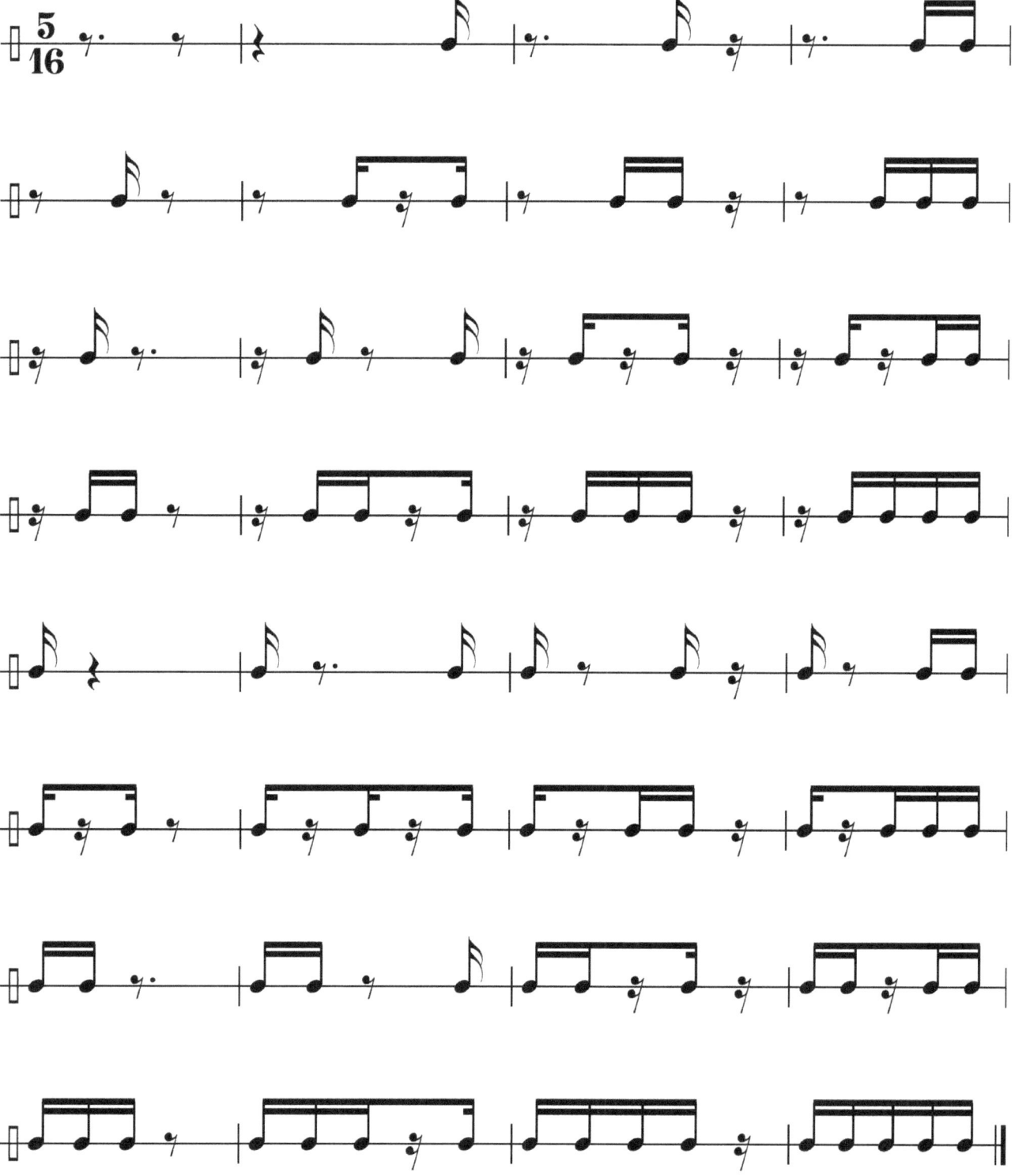

Level 5 Event Point Patterns
Beat - 5/32

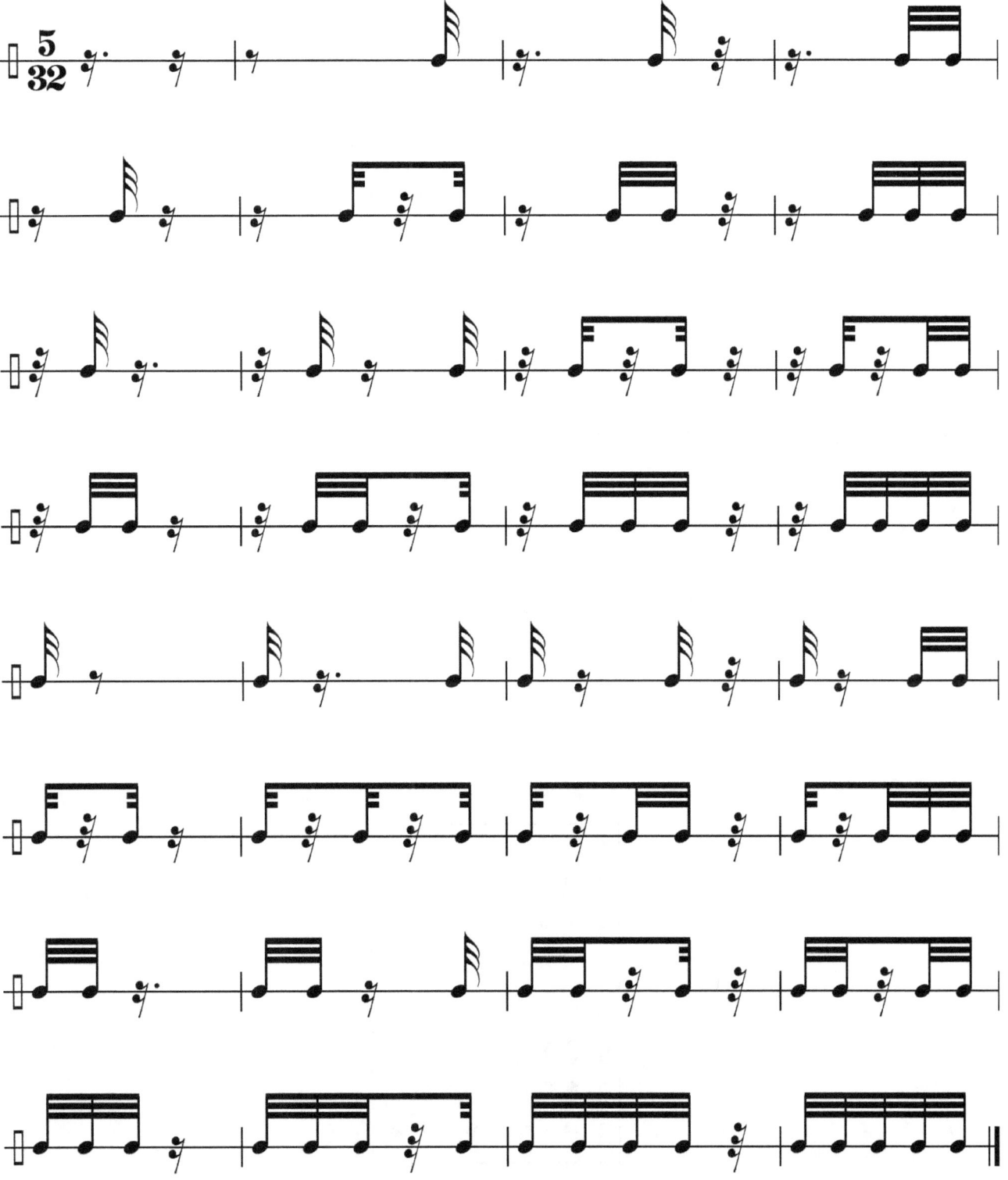

Level 6
Event Point Patterns

In this section, we will:

- create the event point possibilities for Level 6 by systematically pairing 0's and 1's in two binary combination tables with the Level 5 possibilities

- substitute the 0/1 combinations with five beat note values (half, quarter, eighth, sixteenth and thirty-second) in two sets of binary combination tables for **compound beat** and **simple beat division** contexts

- place these re-written patterns in their respective music measure formats for reading/practice in 6/2, 6/4, 6/8, 6/16, 6/32 (compound beat), and in 3/2, 3/4, 3/8, 3/16, 3/32 (simple beat division)

There are **64** Level 6 Event Point Patterns.

```
1 *
2 * *
3 * * *
4 * * * *
5 * * * * *
6 0 1 1 0 1 0
7 * * * * * *
8 * * * * * * *
```

Level 6 Event Point Patterns - Discussion

For the next level of rhythm pattern development, we are appending 0's and 1's to the previous Level 5 event point pattern possibilities. This creates the identical number of 0/1 combinations for both the **compound beat** and **simple beat division** patterns in Level 6.

When we re-write the patterns using conventional music notation, we distinguish the two metric contexts in two sets of combination tables. We beam the **three**-note groupings for the **compound** meters, and we beam the **two**-note groupings for the **simple beat division** meters.

By doing so, the logical order in which the patterns evolve remains the same for both groups. This ensures that our Binary Rhythm Pattern Indexing System's numbering method remains sequential, accurate, and consistent.

As mentioned, six-note patterns are beamed and phrased differently in 6/8 than in 3/4. However, we are numbering the patterns based on their evolving order combinations of silence and sound, rather than the two different ways they can be beamed.

Level 6 event point patterns occur in three formats:

- **Sextuplets** - with **varying** note values and groupings (e.g., quarter, eight, sixteenth)

- **Compound meters** - with **two** primary pulses, each initially divided into **three** parts

- **Simple meters** - with **three** beats, each initially divided into **two** parts

Figure 28. *Sextuplets in 4/4*

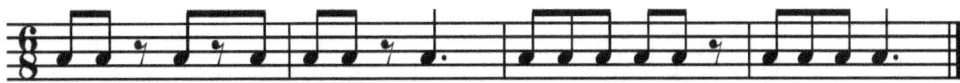

Figure 29. *Compound Meter (6/8)*

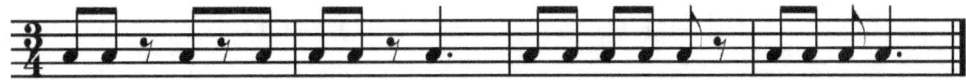

Figure 30. *Simple Beat Division Meter (3/4)*

Note: While the fundamental grouping of rests and notes may differ in these contexts, the number of event point possibilities (64) remains identical.

Level 6 Event Point Patterns
0/1

	0	1
0 0 0 0 0	$000000_{6.1}$	$000001_{6.2}$
0 0 0 0 1	$000010_{6.3}$	$000011_{6.4}$
0 0 0 1 0	$000100_{6.5}$	$000101_{6.6}$
0 0 0 1 1	$000110_{6.7}$	$000111_{6.8}$
0 0 1 0 0	$001000_{6.9}$	$001001_{6.10}$
0 0 1 0 1	$001010_{6.11}$	$001011_{6.12}$
0 0 1 1 0	$001100_{6.13}$	$001101_{6.14}$
0 0 1 1 1	$001110_{6.15}$	$001111_{6.16}$
0 1 0 0 0	$010000_{6.17}$	$010001_{6.18}$
0 1 0 0 1	$010010_{6.19}$	$010011_{6.20}$
0 1 0 1 0	$010100_{6.21}$	$010101_{6.22}$
0 1 0 1 1	$010110_{6.23}$	$010111_{6.24}$
0 1 1 0 0	$011000_{6.25}$	$011001_{6.26}$
0 1 1 0 1	$011010_{6.27}$	$011011_{6.28}$
0 1 1 1 0	$011100_{6.29}$	$011101_{6.30}$
0 1 1 1 1	$011110_{6.31}$	$011111_{6.32}$

Level 6 Event Point Patterns
0/1 (cont'd)

	0	1
1 0 0 0 0	$100000_{6.33}$	$100001_{6.34}$
1 0 0 0 1	$100010_{6.35}$	$100011_{6.36}$
1 0 0 1 0	$100100_{6.37}$	$100101_{6.38}$
1 0 0 1 1	$100110_{6.39}$	$100111_{6.40}$
1 0 1 0 0	$101000_{6.41}$	$101001_{6.42}$
1 0 1 0 1	$101010_{6.43}$	$101011_{6.44}$
1 0 1 1 0	$101100_{6.45}$	$101101_{6.46}$
1 0 1 1 1	$101110_{6.47}$	$101111_{6.48}$
1 1 0 0 0	$110000_{6.49}$	$110001_{6.50}$
1 1 0 0 1	$110010_{6.51}$	$110011_{6.52}$
1 1 0 1 0	$110100_{6.53}$	$110101_{6.54}$
1 1 0 1 1	$110110_{6.55}$	$110111_{6.56}$
1 1 1 0 0	$111000_{6.57}$	$111001_{6.58}$
1 1 1 0 1	$111010_{6.59}$	$111011_{6.60}$
1 1 1 1 0	$111100_{6.61}$	$111101_{6.62}$
1 1 1 1 1	$111110_{6.63}$	$111111_{6.64}$

Level 6 Event Point Patterns in Compound Meters

The following groups of patterns are the Level 6 event point possibilities as they occur in compound meters (consisting of **two** beat notes, each divided into **three** initial parts).

They are re-written in the contexts of 6/2, 6/4, 6/8, 6/16 and 6/32.

The Binary Rhythm Indexing System
Applied to Level 6 Event Point Patterns

Compound Beat

We previously discussed the relative aspect of the Binary Rhythm Pattern Indexing System in Part II, page 30. Applied to the compound beat versions of the Level 6 event point patterns, we experience them in the context of **two** beat notes, each divided into **three** initial parts.

The BIN's (binary indexing numbers) assigned to the following group of patterns do not specify sextuplet, compound beat, or simple beat division contexts. They are used to identify the event point level and the sequence in which the rest/note combinations are generated.

Level 6 Event Point Patterns
Half Rest/Note - 6/2

Level 6 Event Point Patterns
Half Rest/Note - 6/2 (cont'd)

Level 6 Event Point Patterns
Quarter Rest/Note - 6/4

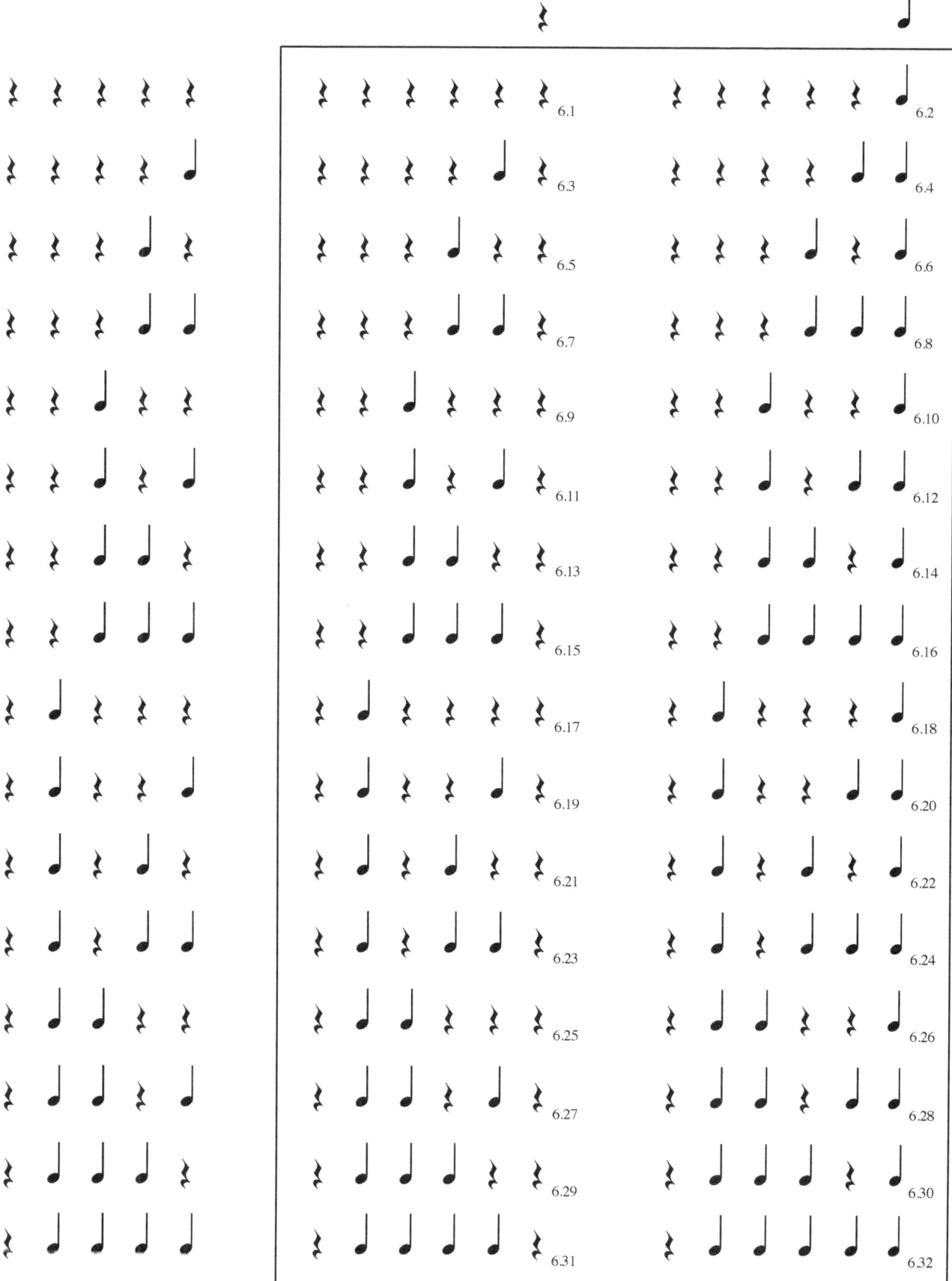

Level 6 Event Point Patterns
Quarter Rest/Note - 6/4 (cont'd)

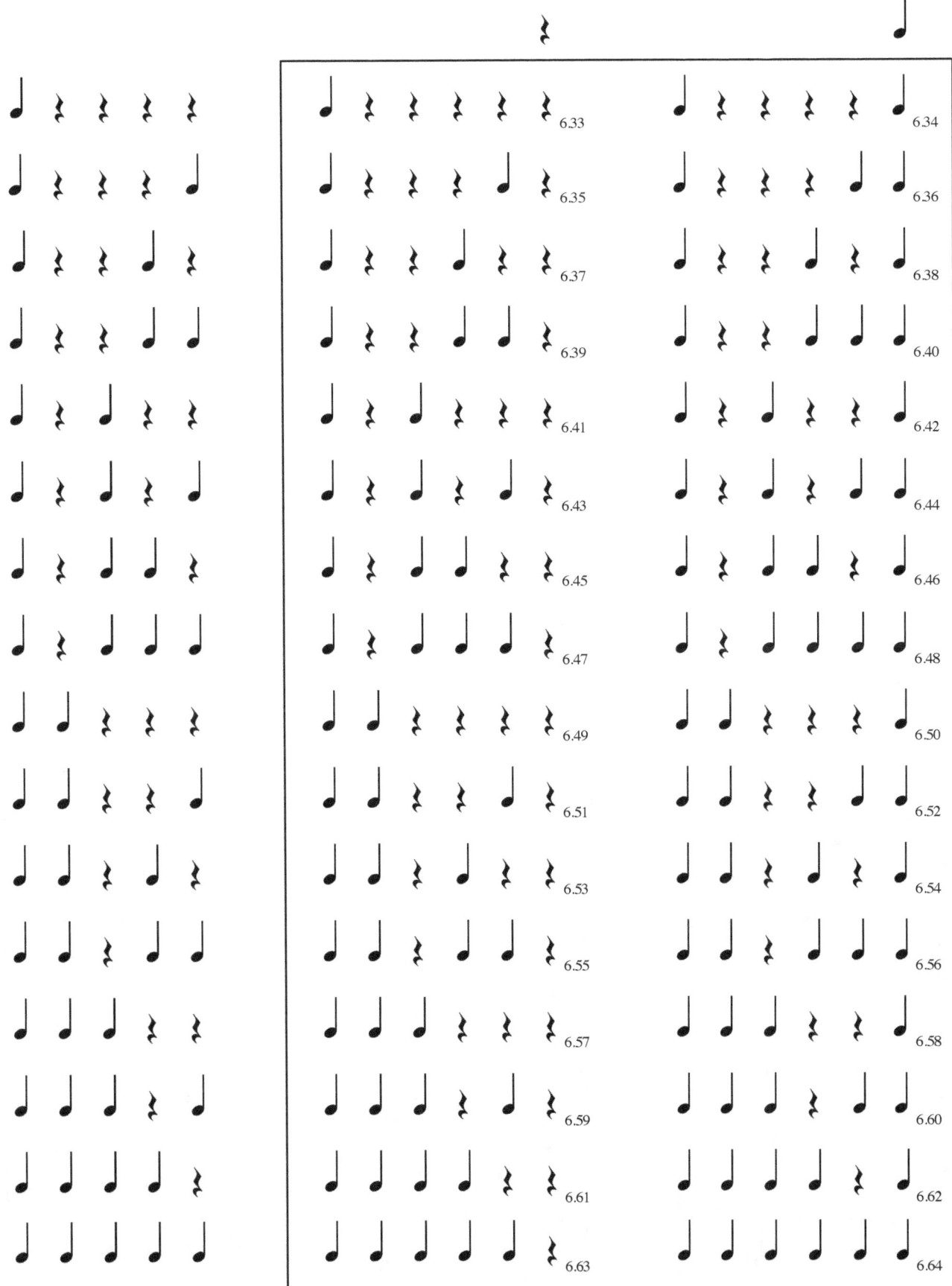

Level 6 Event Point Patterns
Eighth Rest/Note - 6/8

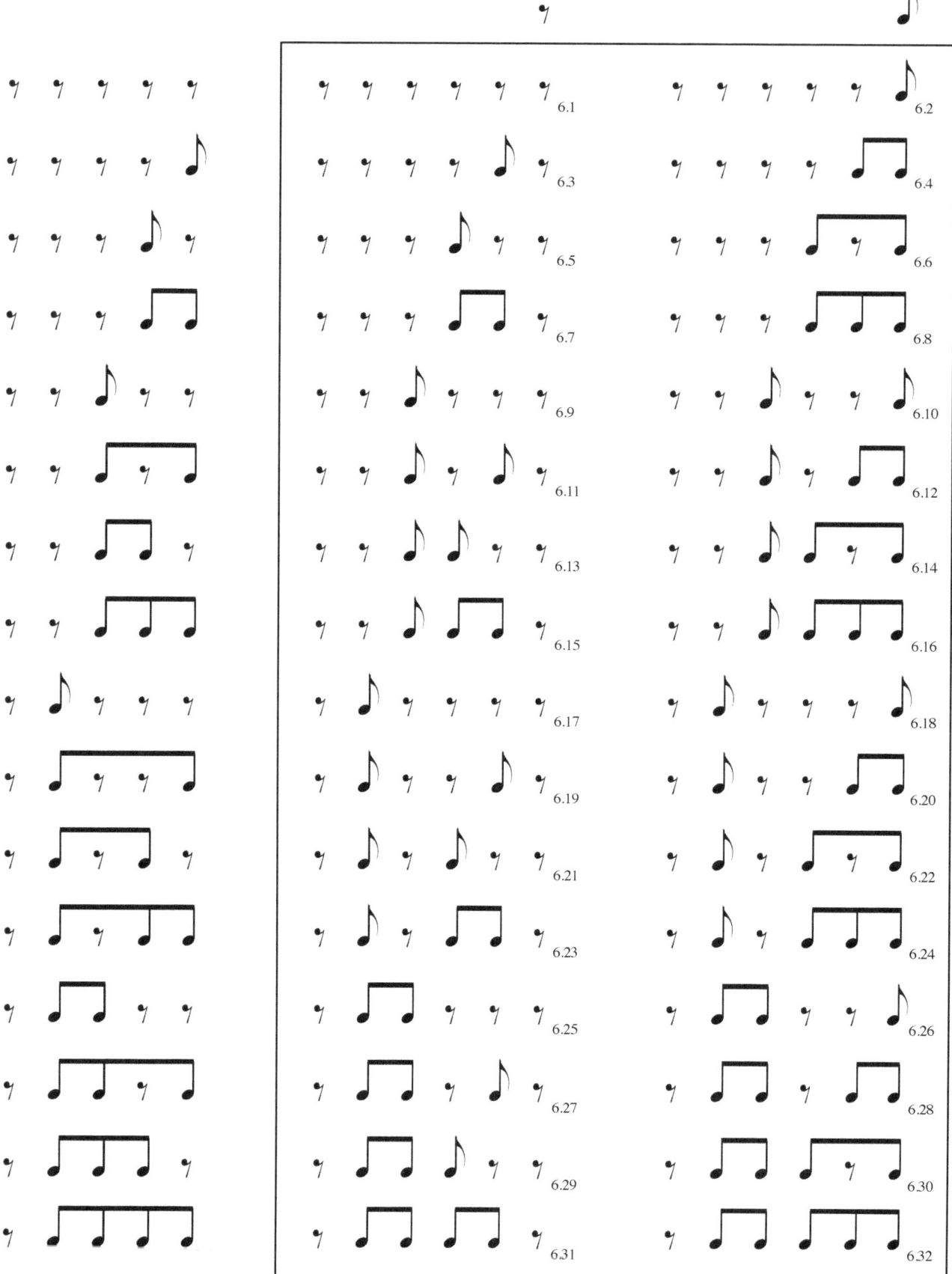

Level 6 Event Point Patterns
Eighth Rest/Note - 6/8 (cont'd)

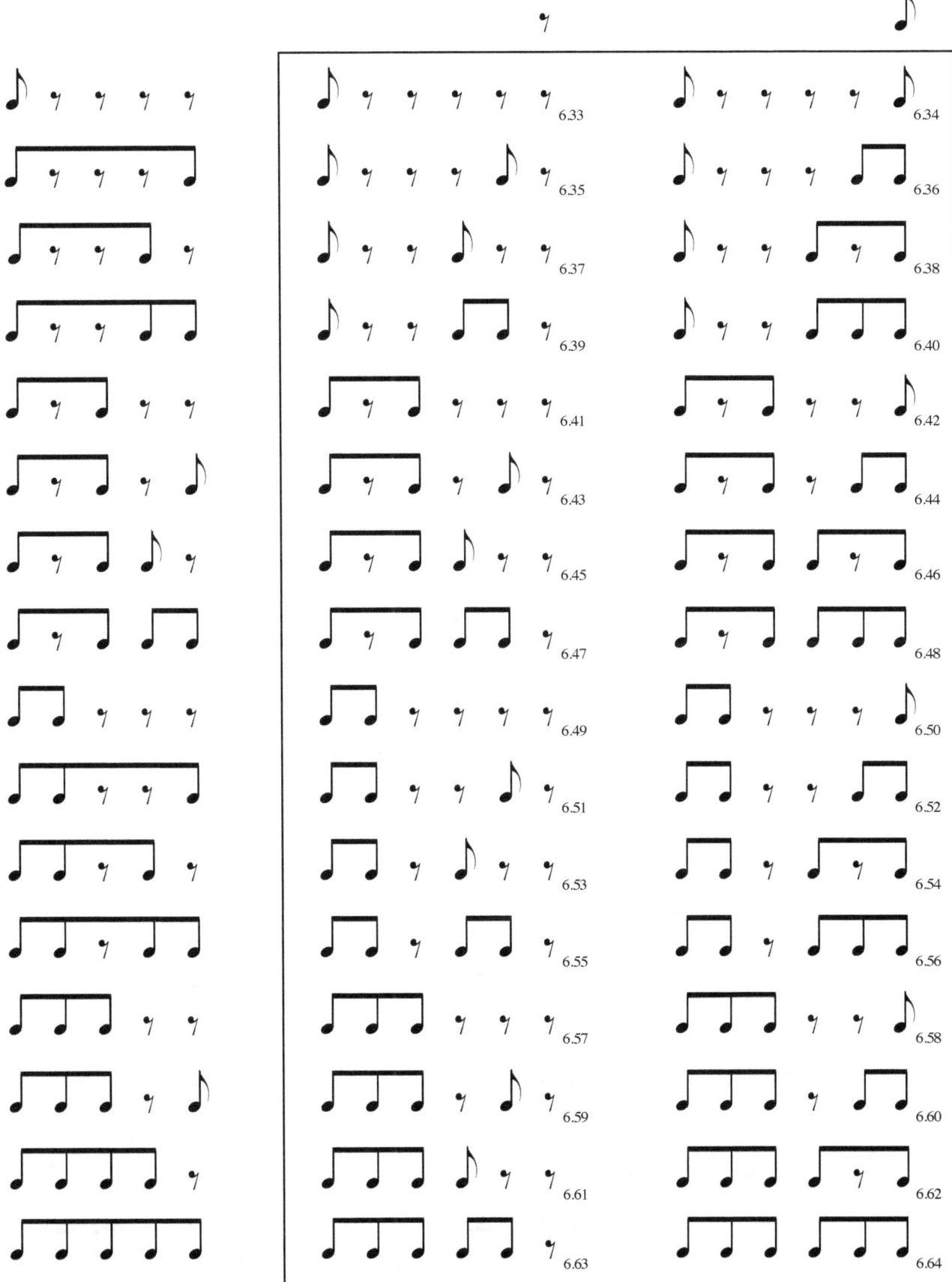

Level 6 Event Point Patterns
Sixteenth Rest/Note - 6/16

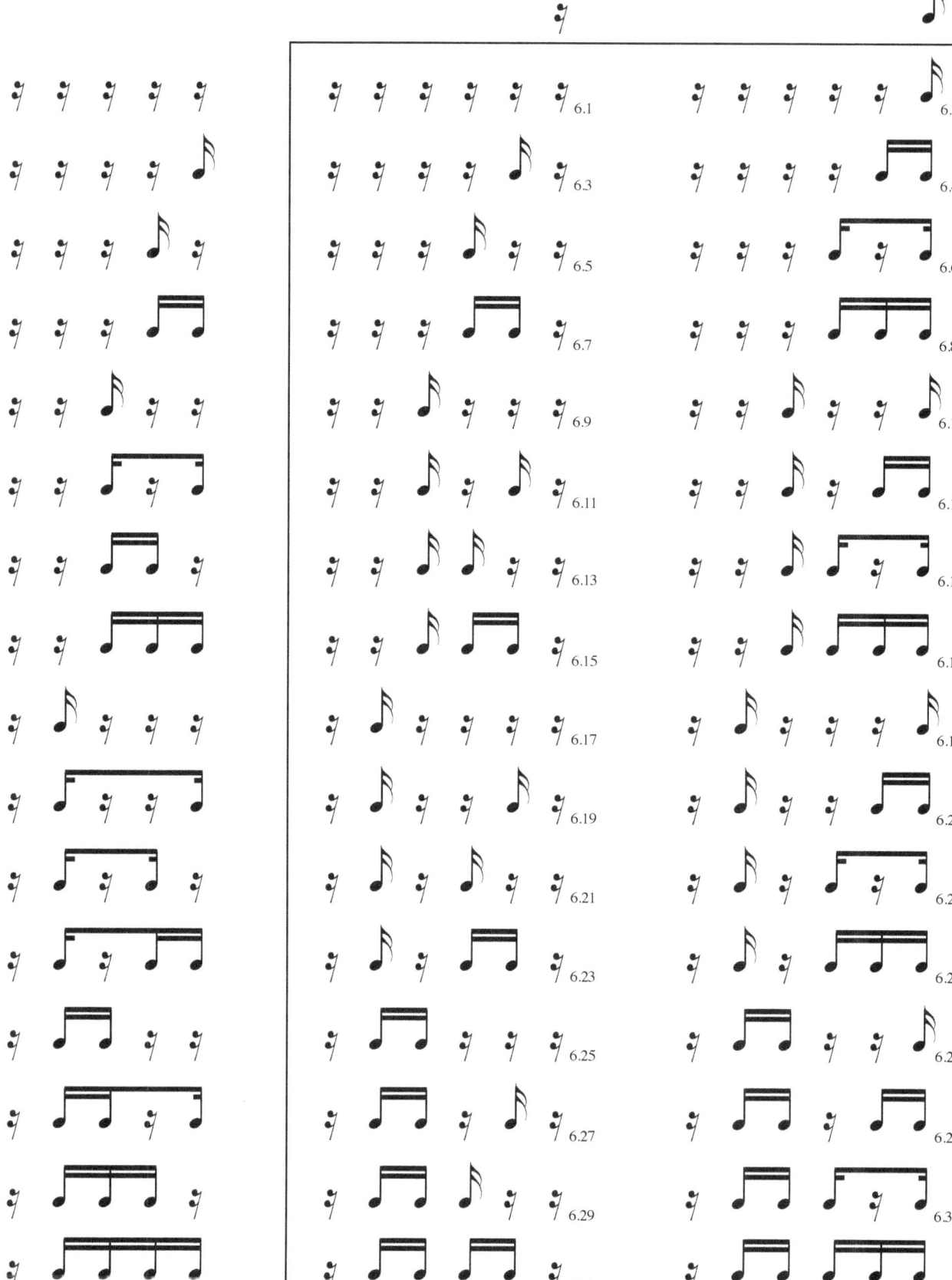

Level 6 Event Point Patterns
Sixteenth Rest/Note - 6/16 (cont'd)

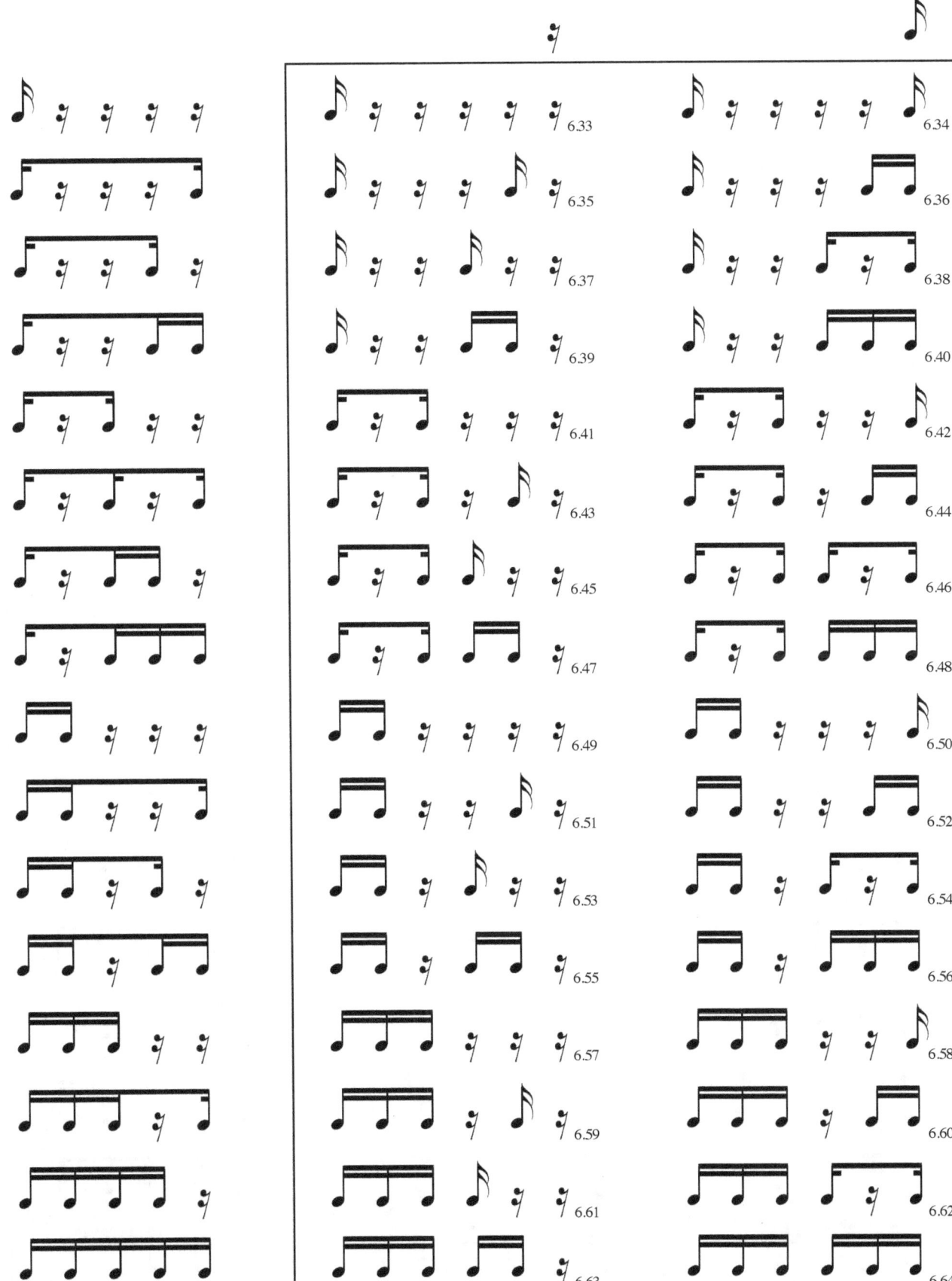

Level 6 Event Point Patterns
Thirty-second Rest/Note - 6/32

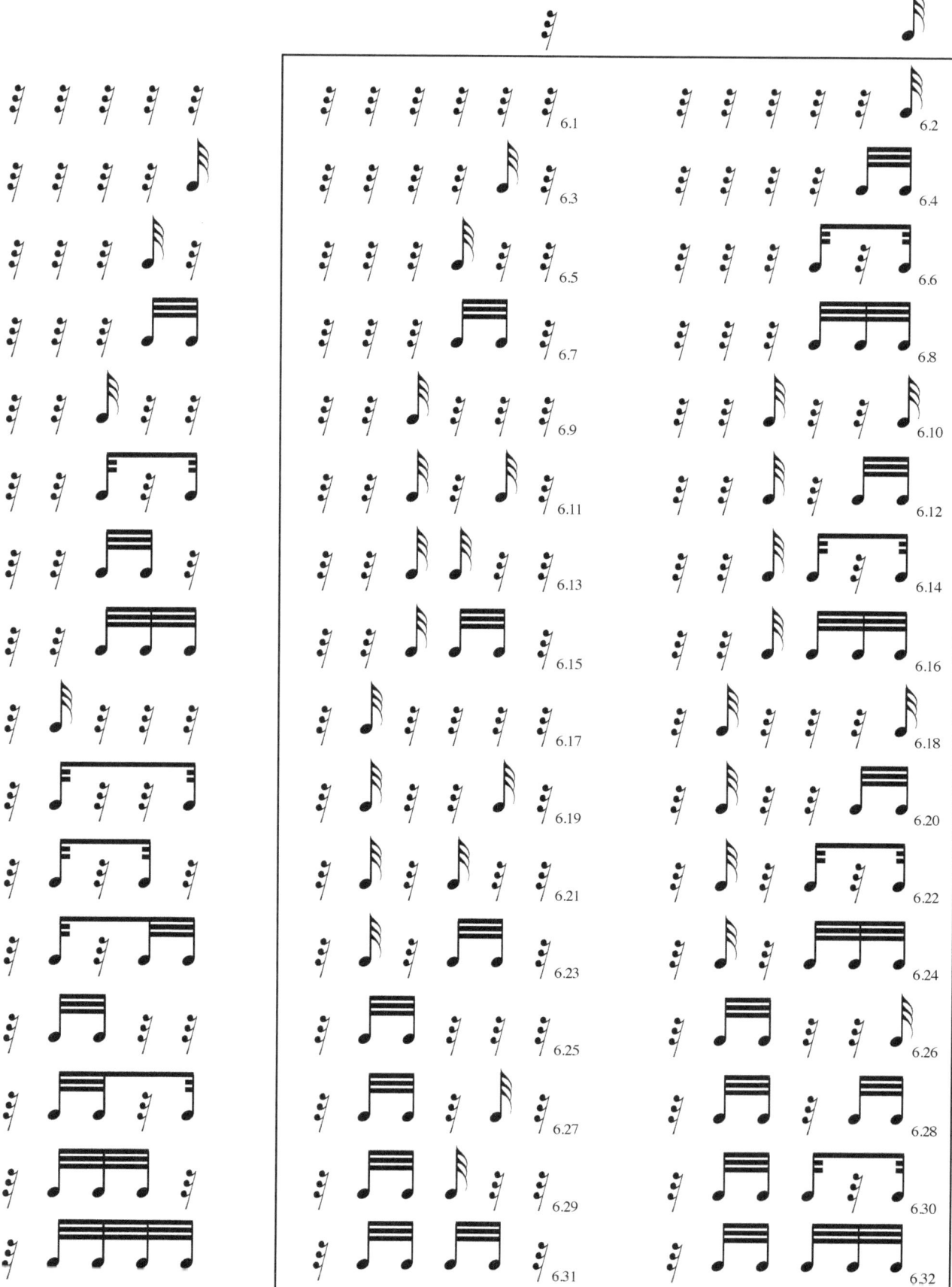

Level 6 Event Point Patterns
Thirty-second Rest/Note - 6/32 (cont'd)

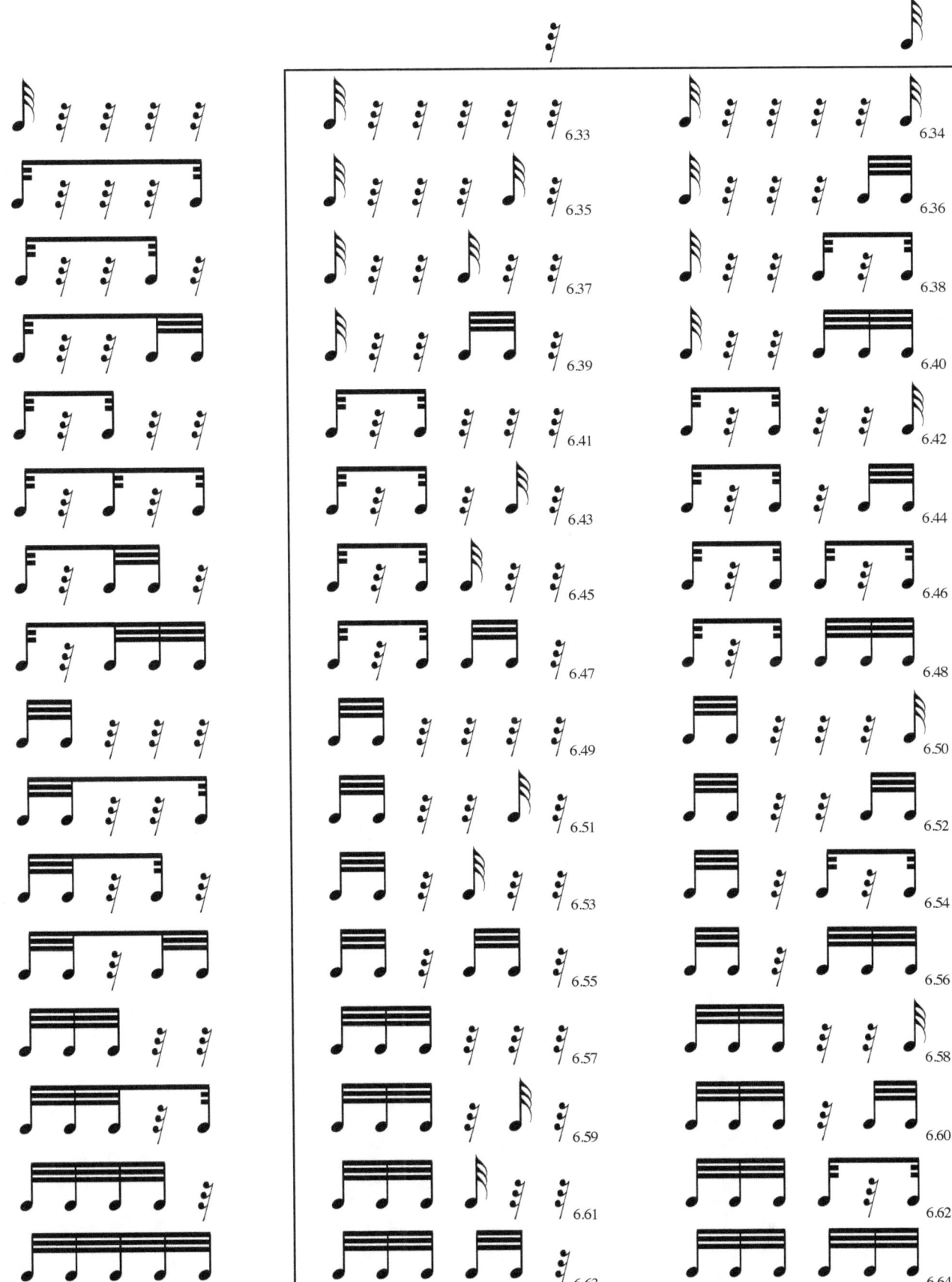

Music Measure Presentation of the Level 6 Event Point Patterns in Compound Meters

The following group of patterns are the Level 6 event point possibilities as they occur in compound meters (consisting of **two** beat notes, each divided into **three** initial parts).

They are presented in their respective music measure contexts of 6/2, 6/4, 6/8, 6/16 and 6/32.

For practical reading purposes, we are dotting beat rests and notes to re-enforce the compound beat context and to reduce the number of individual rests.

Doing so does change the note duration, but not the initial location in time **where** the sound event occurs. This perspective remains our primary emphasis. The more exact and literal versions of the patterns are found in the preceding binary combination tables (pp. 76-85).

To apply the practice methods discussed on page 35:

- **Read and Play** the patterns

- **Sing** the patterns

- **Audiate** (generate the sound in your mind) and **Visualize** performing the patterns

A Useful Practice Application of the 6/8 Patterns

There are sixty-four basic 6/8 event point possibilities at the beat level. The number of 9/8 beat patterns expand to 512, and the 12/8 beat possibilities grow to 4,096.

While the 9/8 and 12/8 combinations exceed the limits of this book, you can use the two pages of 6/8 patterns to practice these larger meters. Simply choose either one or two measures, and combine them with any one of the 6/8 measures.

For **all instruments**, this simple exercise can use used to develop rhythmic improvisation skills.

For **drummers**, the patterns can be used as accents to build fills around. Additionally, doubling, tripling or even quadrupling single-stroke rolls using these patterns will provide a great deal of material for explorations.

Level 6 Event Point Patterns
Compound Beat - 6/2

Level 6 Event Point Patterns
Compound Beat - 6/2 (cont'd)

Level 6 Event Point Patterns
Compound Beat - 6/4

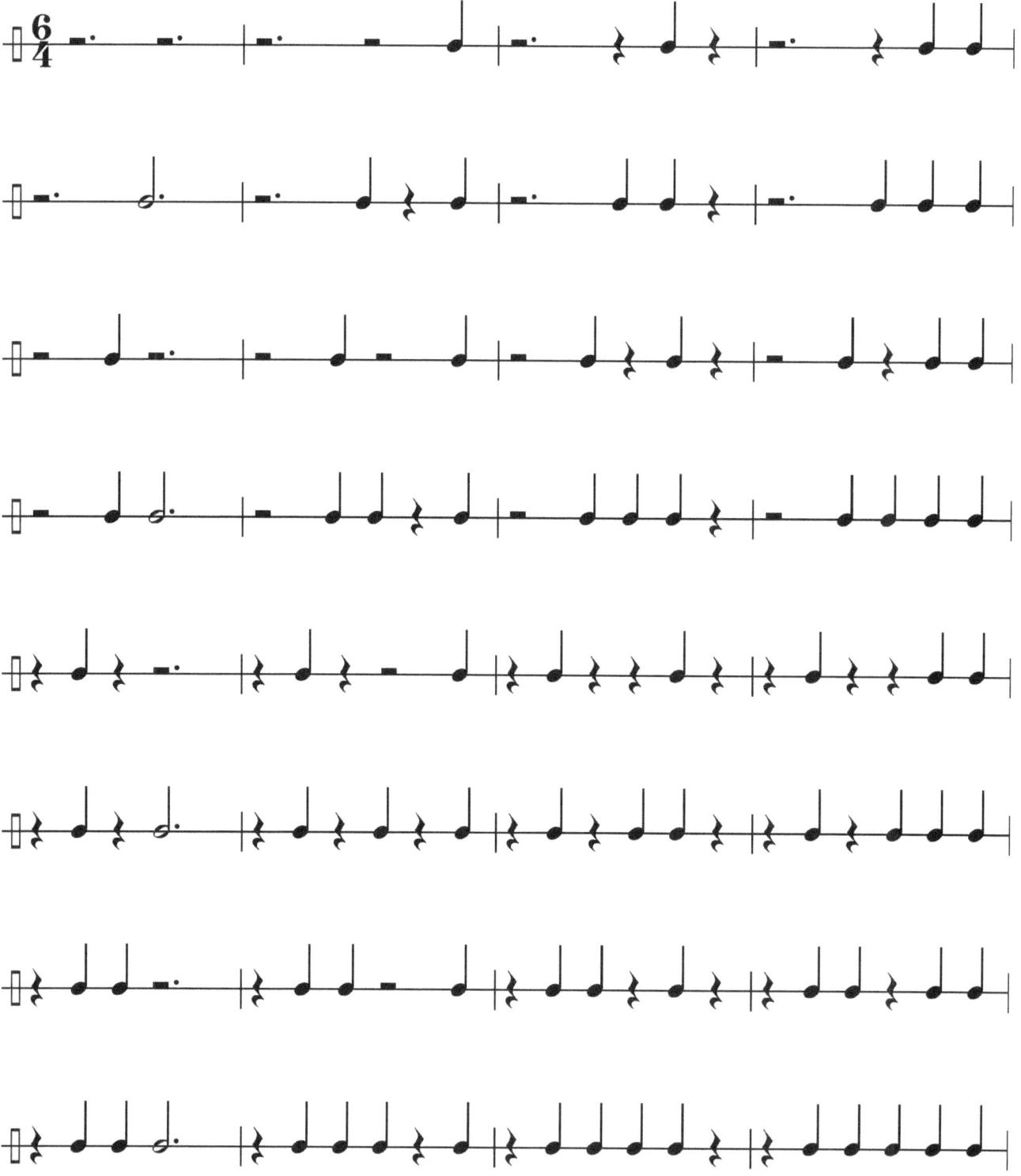

Level 6 Event Point Patterns
Compound Beat - 6/4 (cont'd)

Level 6 Event Point Patterns
Compound Beat - 6/8

Level 6 Event Point Patterns
Compound Beat - 6/8 (cont'd)

Level 6 Event Point Patterns
Compound Beat - 6/16

Level 6 Event Point Patterns
Compound Beat - 6/16 (cont'd)

Level 6 Event Point Patterns
Compound Beat - 6/32

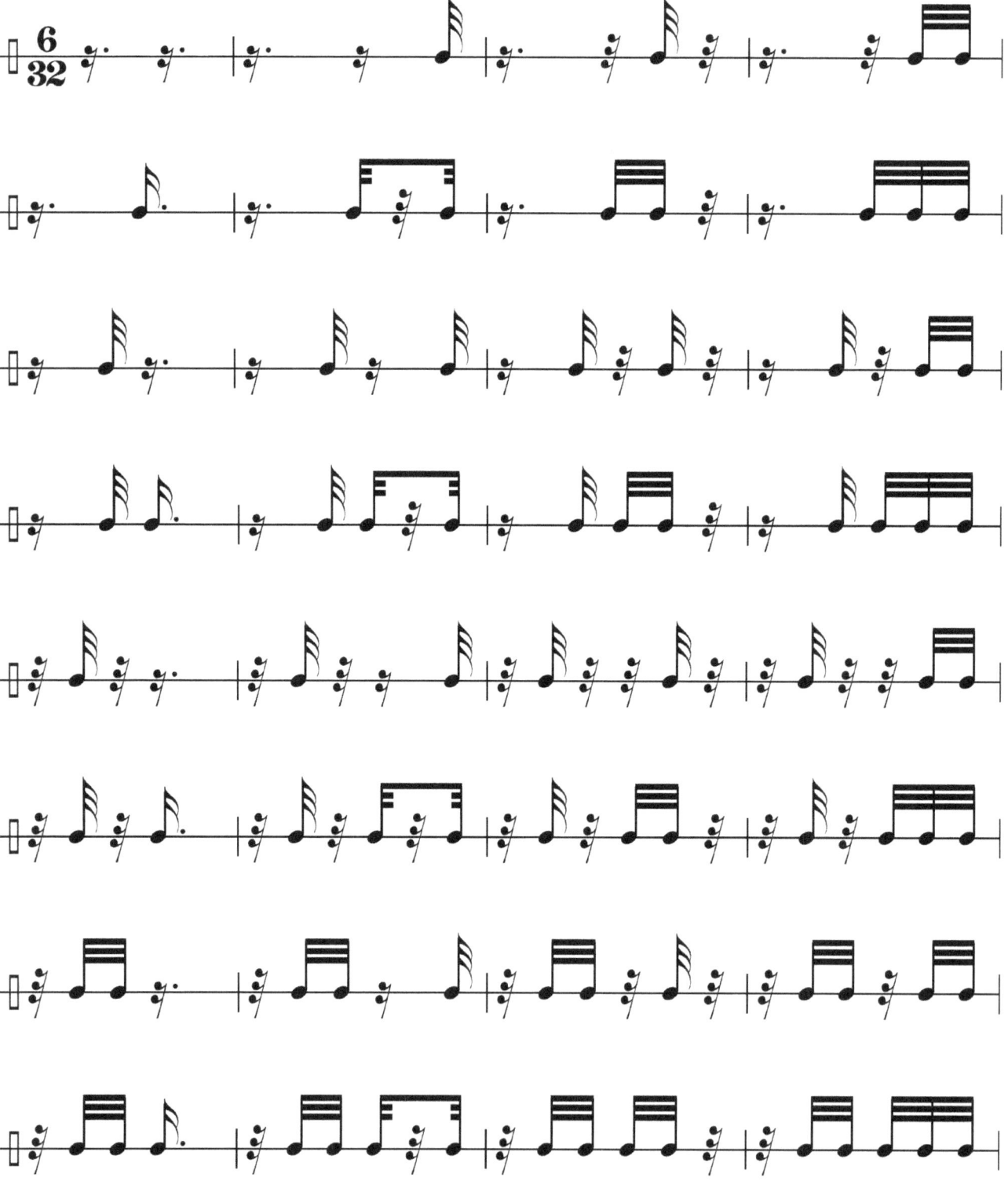

Level 6 Event Point Patterns
Compound Beat - 6/32 (cont'd)

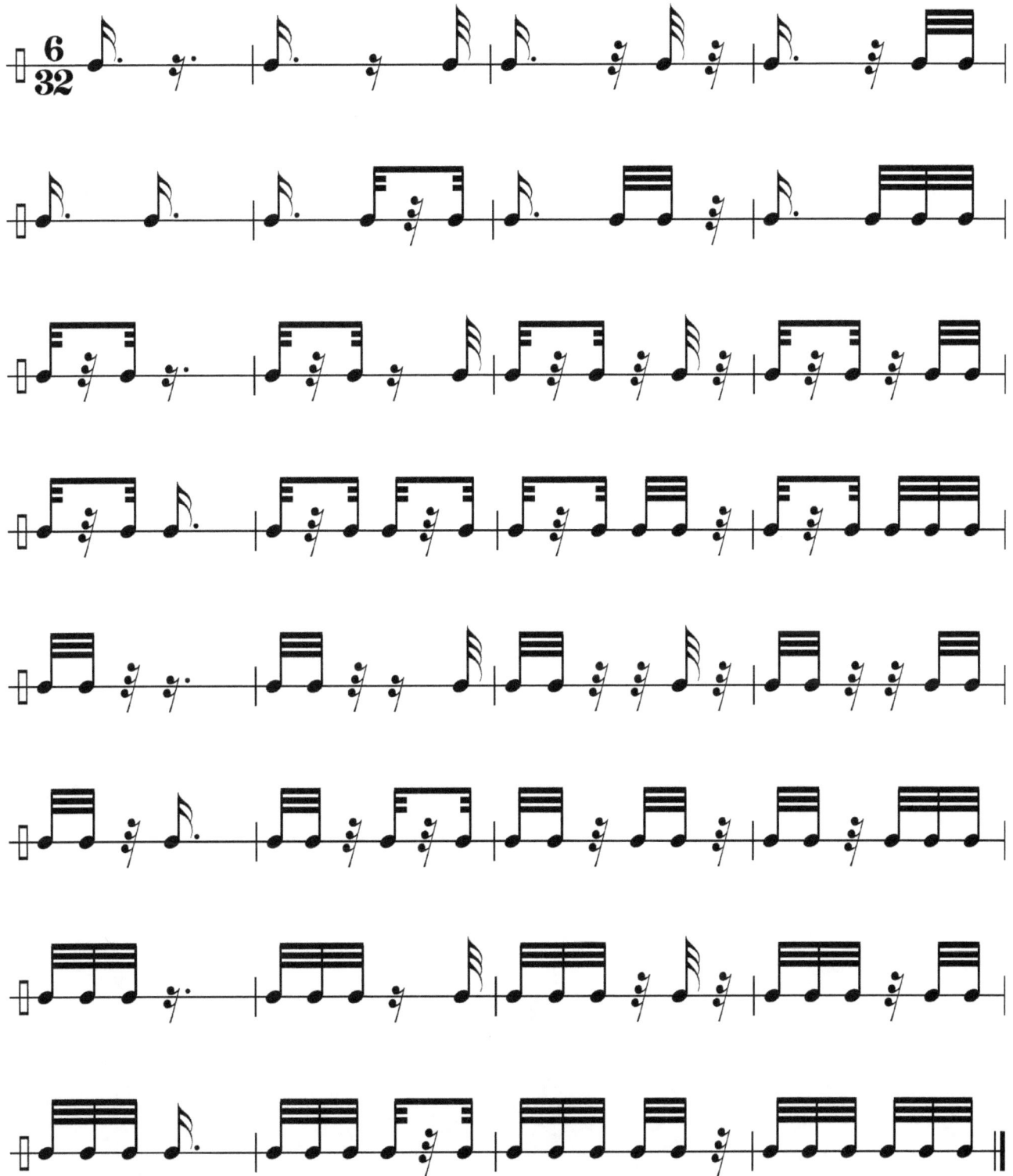

Level 6 Event Point Patterns as Simple Beat Divisions

The following group of patterns are the Level 6 event point possibilities occurring as simple beat divisions (consisting of **three** beat notes, each divided into **two** initial parts).

We will be beaming the divided beats to emphasize their **duple** groupings. While this does change the overall contour of the patterns compared to what we saw in the compound beat context, the number of event point possibilities (64) remains identical to those found in the compound beat tables.

The Binary Rhythm Indexing System
Applied to Level 6 Event Point Patterns

Simple Beat Division

We previously discussed the relative aspect of the Binary Rhythm Pattern Indexing System in Part II, page 30. Applied to the simple beat division version of the Level 6 event point patterns, we experience them in the context of **three** beat notes, each divided into **two** initial parts.

The BIN's (binary indexing numbers) assigned to the following group of patterns do not specify sextuplet, compound beat, or simple beat division contexts. They are used to identify the event point level and the sequence in which the rest/note combinations are generated.

Level 6 Event Point Patterns
Simple Beat Division - 3/2

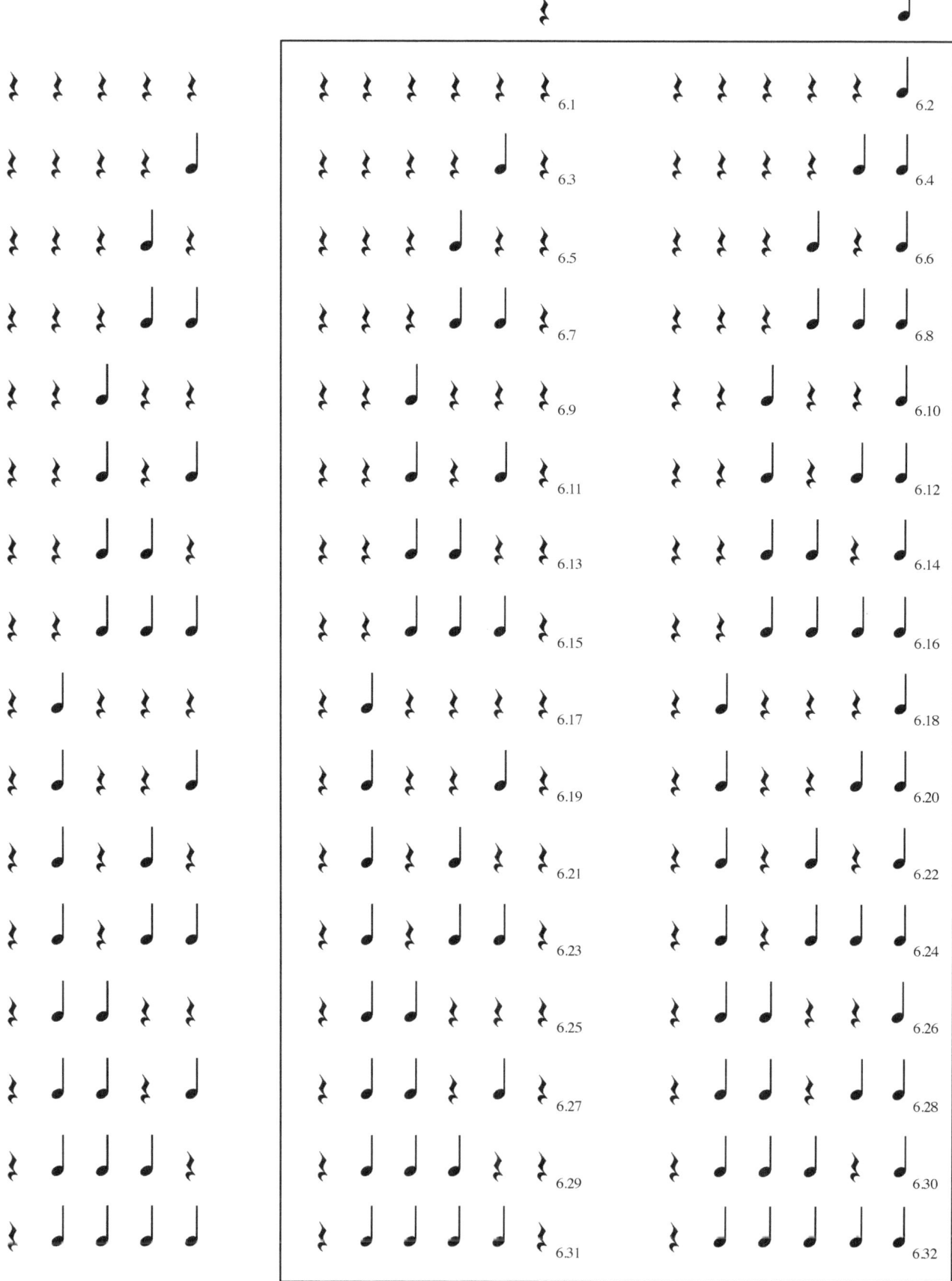

Level 6 Event Point Patterns
Simple Beat Division - 3/2 (cont'd)

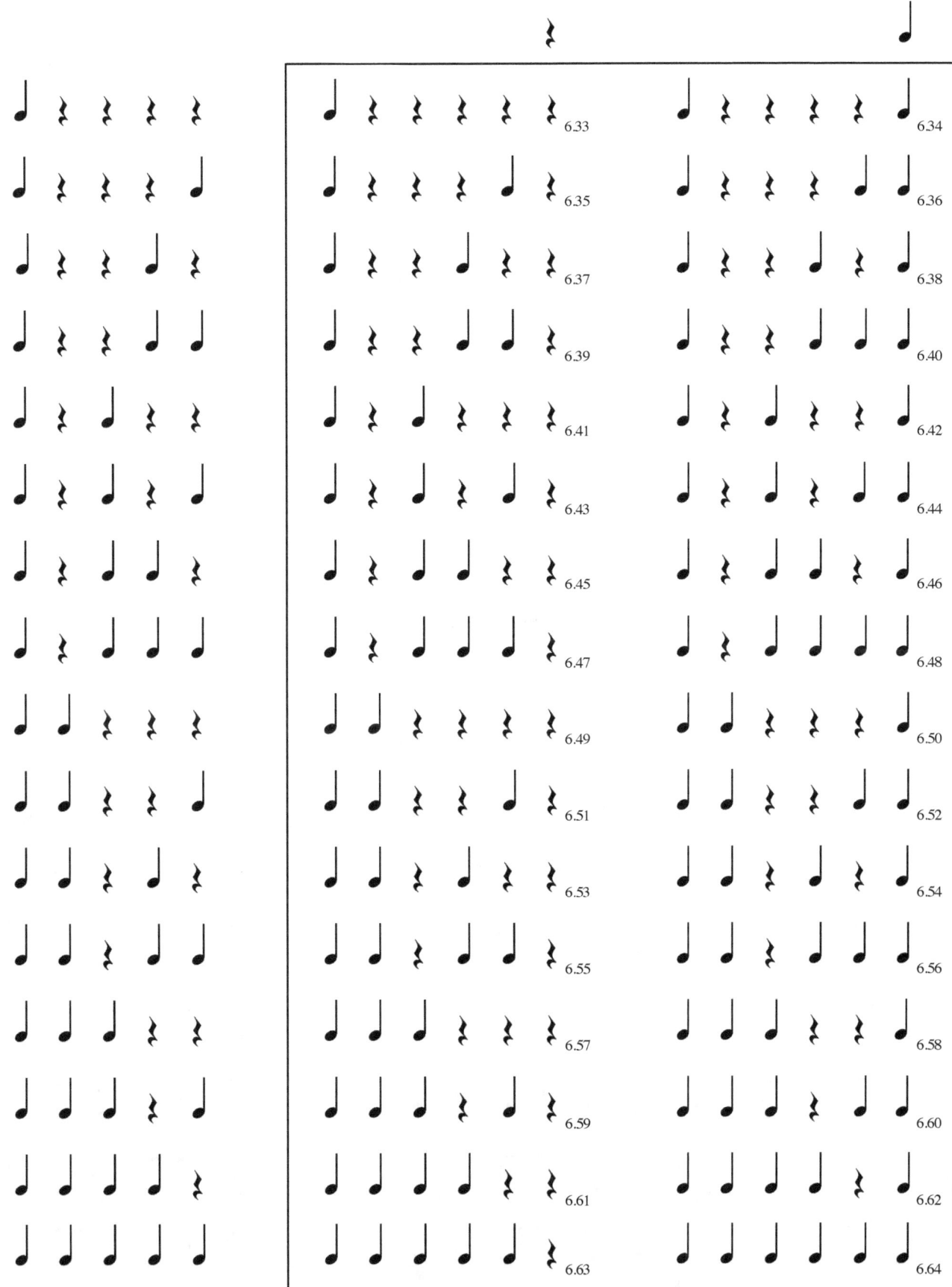

Level 6 Event Point Patterns
Simple Beat Division - 3/4

Level 6 Event Point Patterns
Simple Beat Division - 3/4 (cont'd)

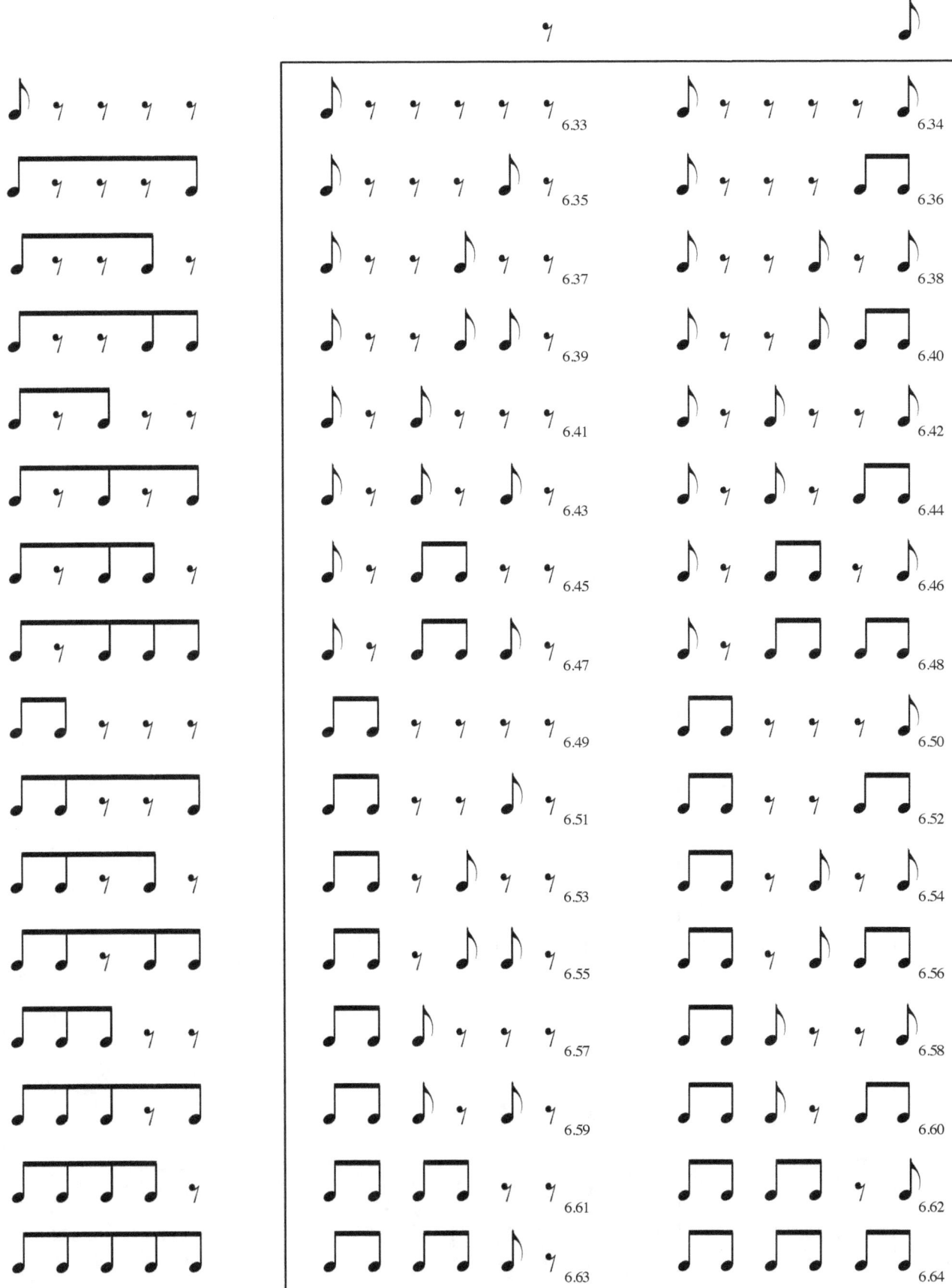

Level 6 Event Point Patterns
Simple Beat Division - 3/8

Level 6 Event Point Patterns
Simple Beat Division - 3/8 (cont'd)

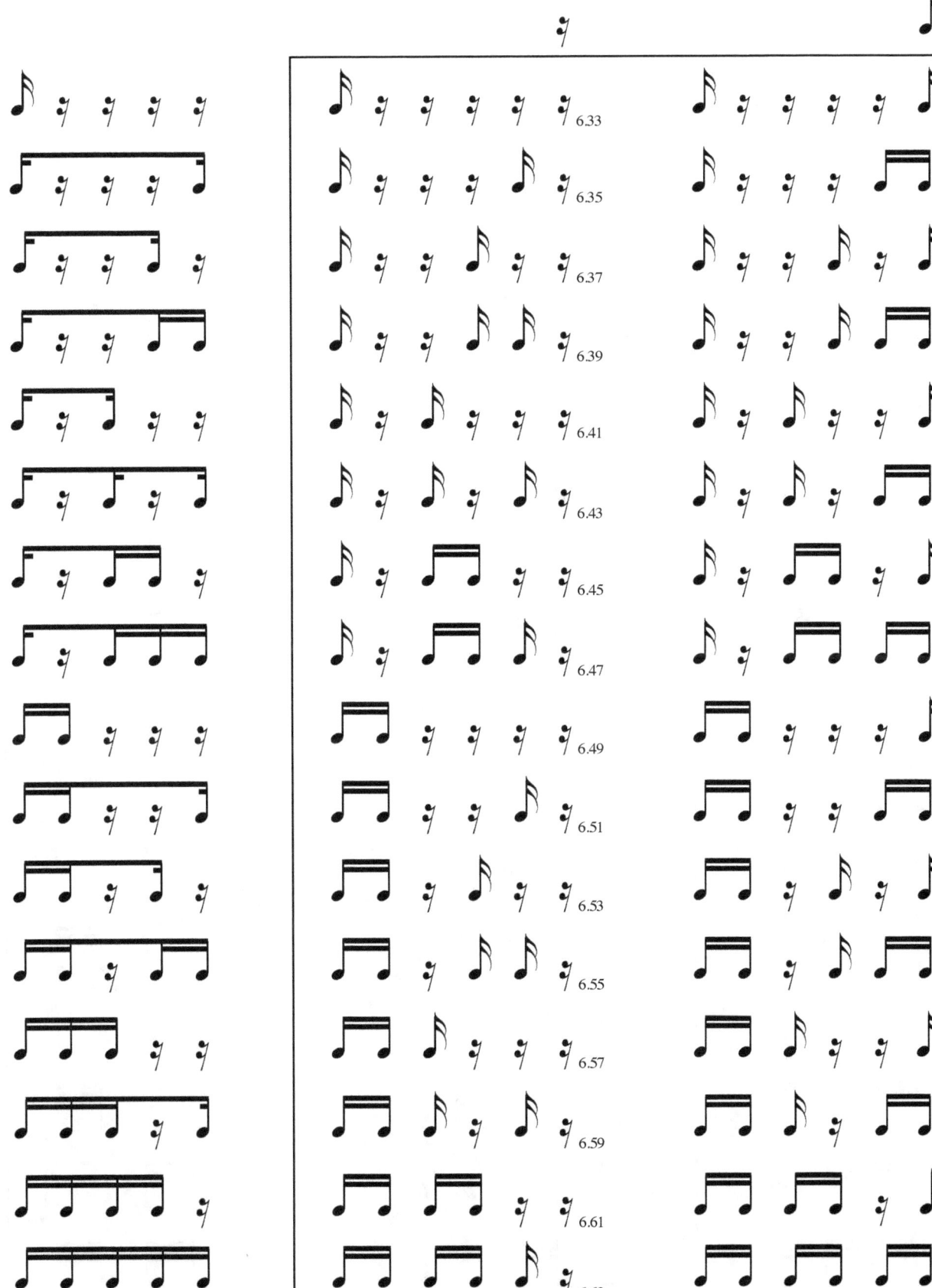

Level 6 Event Point Patterns
Simple Beat Division - 3/16

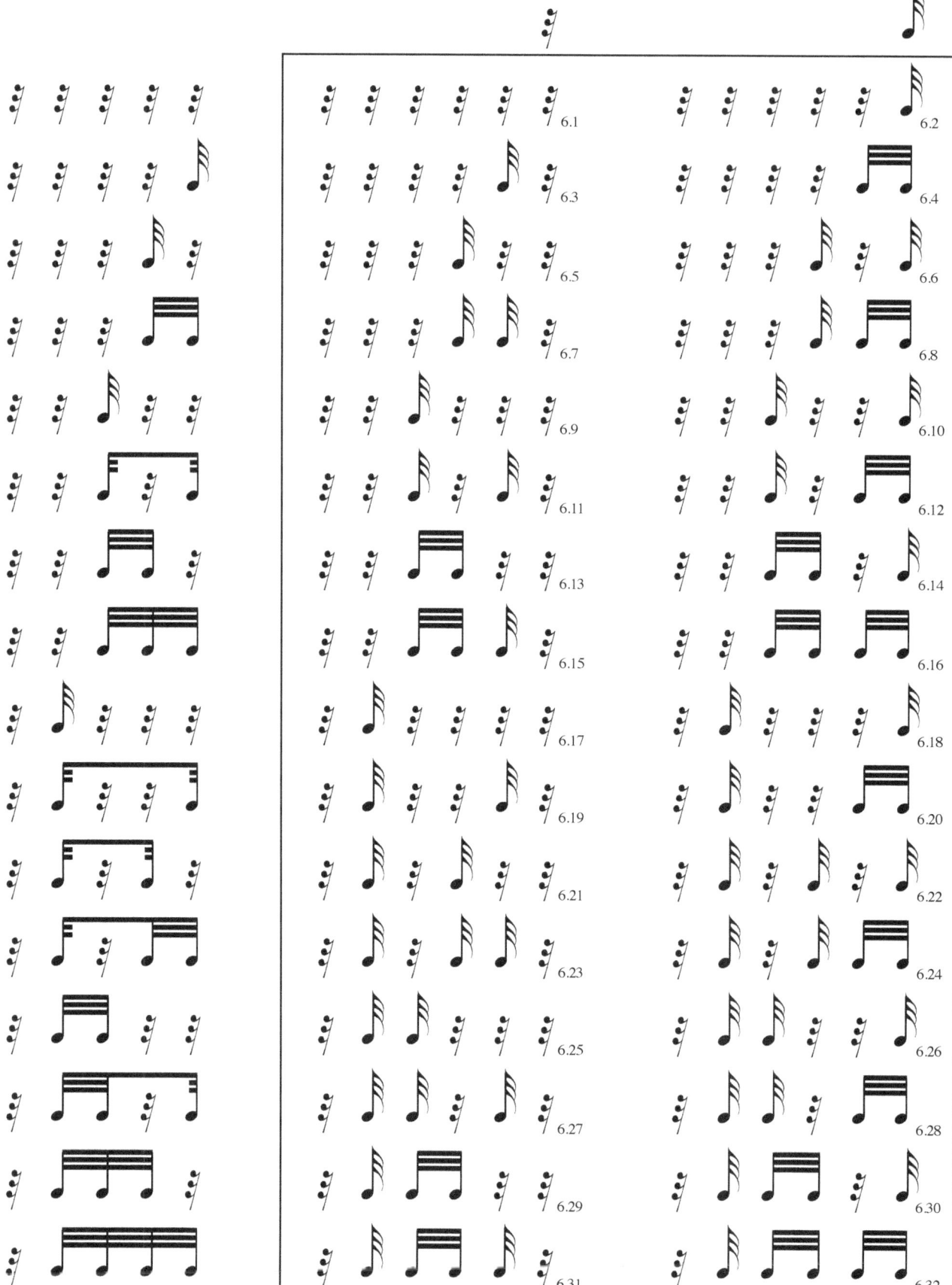

Level 6 Event Point Patterns
Simple Beat Division - 3/16 (cont'd)

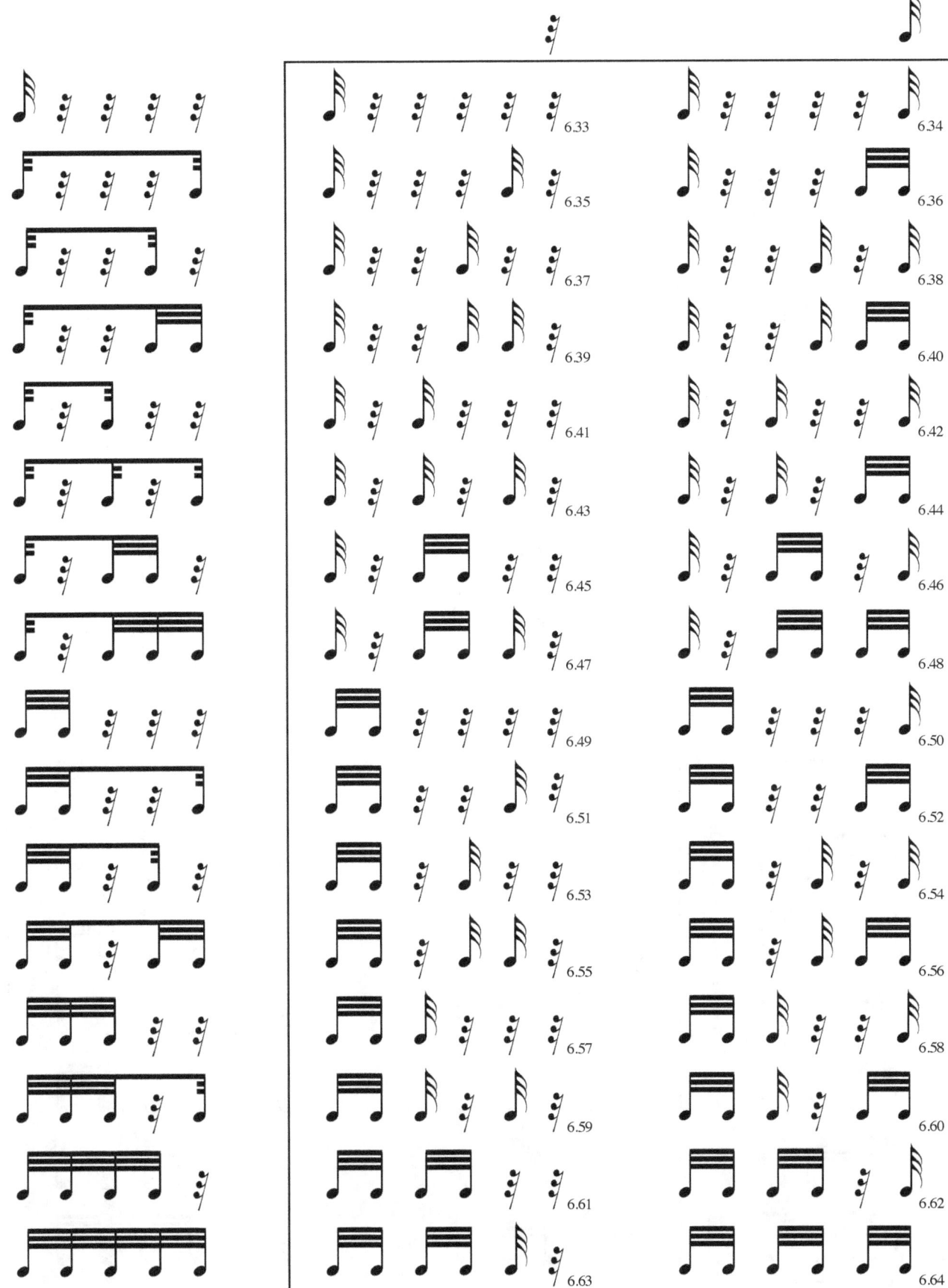

Level 6 Event Point Patterns
Simple Beat Division - 3/32

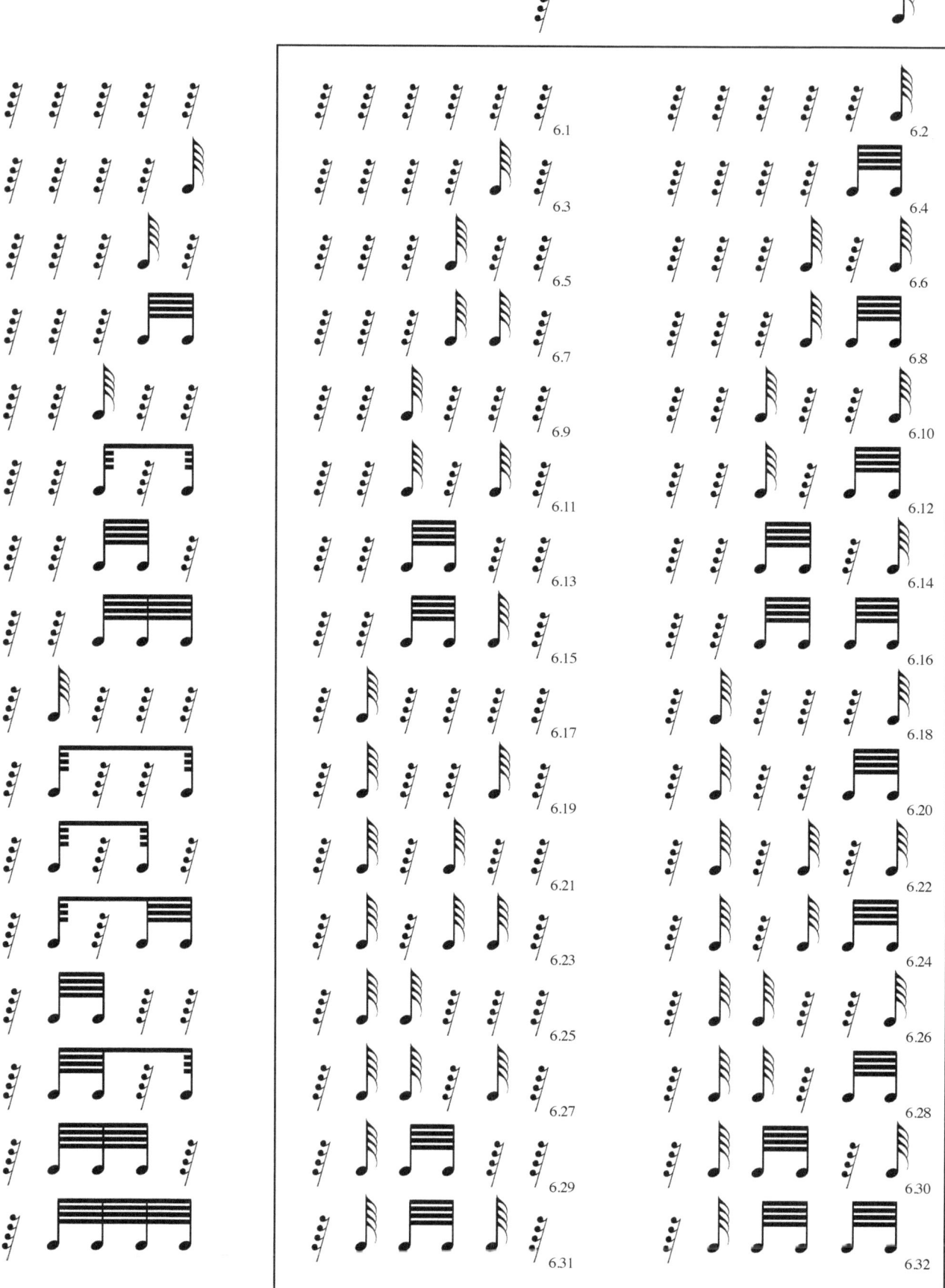

Level 6 Event Point Patterns
Simple Beat Division - 3/32 (cont'd)

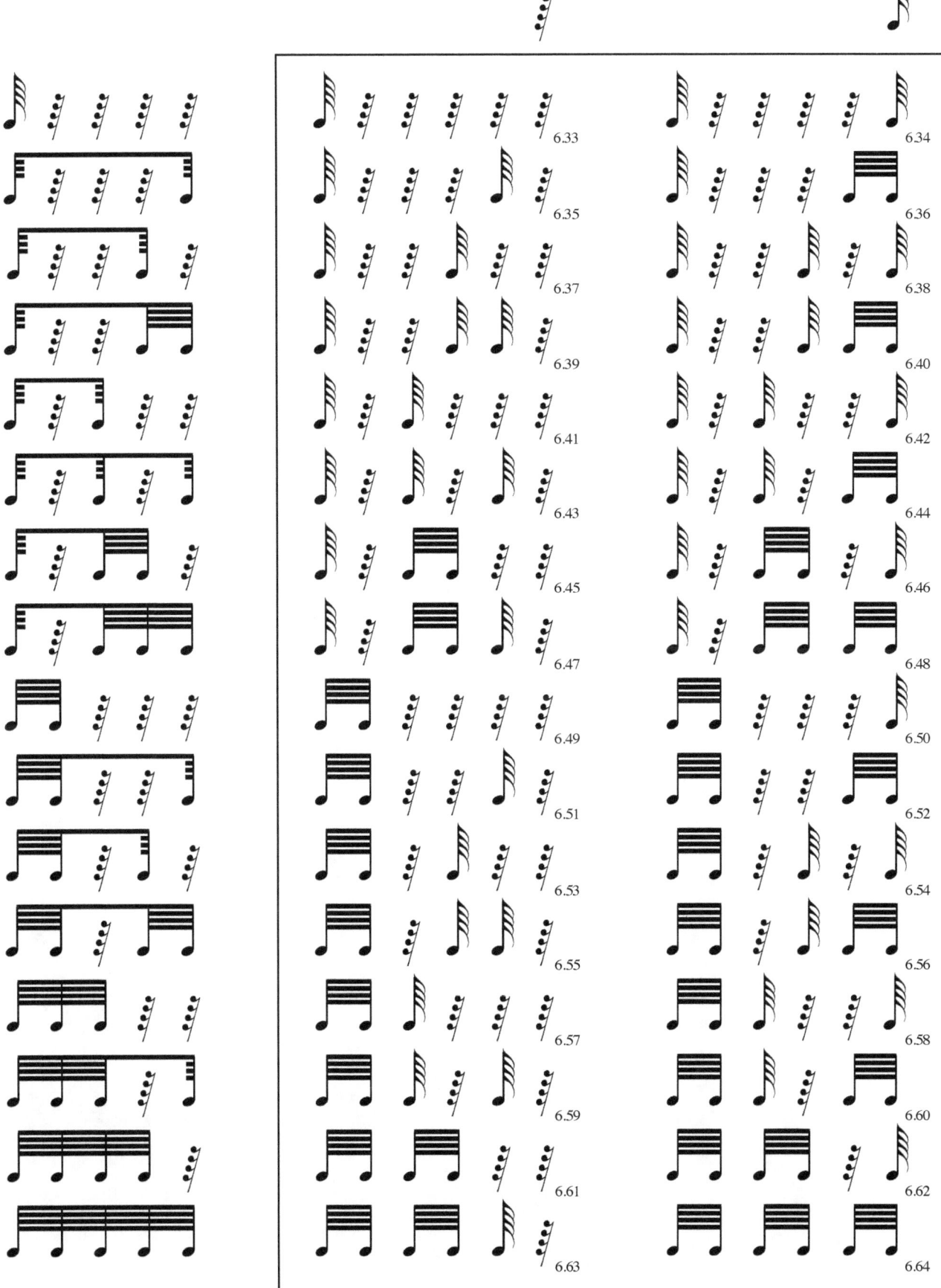

Music Measure Presentation of the Level 6 Event Point Patterns as Simple Beat Divisions

The following group of patterns are the Level 6 event point possibilities as they occur in simple beat division meters (consisting of **three** beat notes, each divided into **two** initial parts).

They are presented in their respective music measure contexts of 3/2, 3/4, 3/8, 3/16 and 3/32.

For practical reading purposes, we are grouping the individual rests where possible (e.g., two successive eighth rests starting on the beat become one quarter rest).

The more exact and literal versions of the patterns are found in the preceding binary combination tables (pp. 100-109).

To apply the practice methods discussed on page 35:

- **Read and Play** the patterns

- **Sing** the patterns

- **Audiate** (generate the sound in your mind) and **Visualize** performing the patterns

Some Thoughts About the Extended Value of 3/4

The simple beat divisions of the Level 6 event point pattern possibilities have very useful applications when presented in the context of 3/4. Jazz and Latin musicians will discover the core patterns are invaluable for developing standard phrase recognition and improvisational skills.

But there's also an extended value to 3/4, one which may be used by **all** players who want to explore advanced odd meter contexts.

Every odd time signature grouping consist of two and three-beat meter combinations. Master the patterns in 2/4 and 3/4, and you've seen all the elements in 5/4. Add another measure of 2/4, and you've covered the essential combinations in 7/4. Regardless of how you combine the groups of two and three beats, you will have seen the fundamental odd meter building blocks.

Additional mastering of the other simple beat division contexts (3/2, 3/8, 3/16, 3/32) will lay foundation for exploring more advanced, complex odd meters. The further you can move beyond the traditional constraints of 4/4, the broader your rhythmic experiences can become. The simplicity of 3/4 serves as a powerful gateway to that liberation.

Level 6 Event Point Patterns
Simple Beat Division - 3/2

Level 6 Event Point Patterns
Simple Beat Division - 3/2 (cont'd)

Level 6 Event Point Patterns
Simple Beat Division - 3/4

Level 6 Event Point Patterns
Simple Beat Division - 3/4 (cont'd)

Level 6 Event Point Patterns
Simple Beat Division - 3/8

Level 6 Event Point Patterns
Simple Beat Division - 3/8 (cont'd)

Level 6 Event Point Patterns
Simple Beat Division - 3/16

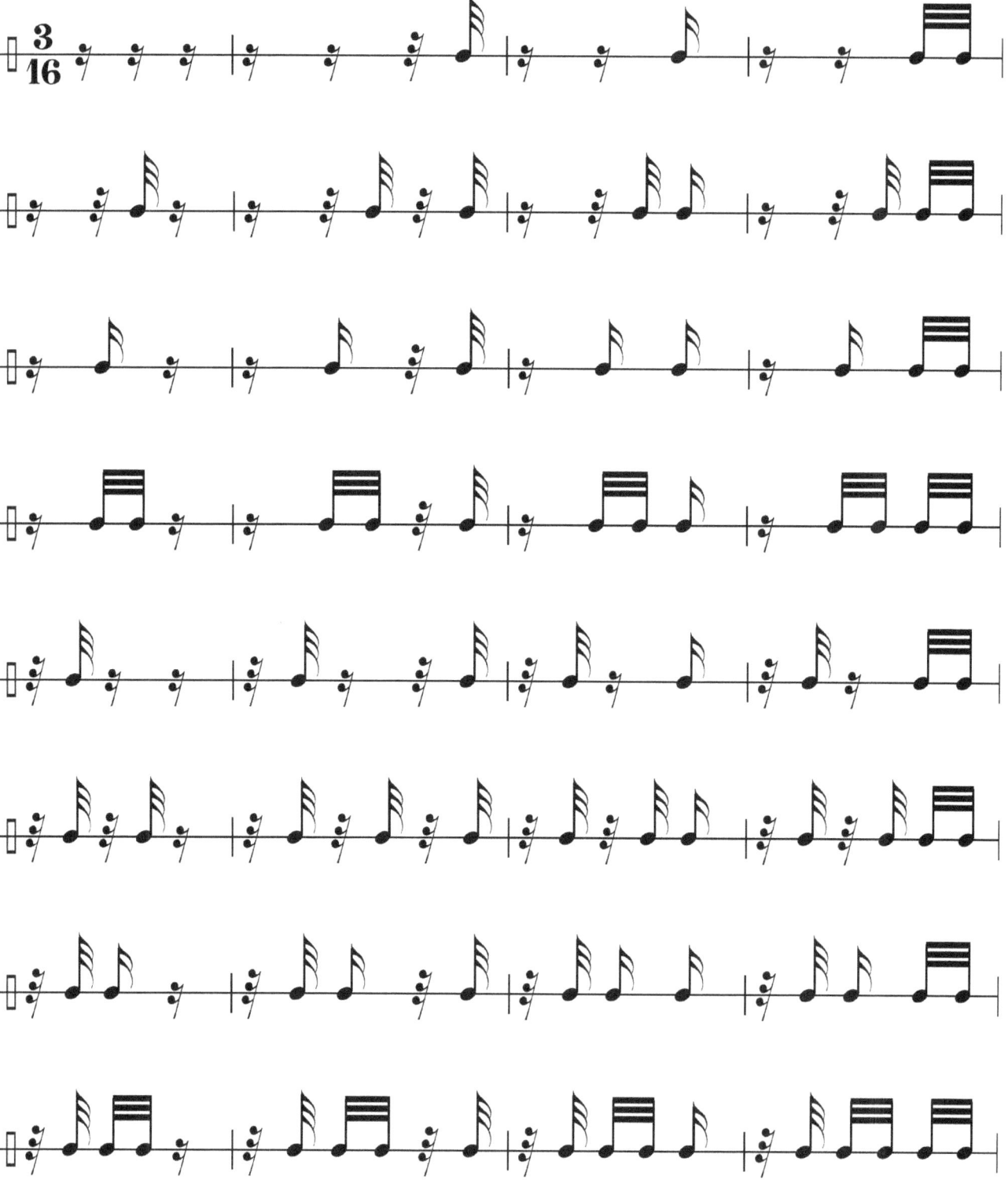

Level 6 Event Point Patterns
Simple Beat Division - 3/16 (cont'd)

Level 6 Event Point Patterns
Simple Beat Division - 3/32

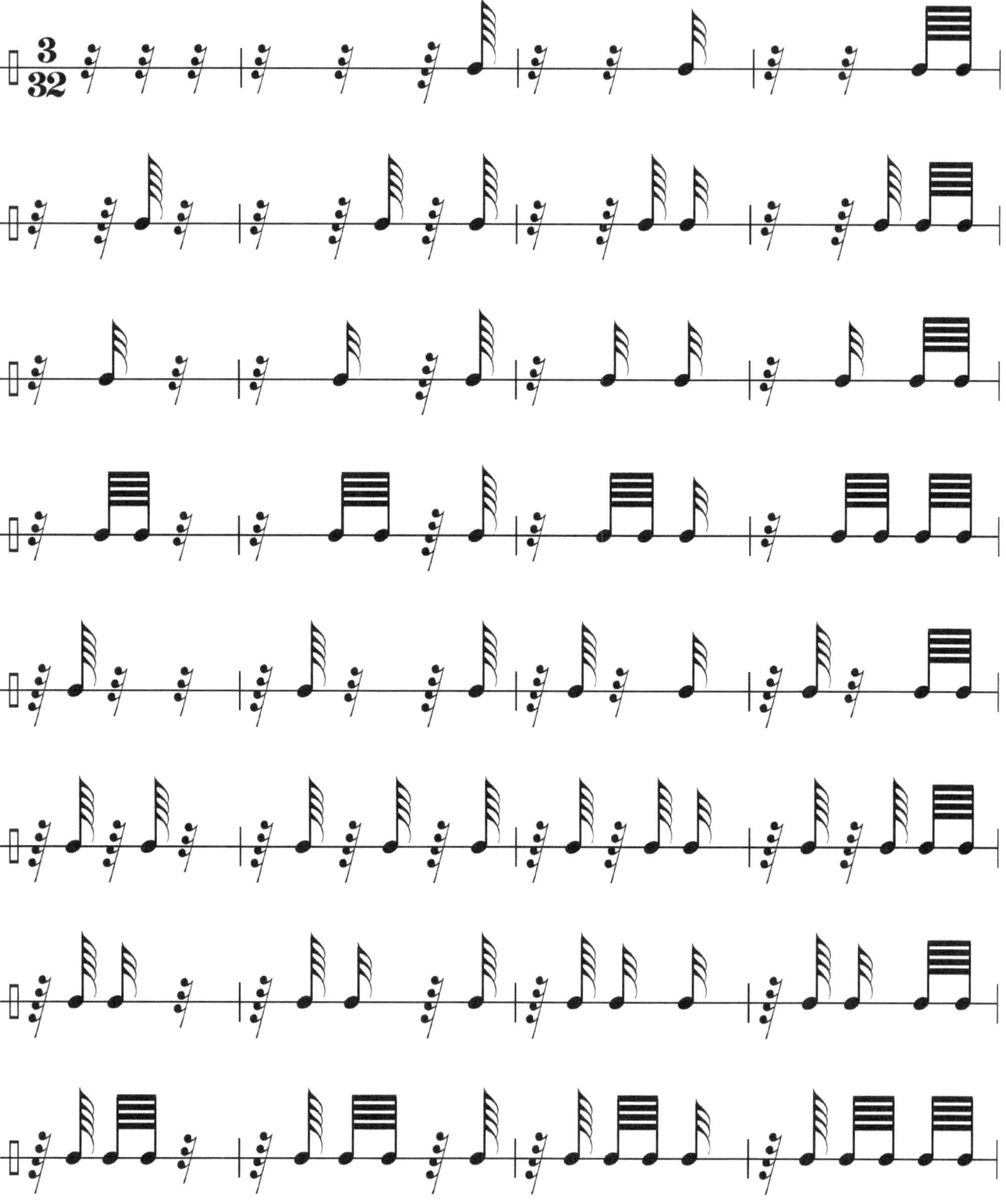

Level 6 Event Point Patterns
Simple Beat Division - 3/32 (cont'd)

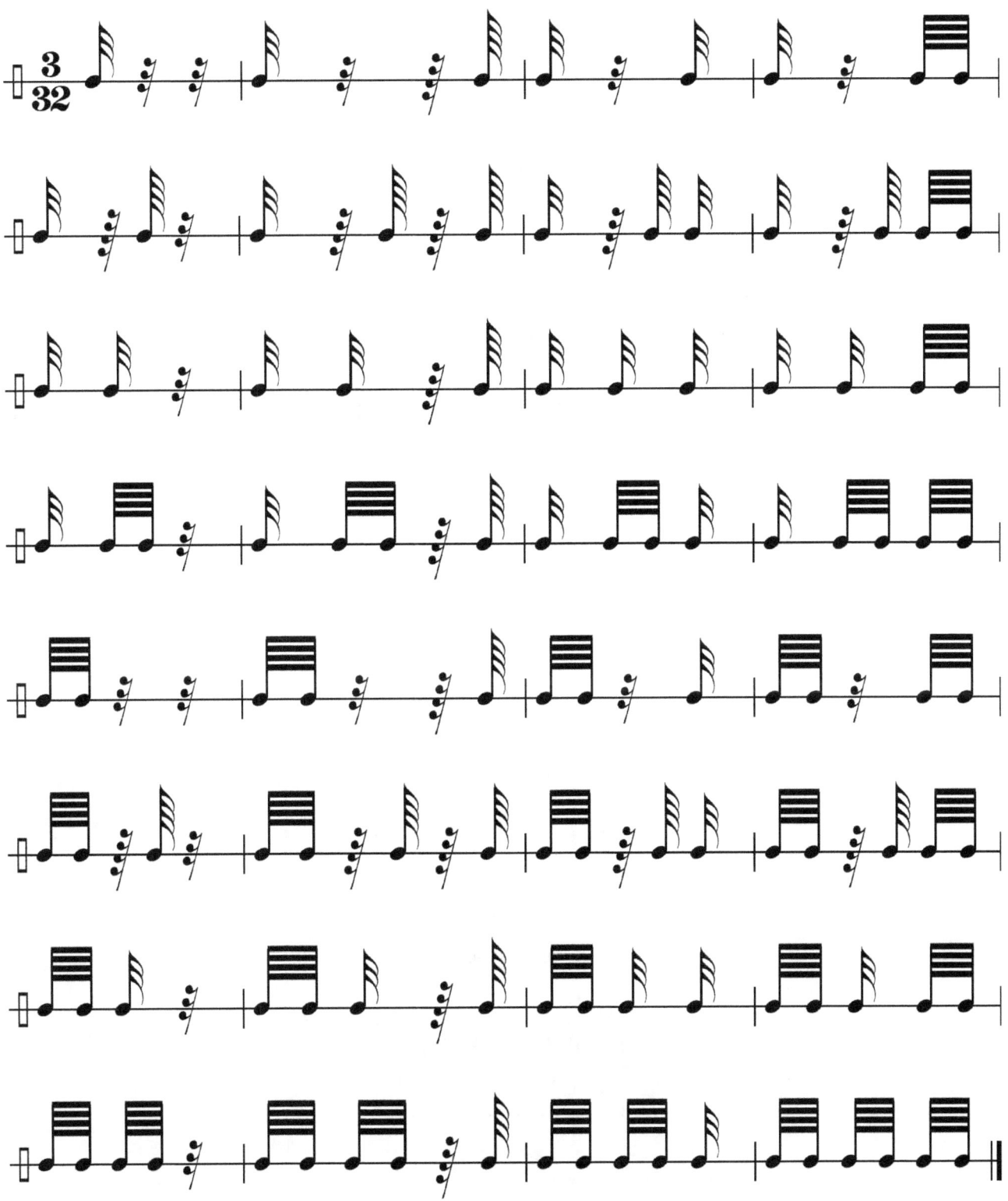

Level 7
Event Point Patterns

In this section, we will:

- create the event point possibilities for Level 7 by systematically pairing 0's and 1's in four binary combination tables with the Level 6 possibilities

- substitute the 0/1 combinations with five beat note values (half, quarter, eighth, sixteenth and thirty-second)

- place these re-written patterns in their respective music measure formats for reading/practice in 7/2, 7/4, 7/8, 7/16 and 7/32

There are **128** Level 7 Event Point Patterns.

```
1  *
2  * *
3  * * *
4  * * * *
5  * * * * *
6  * * * * * *
7  0 1 1 0 1 0 1
8  * * * * * * * *
```

Level 7 Event Point Patterns - Discussion

We can become familiar with how to conceive and play our seven-note groupings by first viewing them as beat notes in various metric contexts. We can then practice them as polyrhythms (septuplets), using a variation on the method that we explored (p. 53) with our five-note groupings (quintuplets):

- Play all the patterns in the following section, emphasizing the first beat of each measure

- Play each measure **twice**, counting them as **1**-2-3-4-5-6-7, **2**-2-3-4-5-6-7

As a result, by performing two measures of 16th beat notes of 7/16 in **Figure 31**...

Figure 31. *Sixteenth Notes as Beat Notes in 7/16*

... you are also, in effect, practicing and performing two groups of septuplets in one measure of 2/4, seen in **Figure 32**. Emphasizing the first beat in both figures helps you develop a feel for the initial note that the polyrhythm version occurs over. If the sixteenth notes in these figures are played at the same tempo, they sound identical, despite occurring in different metric contexts.

Figure 32. *Sixteenth Notes as Accented Septuplets in 2/4*

This approach also applies to mastering more complex patterns. If you can progress from quarter notes, to eighths and then sixteenths, as in the **Figure 33** sequence...

Figure 33. *Identical Sounding Seven-note Patterns Written in 7/4, 7/8, 7/16*

... you can eventually advance to versions of the same pattern in **Figure 34**. The first 7:4 ratio means "seven sixteenth notes played in the space of four sixteenth notes," and the second 7:4 ratio means "seven eighth notes played in the space of four eighth notes."

Figure 34. *Identically Shaped Septuplets Played Over Groups of 1 and 2 Beat Notes in 3/4*

Exercise # 5

Figures 35-37 let you play and hear septuplets as ratios of 7 against 2, 7 against 3, and 7 against 4. The 7/4 measures provide an easy-to-read method of conceptualizing the ratios, followed by groups of septuplets depicting how the notes in the ratios occur in relation to each other. Tap the top notes of each measure with your right hand and the bottom notes with your left hand. The tempo of the top notes in the 7/4 measures can be used as the tempo of the septuplet notes in the respective 2/4, 3/4, and 4/4 measures, making both examples sound identical.

[*Author's note: You can hear these three sets of ratios played using Wolfram Winkel's* Polyrhythm *app for your iPod, iPhone or iPad, or by visiting his book site,* www.fiveoverthree.com]

The Sound of 7 against 2

Figure 35. *Septuplet Sound Played in the Space of 2 Notes*

The Sound of 7 against 3

Figure 36. *Septuplet Sound Played in the Space of 3 Notes*

The Sound of 7 against 4

Figure 37. *Septuplet Sound Played in the Space of 4 Notes*

As with the quintuplet exercises on page 55, playing the patterns against 2, 3, and 4 beat groupings of beat notes lays the foundation for very complex polyrhythm exploration and improvisation.

Exercise # 6

The next skill we want to master is playing simple septuplets shifted across the measure. **Figures 38-43** depict polyrhythms using ratios based on note values. In **Figure 38**, the 7:4 ratio literally means, "Seven eighth notes played in the space of four eighth notes." However, you could also **hear** it as seven eighth notes played in the space of two quarter notes or even eight sixteenth notes. The mathematics of any polyrhythm is relative to the notation used to express it, but its sound shape remains absolute.

7 against 2 Beat Notes

Figure 38. *Septuplet Played Over Beats 1 and 2 in 4/4*

Figure 39. *Septuplet Played Over Beats 2 and 3 in 4/4*

Figure 40. Septuplet Played Over Beats 3 and 4 in 4/4

7 against 3 Beat Notes

Figure 41. *Septuplet Played Over Beats 1, 2 and 3 in 4/4*

Figure 42. *Septuplet Played Over Beats 2, 3, and 4 in 4/4*

7 against 4 Beat Notes

Figure 43. *Septuplet Played Over Beats 1, 2, 3 and 4 in 4/4*

When these six exercises are mastered, you can advance to playing all 128 seven-note possibilities within these ratios. You can also apply the doubling and tripling of the initial notes, as explained on page 57.

Level 7 Event Point Patterns
0/1

	0	1
0 0 0 0 0 0	$0000000_{7.1}$	$0000001_{7.2}$
0 0 0 0 0 1	$0000010_{7.3}$	$0000011_{7.4}$
0 0 0 0 1 0	$0000100_{7.5}$	$0000101_{7.6}$
0 0 0 0 1 1	$0000110_{7.7}$	$0000111_{7.8}$
0 0 0 1 0 0	$0001000_{7.9}$	$0001001_{7.10}$
0 0 0 1 0 1	$0001010_{7.11}$	$0001011_{7.12}$
0 0 0 1 1 0	$0001100_{7.13}$	$0001101_{7.14}$
0 0 0 1 1 1	$0001110_{7.15}$	$0001111_{7.16}$
0 0 1 0 0 0	$0010000_{7.17}$	$0010001_{7.18}$
0 0 1 0 0 1	$0010010_{7.19}$	$0010011_{7.20}$
0 0 1 0 1 0	$0010100_{7.21}$	$0010101_{7.22}$
0 0 1 0 1 1	$0010110_{7.23}$	$0010111_{7.24}$
0 0 1 1 0 0	$0011000_{7.25}$	$0011001_{7.26}$
0 0 1 1 0 1	$0011010_{7.27}$	$0011011_{7.28}$
0 0 1 1 1 0	$0011100_{7.29}$	$0011101_{7.30}$
0 0 1 1 1 1	$0011110_{7.31}$	$0011111_{7.32}$

Level 7 Event Point Patterns
0/1 (cont'd)

	0	1
0 1 0 0 0 0	$0100000_{7.33}$	$0100001_{7.34}$
0 1 0 0 0 1	$0100010_{7.35}$	$0100011_{7.36}$
0 1 0 0 1 0	$0100100_{7.37}$	$0100101_{7.38}$
0 1 0 0 1 1	$0100110_{7.39}$	$0100111_{7.40}$
0 1 0 1 0 0	$0101000_{7.41}$	$0101001_{7.42}$
0 1 0 1 0 1	$0101010_{7.43}$	$0101011_{7.44}$
0 1 0 1 1 0	$0101100_{7.45}$	$0101101_{7.46}$
0 1 0 1 1 1	$0101110_{7.47}$	$0101111_{7.48}$
0 1 1 0 0 0	$0110000_{7.49}$	$0110001_{7.50}$
0 1 1 0 0 1	$0110010_{7.51}$	$0110011_{7.52}$
0 1 1 0 1 0	$0110100_{7.53}$	$0110101_{7.54}$
0 1 1 0 1 1	$0110110_{7.55}$	$0110111_{7.56}$
0 1 1 1 0 0	$0111000_{7.57}$	$0111001_{7.58}$
0 1 1 1 0 1	$0111010_{7.59}$	$0111011_{7.60}$
0 1 1 1 1 0	$0111100_{7.61}$	$0111101_{7.62}$
0 1 1 1 1 1	$0111110_{7.63}$	$0111111_{7.64}$

Level 7 Event Point Patterns
0/1 (cont'd)

	0	1
1 0 0 0 0 0	$1000000_{7.65}$	$1000001_{7.66}$
1 0 0 0 0 1	$1000010_{7.67}$	$1000011_{7.68}$
1 0 0 0 1 0	$1000100_{7.69}$	$1000101_{7.70}$
1 0 0 0 1 1	$1000110_{7.71}$	$1000111_{7.72}$
1 0 0 1 0 0	$1001000_{7.73}$	$1001001_{7.74}$
1 0 0 1 0 1	$1001010_{7.75}$	$1001011_{7.76}$
1 0 0 1 1 0	$1001100_{7.77}$	$1001101_{7.78}$
1 0 0 1 1 1	$1001110_{7.79}$	$1001111_{7.80}$
1 0 1 0 0 0	$1010000_{7.81}$	$1010001_{7.82}$
1 0 1 0 0 1	$1010010_{7.83}$	$1010011_{7.84}$
1 0 1 0 1 0	$1010100_{7.85}$	$1010101_{7.86}$
1 0 1 0 1 1	$1010110_{7.87}$	$1010111_{7.88}$
1 0 1 1 0 0	$1011000_{7.89}$	$1011001_{7.90}$
1 0 1 1 0 1	$1011010_{7.91}$	$1011011_{7.92}$
1 0 1 1 1 0	$1011100_{7.93}$	$1011101_{7.94}$
1 0 1 1 1 1	$1011110_{7.95}$	$1011111_{7.96}$

Level 7 Event Point Patterns
0/1 (cont'd)

	0	1
1 1 0 0 0 0	$1100000_{7.97}$	$1100001_{7.98}$
1 1 0 0 0 1	$1100010_{7.99}$	$1100011_{7.100}$
1 1 0 0 1 0	$1100100_{7.101}$	$1100101_{7.102}$
1 1 0 0 1 1	$1100110_{7.103}$	$1100111_{7.104}$
1 1 0 1 0 0	$1101000_{7.105}$	$1101001_{7.106}$
1 1 0 1 0 1	$1101010_{7.107}$	$1101011_{7.108}$
1 1 0 1 1 0	$1101100_{7.109}$	$1101101_{7.110}$
1 1 0 1 1 1	$1101110_{7.111}$	$1101111_{7.112}$
1 1 1 0 0 0	$1110000_{7.113}$	$1110001_{7.114}$
1 1 1 0 0 1	$1110010_{7.115}$	$1110011_{7.116}$
1 1 1 0 1 0	$1110100_{7.117}$	$1110101_{7.118}$
1 1 1 0 1 1	$1110110_{7.119}$	$1110111_{7.120}$
1 1 1 1 0 0	$1111000_{7.121}$	$1111001_{7.122}$
1 1 1 1 0 1	$1111010_{7.123}$	$1111011_{7.124}$
1 1 1 1 1 0	$1111100_{7.125}$	$1111101_{7.126}$
1 1 1 1 1 1	$1111110_{7.127}$	$1111111_{7.128}$

Level 7 Event Point Patterns
Half Rest/Note

Level 7 Event Point Patterns
Half Rest/Note (cont'd)

Level 7 Event Point Patterns
Half Rest/Note (cont'd)

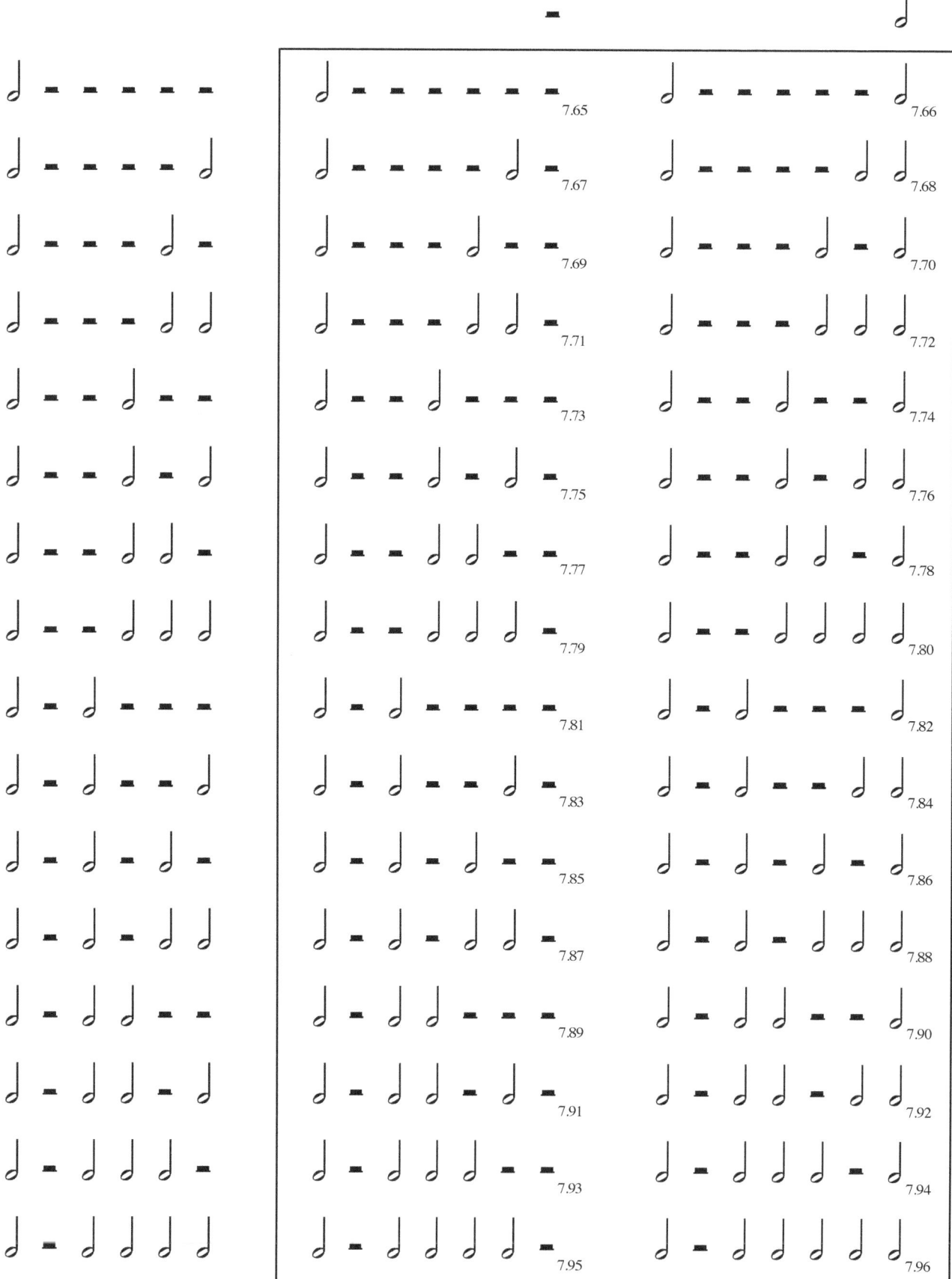

Level 7 Event Point Patterns
Half Rest/Note (cont'd)

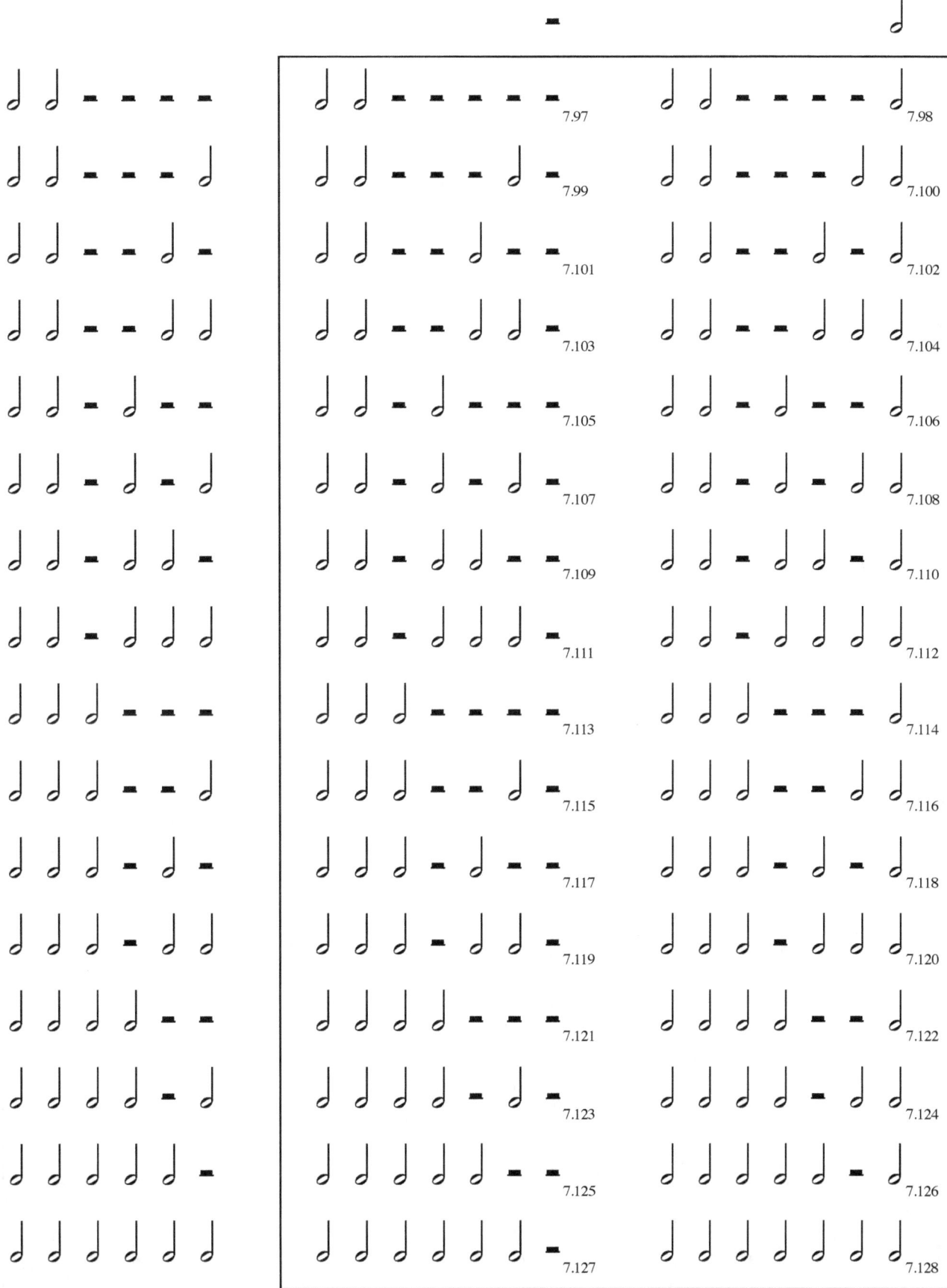

Level 7 Event Point Patterns
Quarter Rest/Note

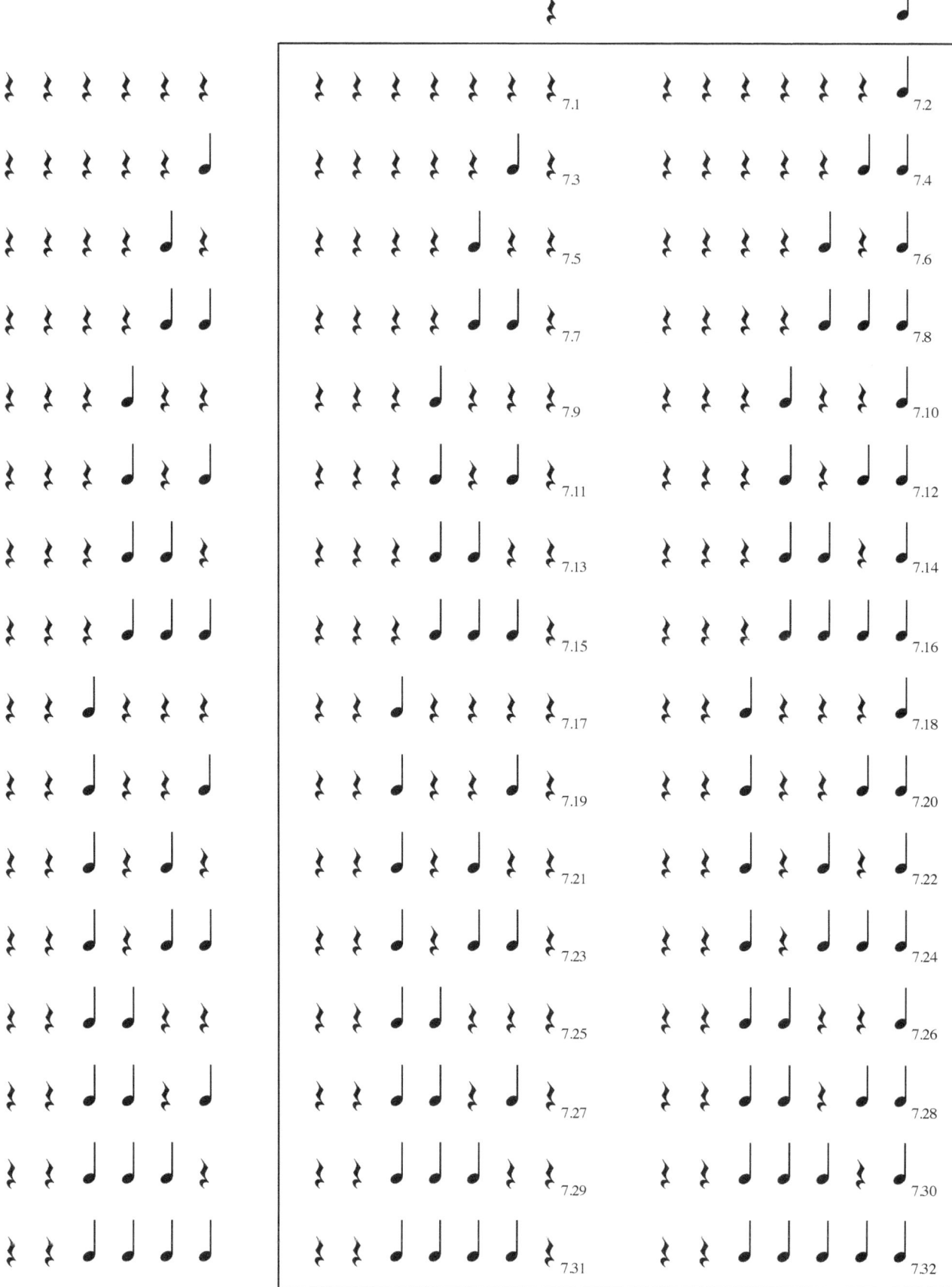

Level 7 Event Point Patterns
Quarter Rest/Note (cont'd)

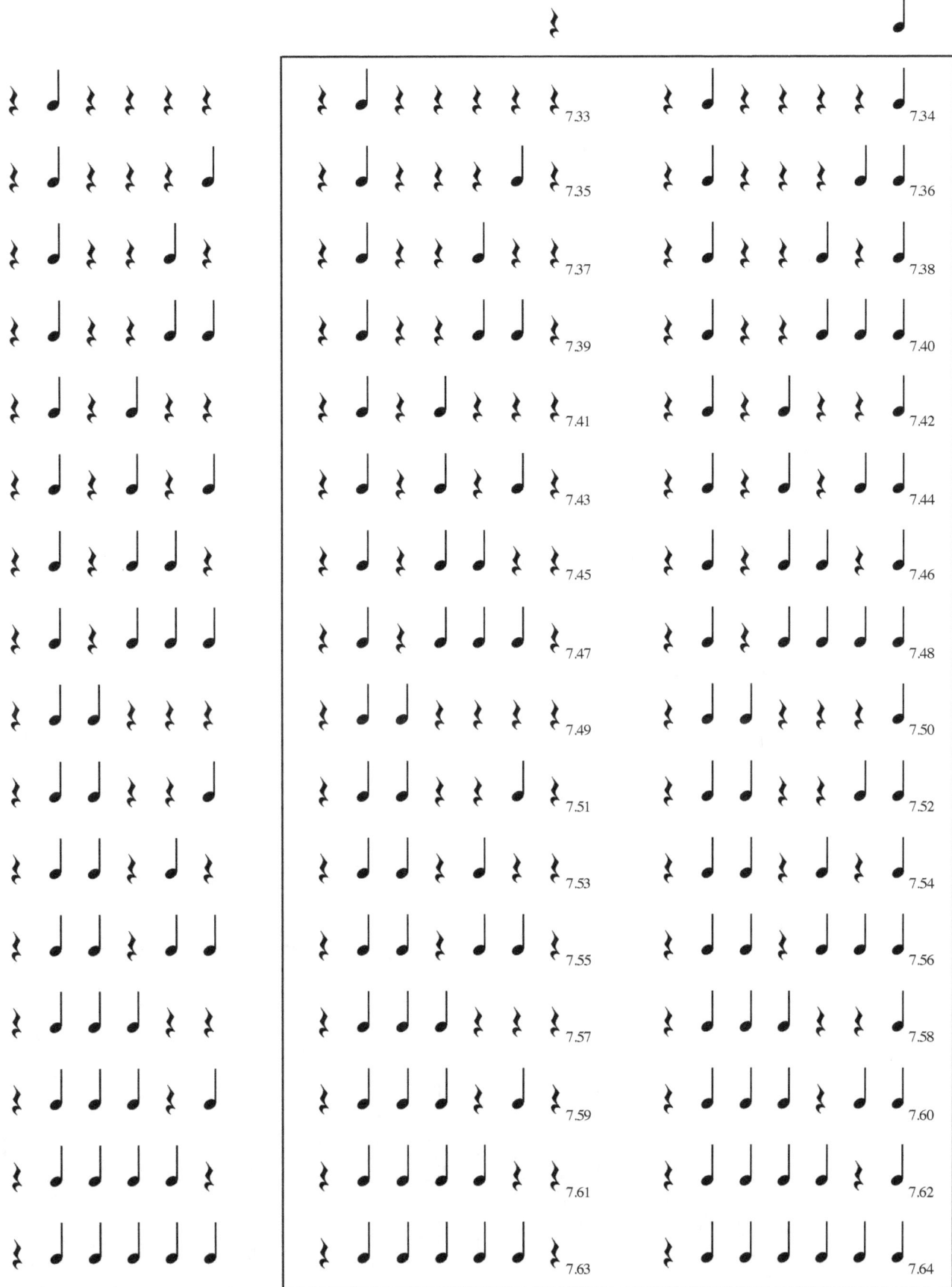

Level 7 Event Point Patterns
Quarter Rest/Note (cont'd)

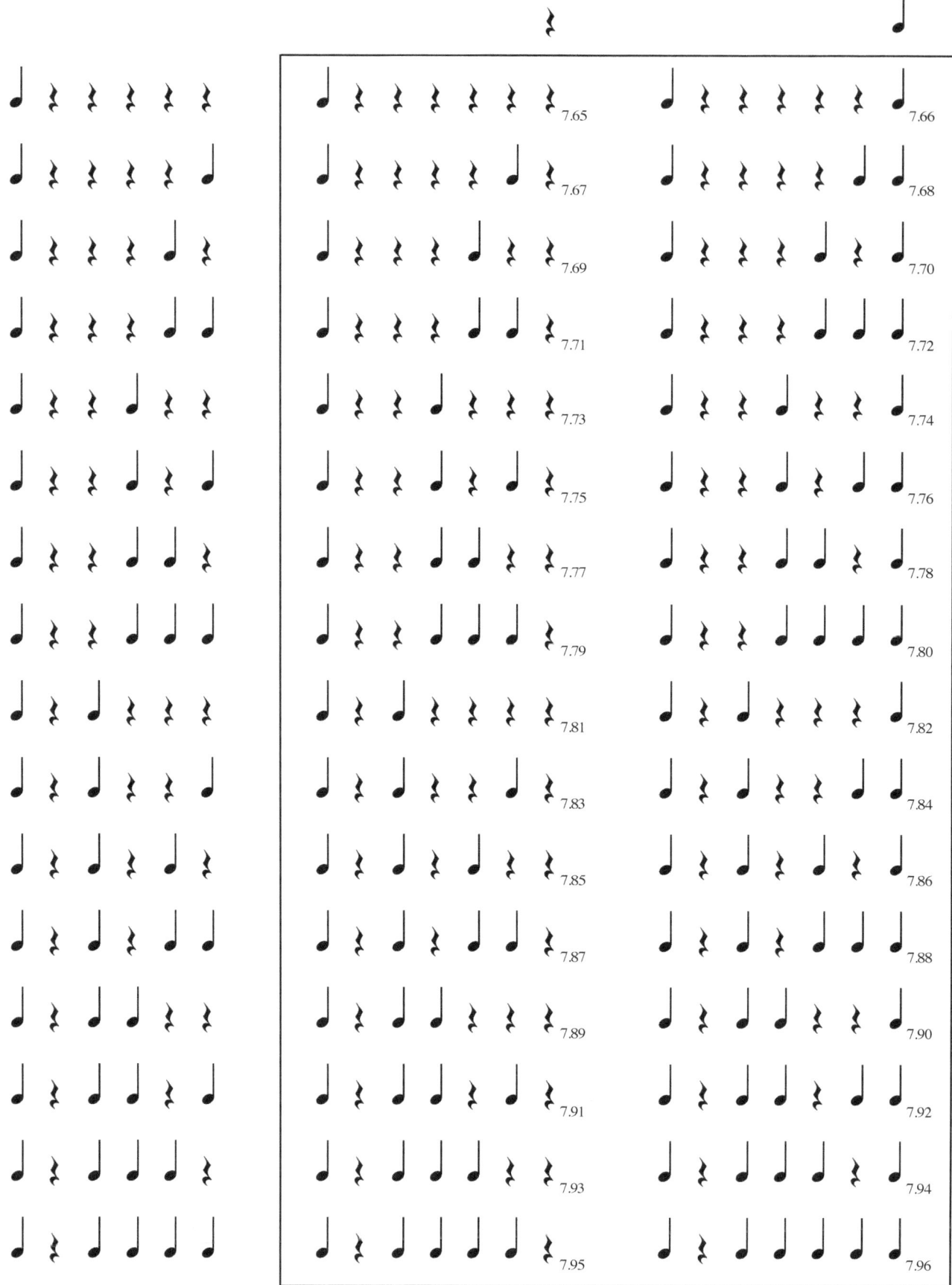

Level 7 Event Point Patterns
Quarter Rest/Note (cont'd)

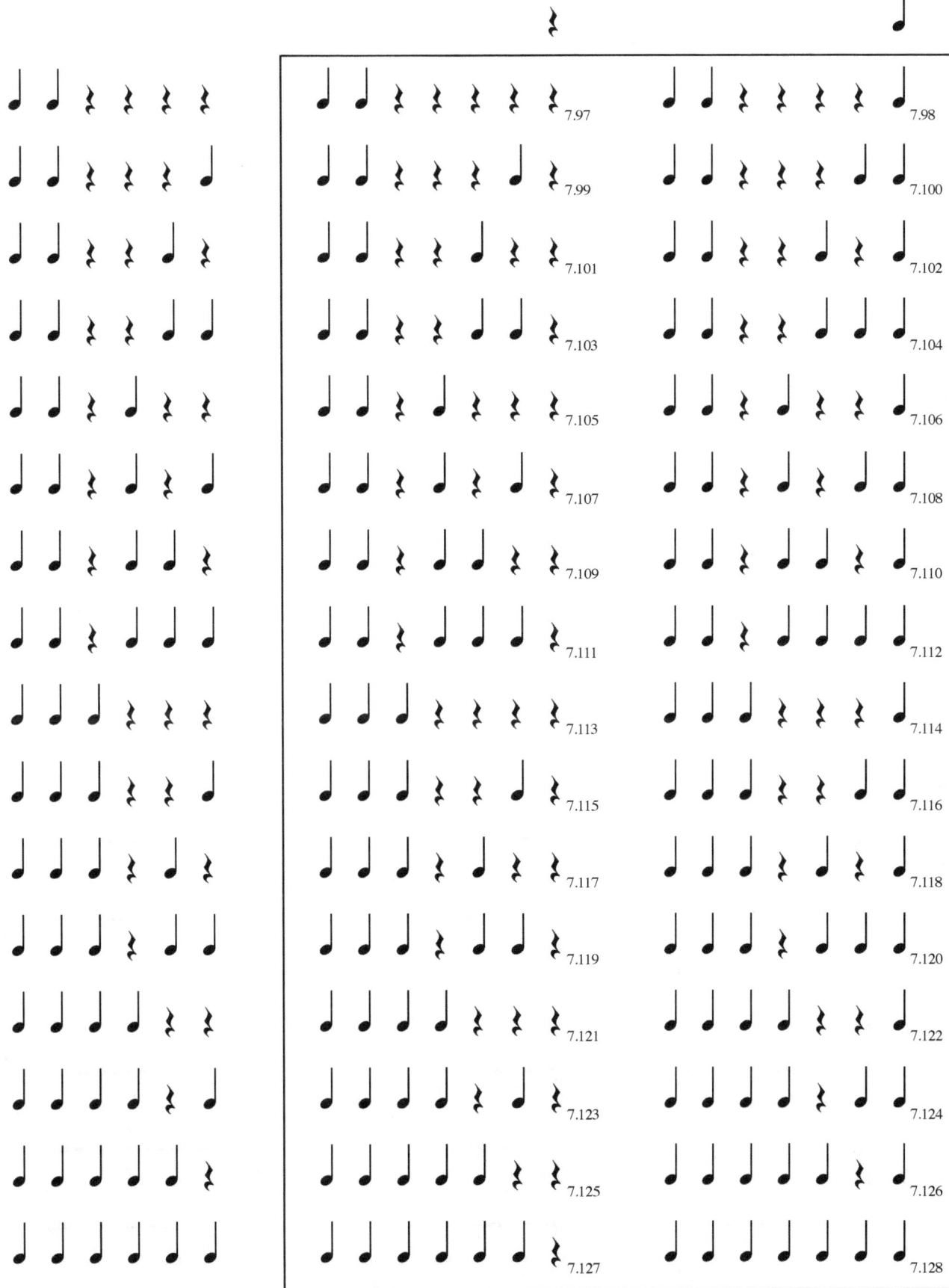

Level 7 Event Point Patterns
Eighth Rest/Note

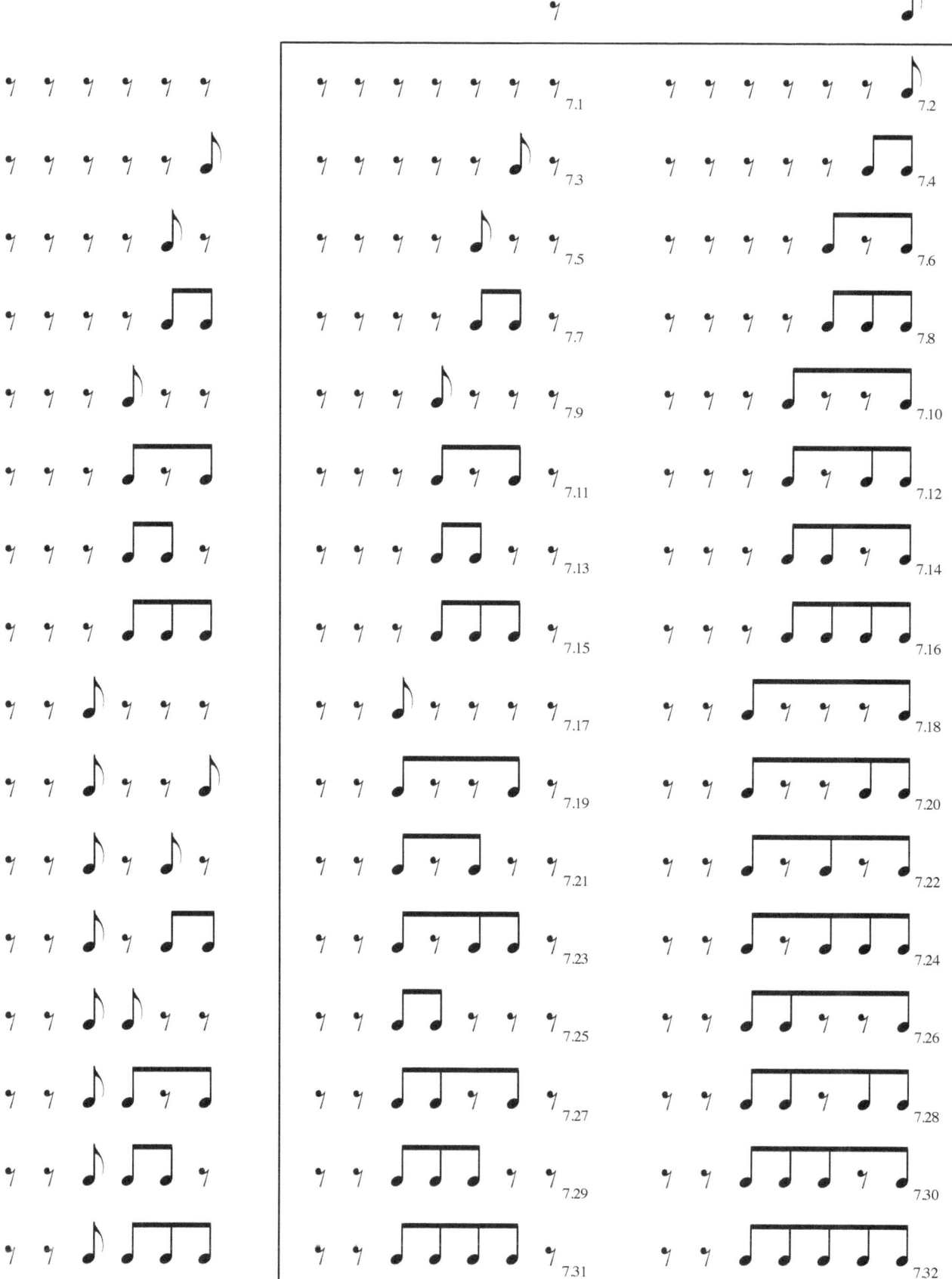

Level 7 Event Point Patterns
Eighth Rest/Note (cont'd)

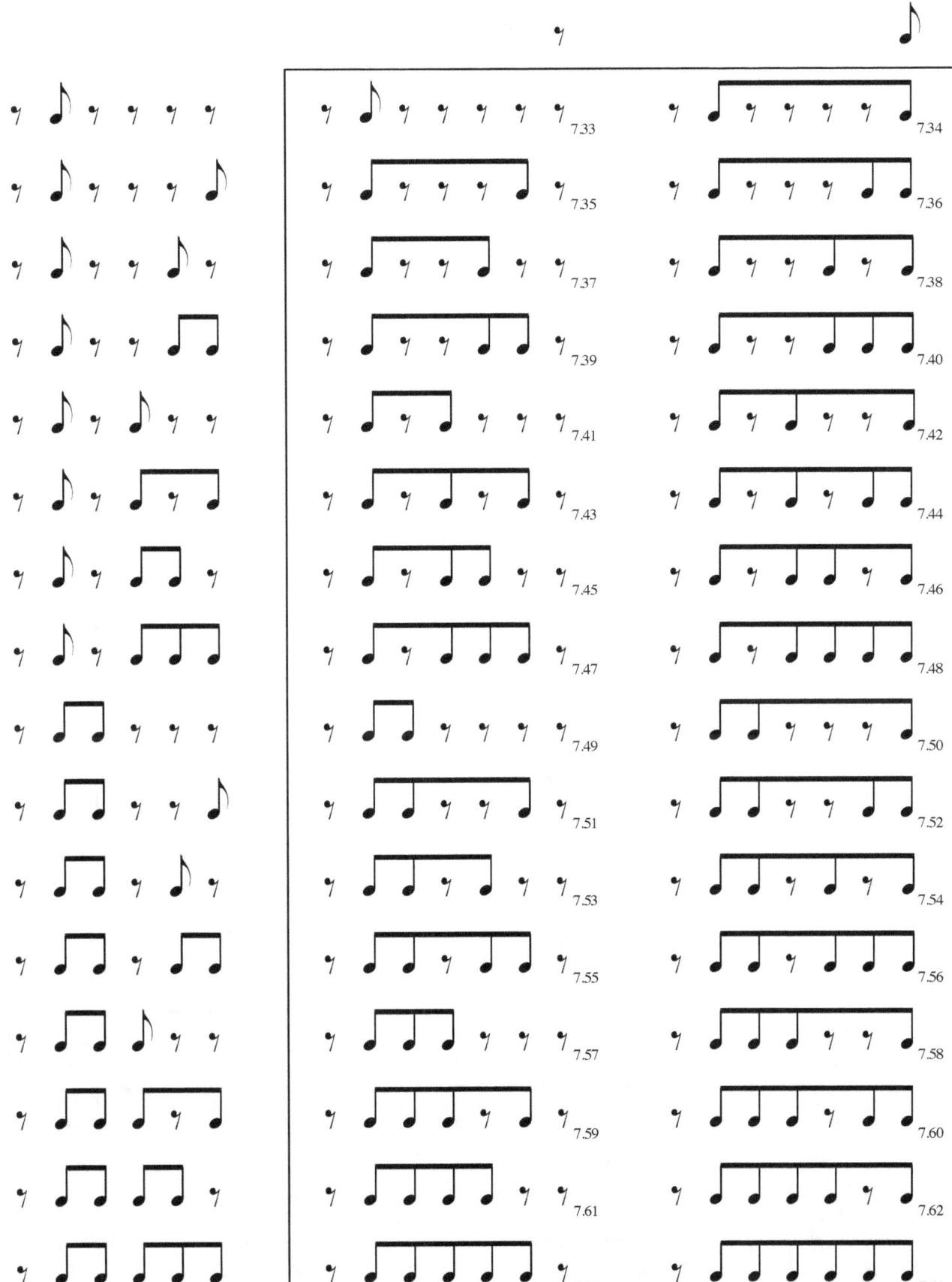

Level 7 Event Point Patterns
Eighth Rest/Note (cont'd)

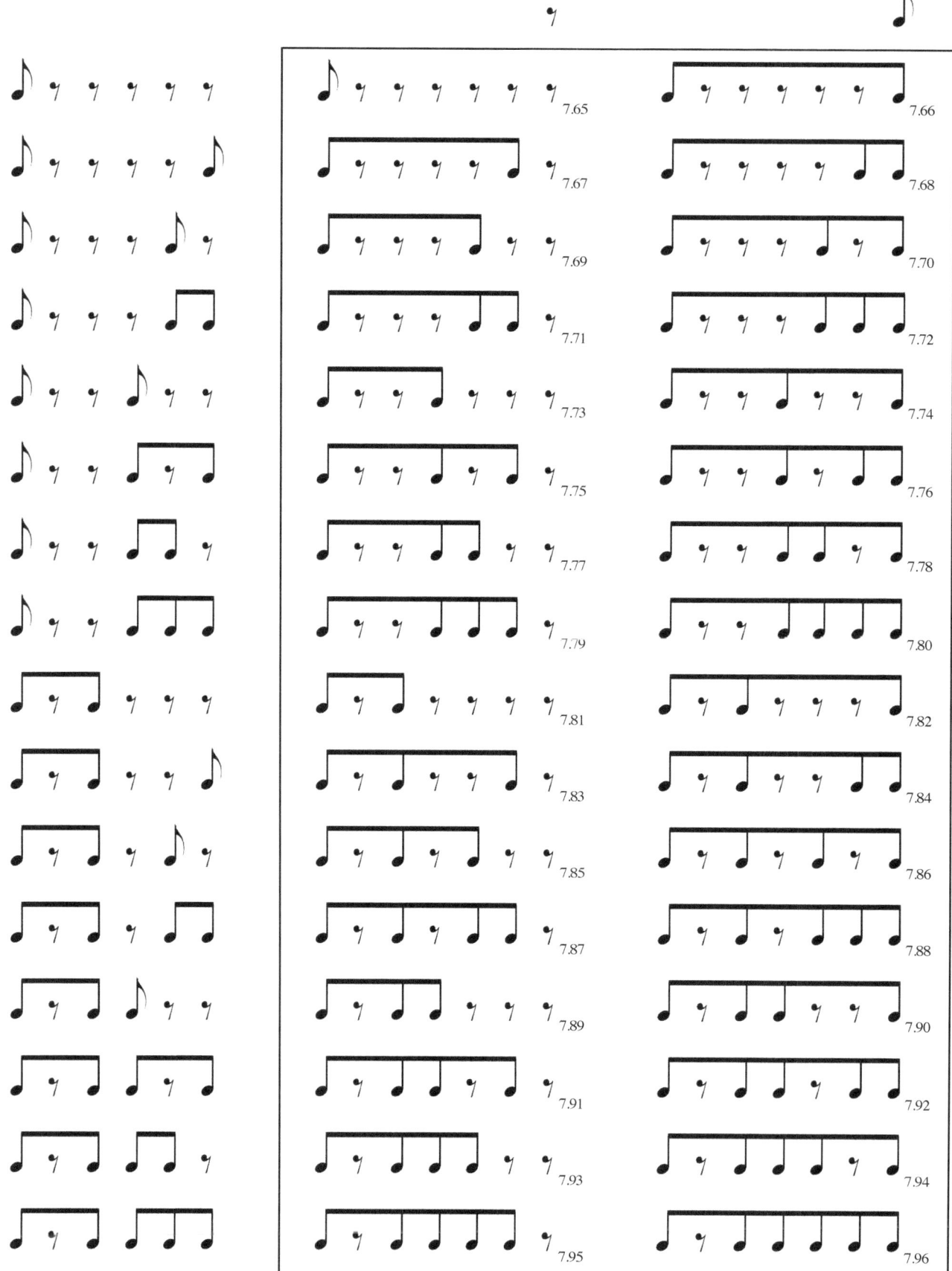

Level 7 Event Point Patterns
Eighth Rest/Note (cont'd)

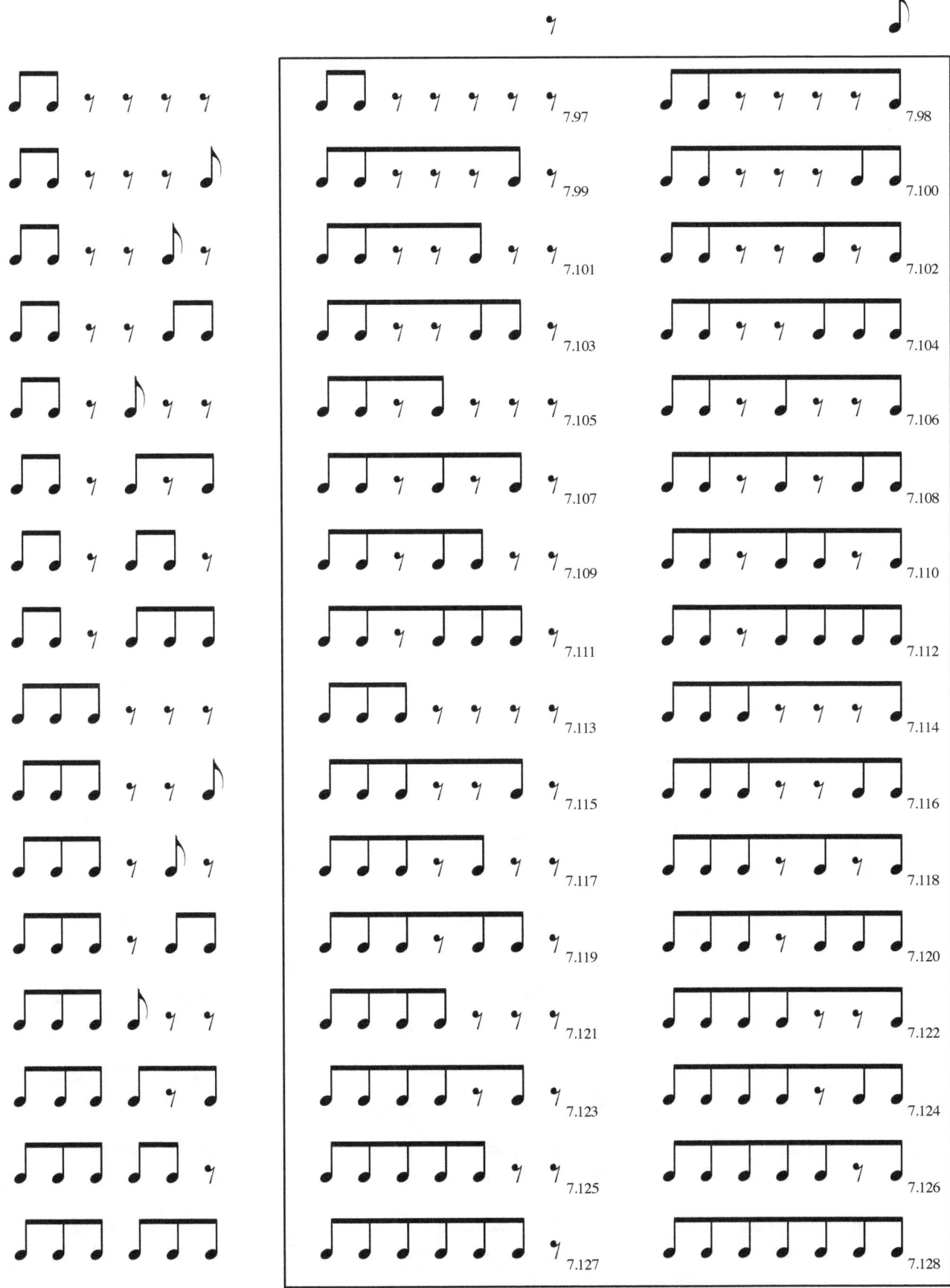

142

Level 7 Event Point Patterns
Sixteenth Rest/Note

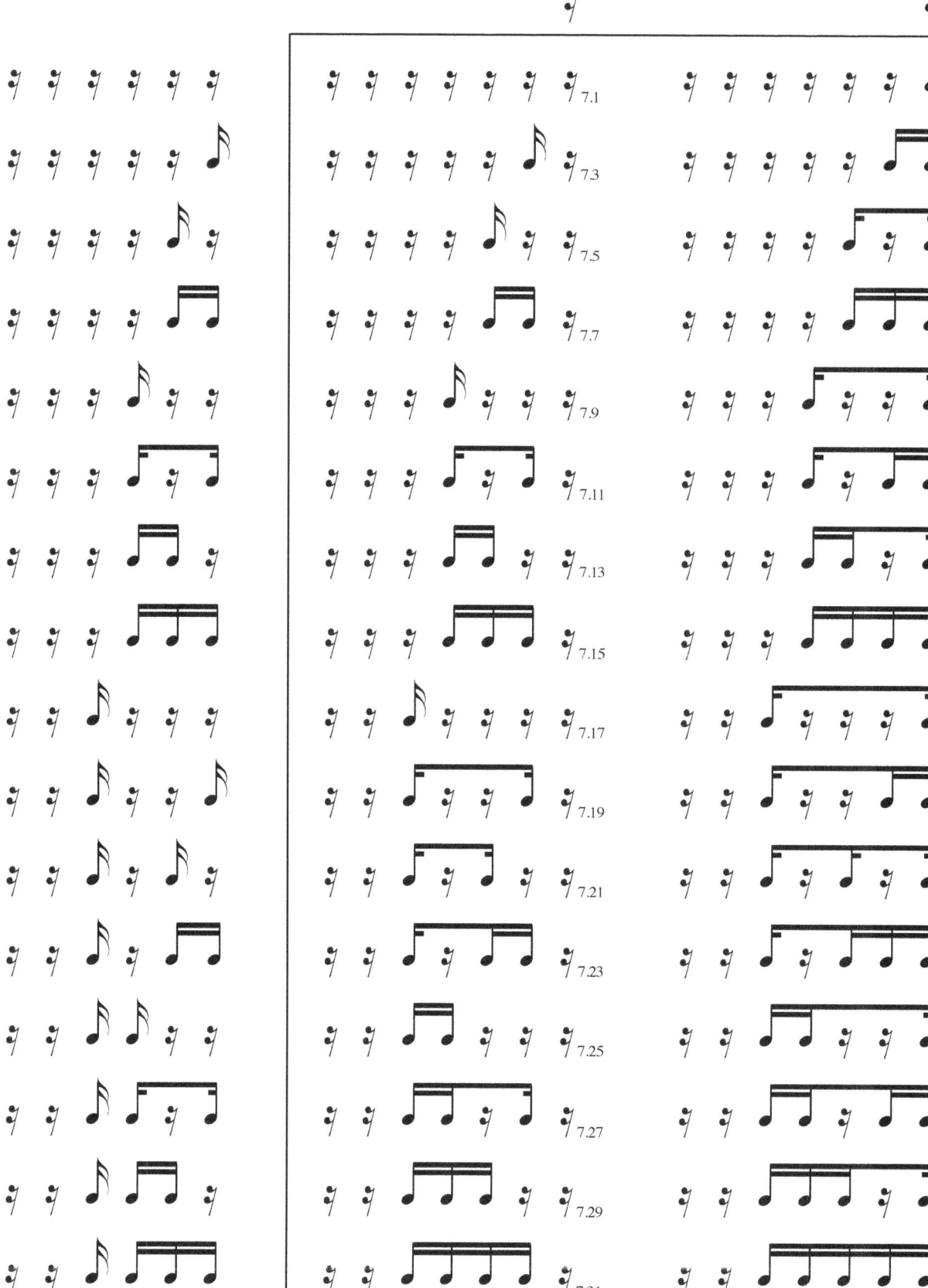

Level 7 Event Point Patterns
Sixteenth Rest/Note (cont'd)

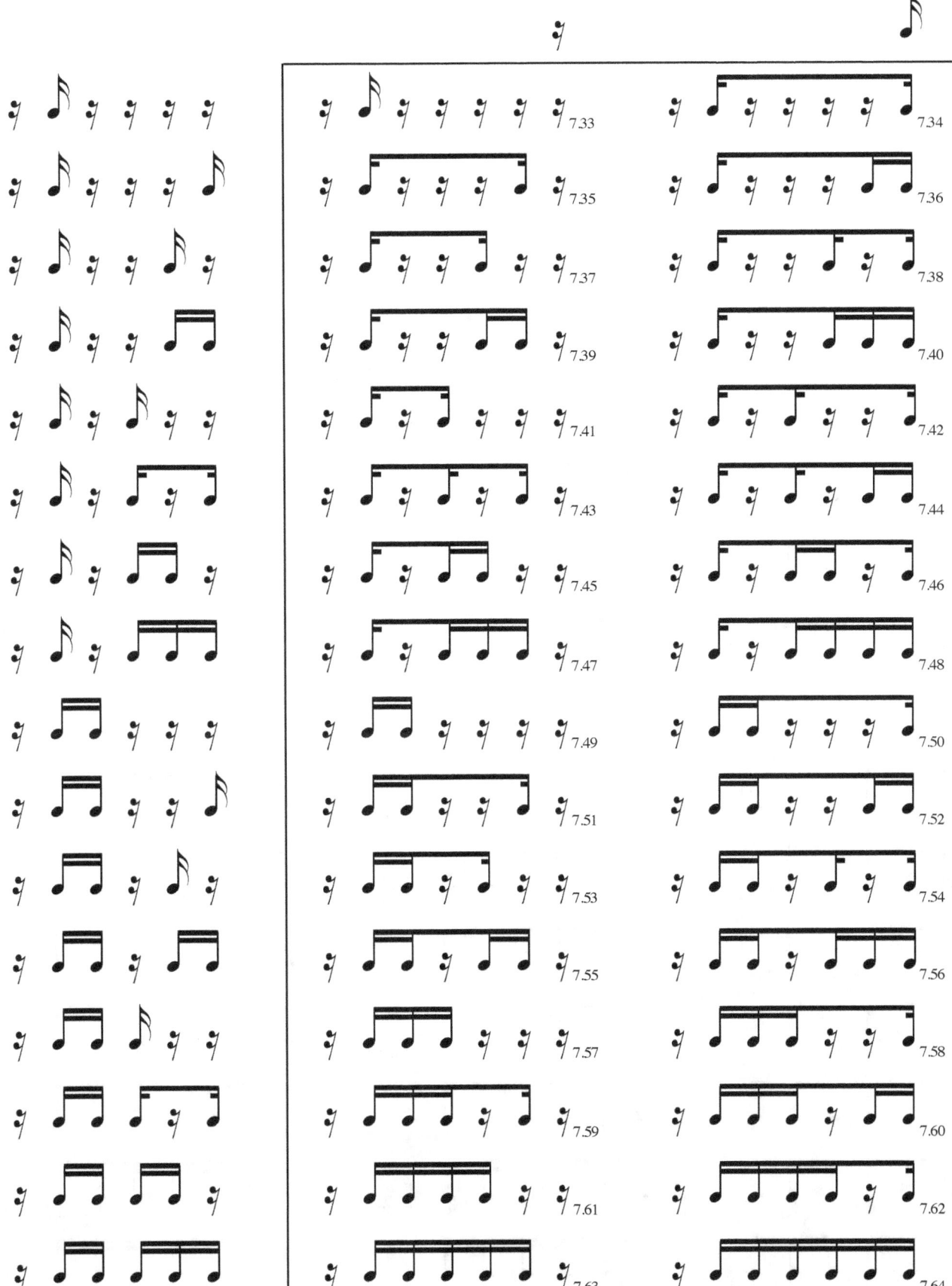

Level 7 Event Point Patterns
Sixteenth Rest/Note (cont'd)

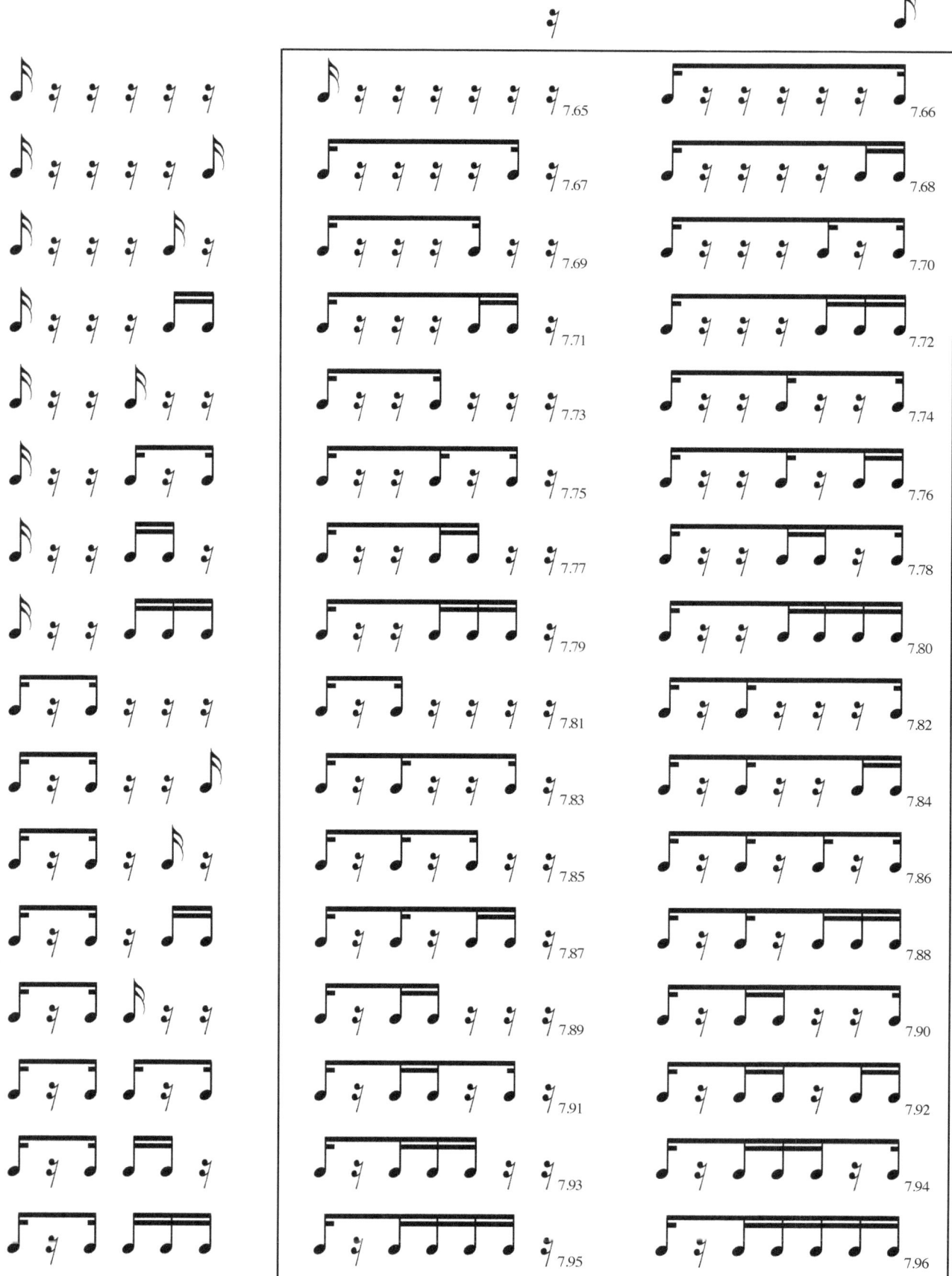

Level 7 Event Point Patterns
Sixteenth Rest/Note (cont'd)

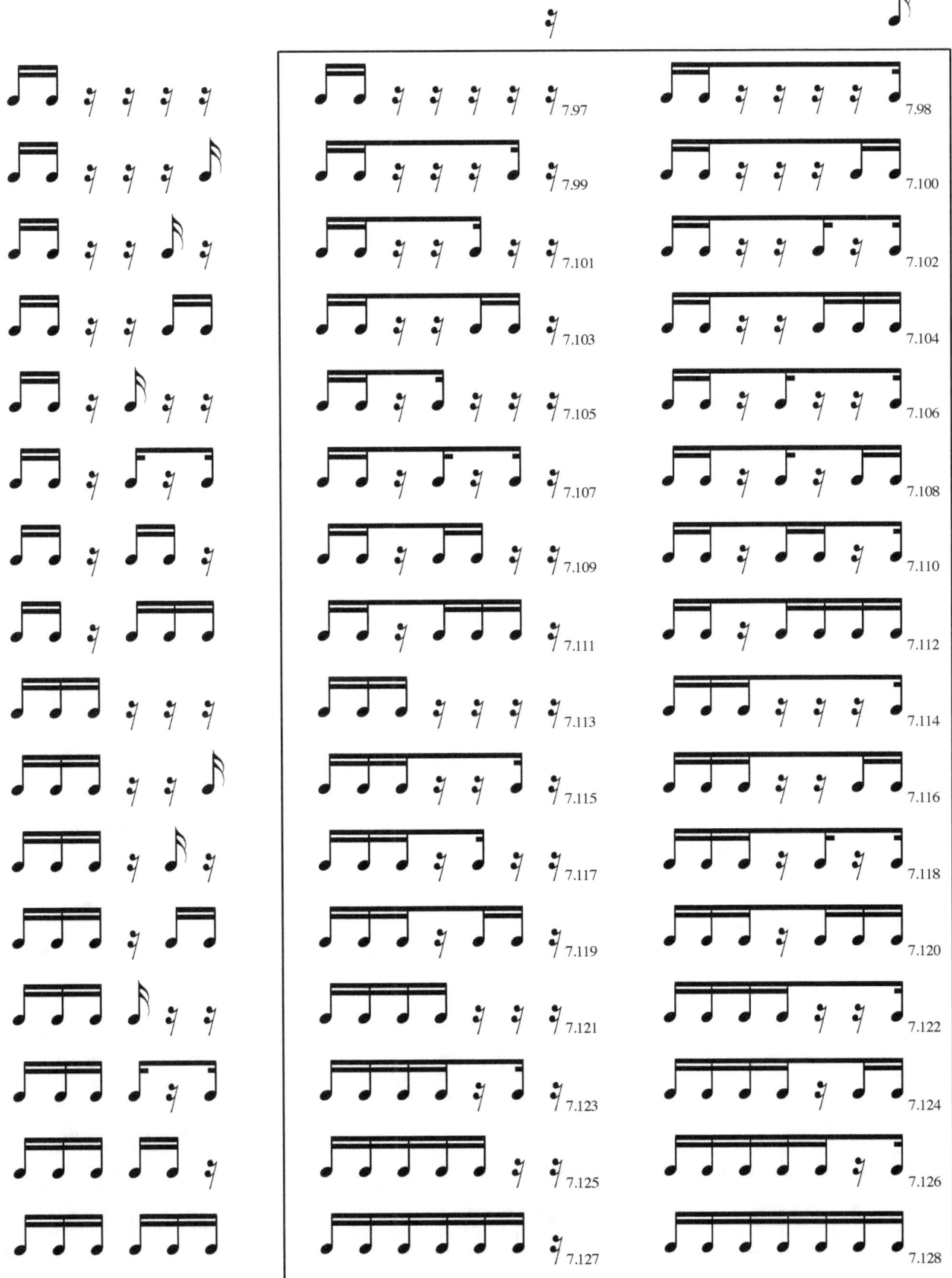

Level 7 Event Point Patterns
Thirty-second Rest/Note

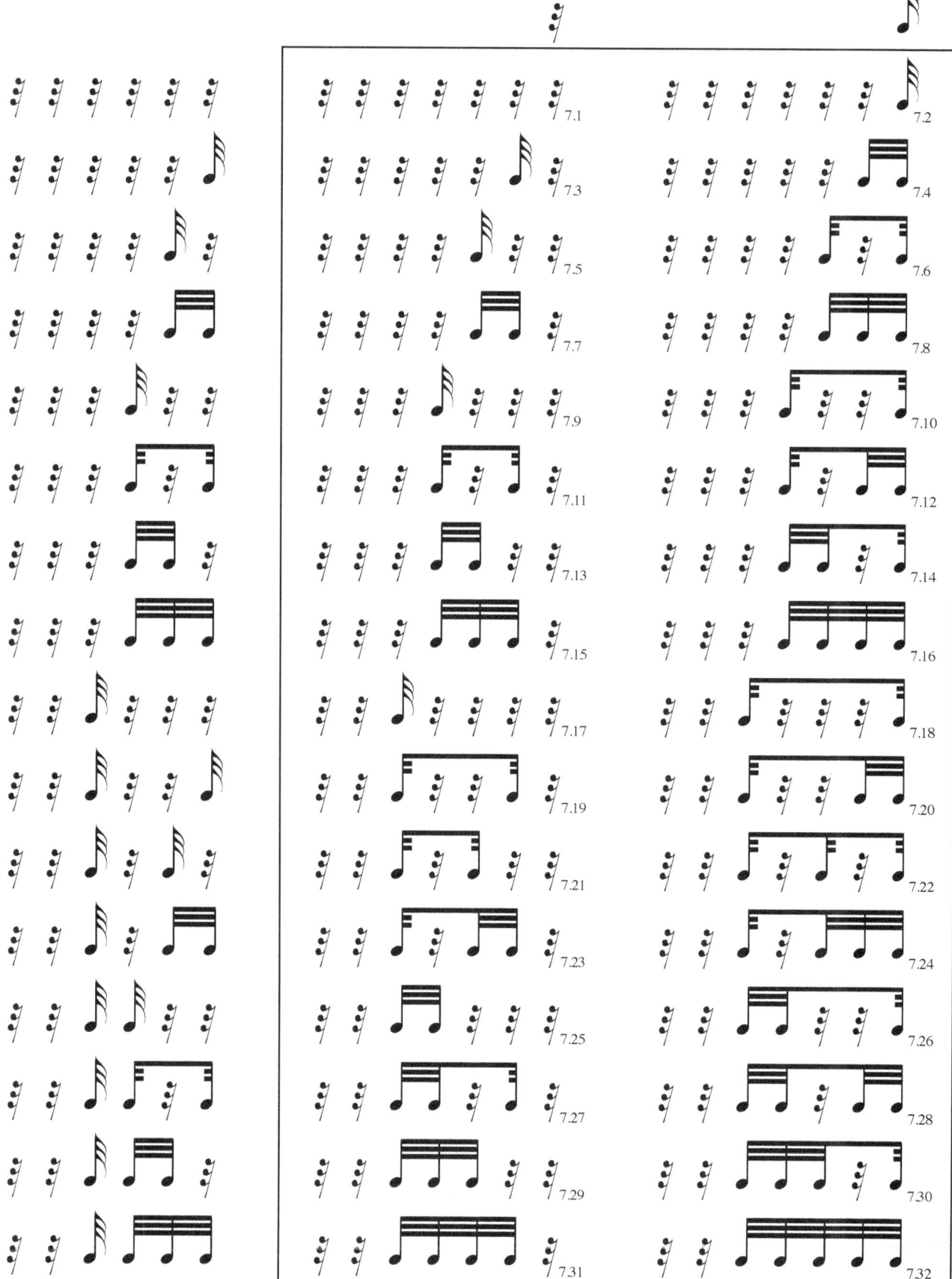

Level 7 Event Point Patterns
Thirty-second Rest/Note (cont'd)

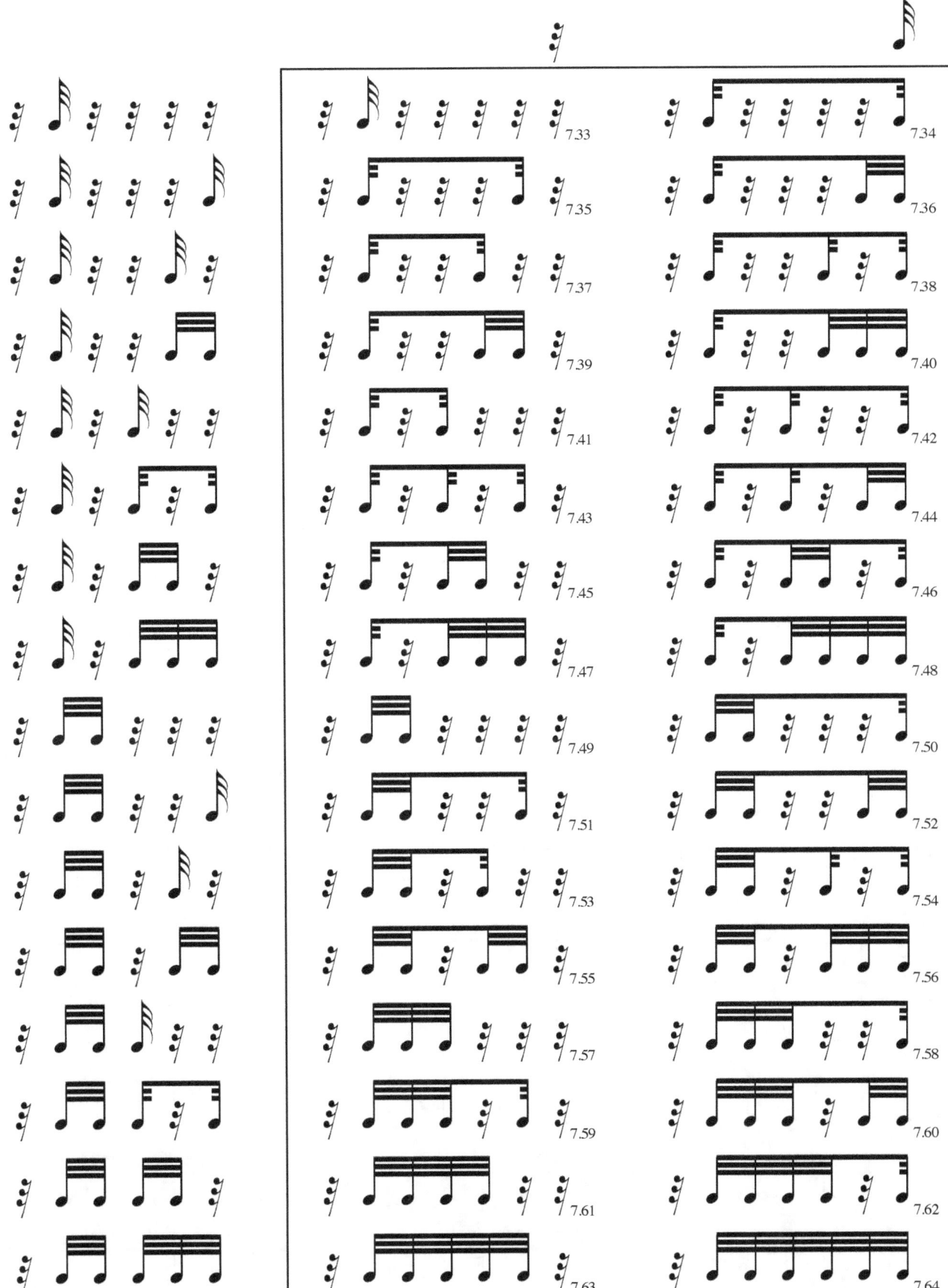

148

Level 7 Event Point Patterns
Thirty-second Rest/Note (cont'd)

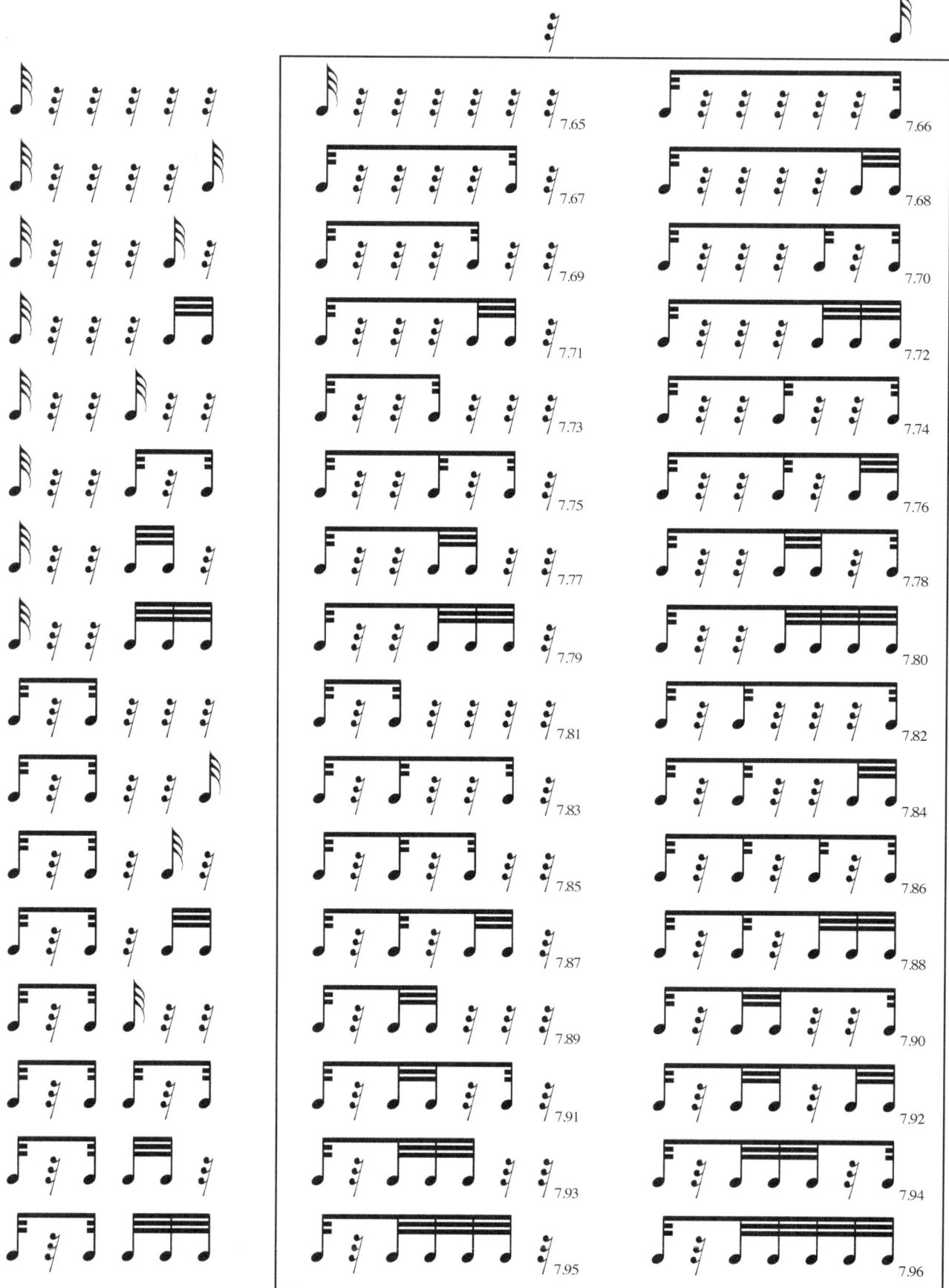

Level 7 Event Point Patterns
Thirty-second Rest/Note (cont'd)

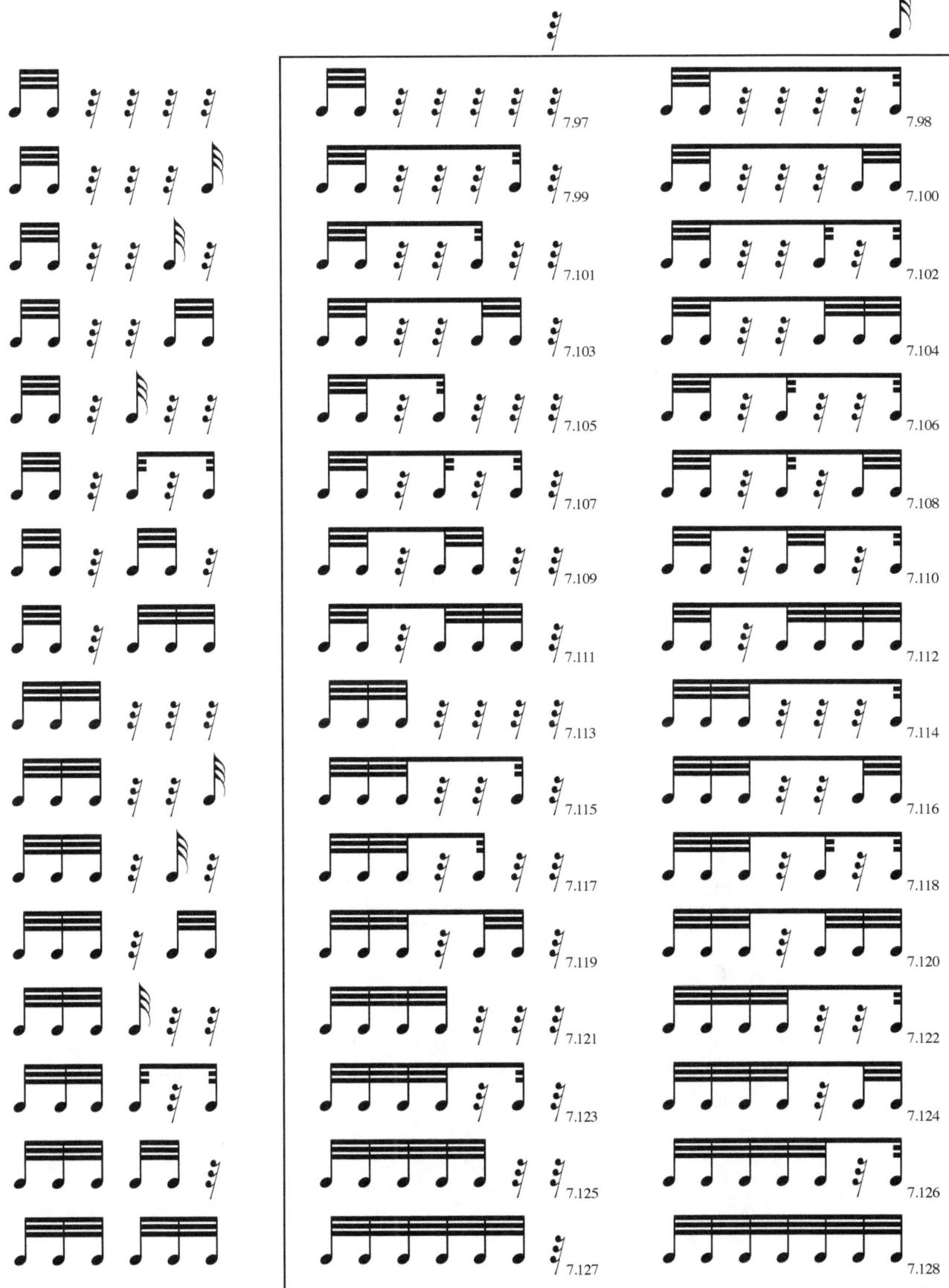

Exercise #7

Advanced Practice Suggestions for Drummers

If you have experimented with odd meters, particularly songs in seven, you can try playing the seven-note patterns as either individual accent groups of seven beat notes, or, as groups of accented divided notes in clusters.

For the first example **(Figure 44)**, we start with a simple two-measure pattern in 7/8:

Figure 44. *Eighth Rests/Notes Played Over Two Measures of 7/8*

Then, in **Figure 45**, we play these patterns **as accents** over two measures of eighth notes in 7/8:

Figure 45. *Septuplets Played as Accented Eighth Notes Over Two Measures of 7/8*

These accents may also be doubled, tripled or quadrupled.

In our second example, we group eighth notes in 7/4 into clusters of 4, 7, and 3, but they are **not** played as polyrhythms. The bracketed numbers are instead used to arrange the eighth notes into the desired clusters. The results create very challenging sound illusions **(Figure 46)**:

Figure 46. *Septuplets Played as Accented Eighth Note Groupings in 7/4*

Tabla drummers excel at this aspect of rhythm manipulation. If you are interested in exploring this approach from an Indian drumming perspective, read Pete Lockett's *Indian Rhythms for Drumset* (Hudson Music, 2008).

Music Measure Presentation of the Level 7 Event Point Patterns as Beat Notes

The following groups of patterns are presented in the beat contexts of 7/2, 7/4, 7/8, 7/16 and 7/32.

The rests have been consolidated to make reading the patterns easier. They are grouped into the largest rest values where possible.

Note value durations remain at the beat note level and have not been altered from the preceding binary combination tables.

To apply the practice methods discussed on page 35:

- **Read and Play** the patterns

- **Sing** the patterns

- **Audiate** (generate the sound in your mind) and **Visualize** performing the patterns

Level 7 Event Point Patterns
7/2 - Beat

Level 7 Event Point Patterns
7/2 - Beat (cont'd)

Level 7 Event Point Patterns
7/2 - Beat (cont'd)

Level 7 Event Point Patterns
7/2 - Beat (cont'd)

Level 7 Event Point Patterns
7/4 - Beat

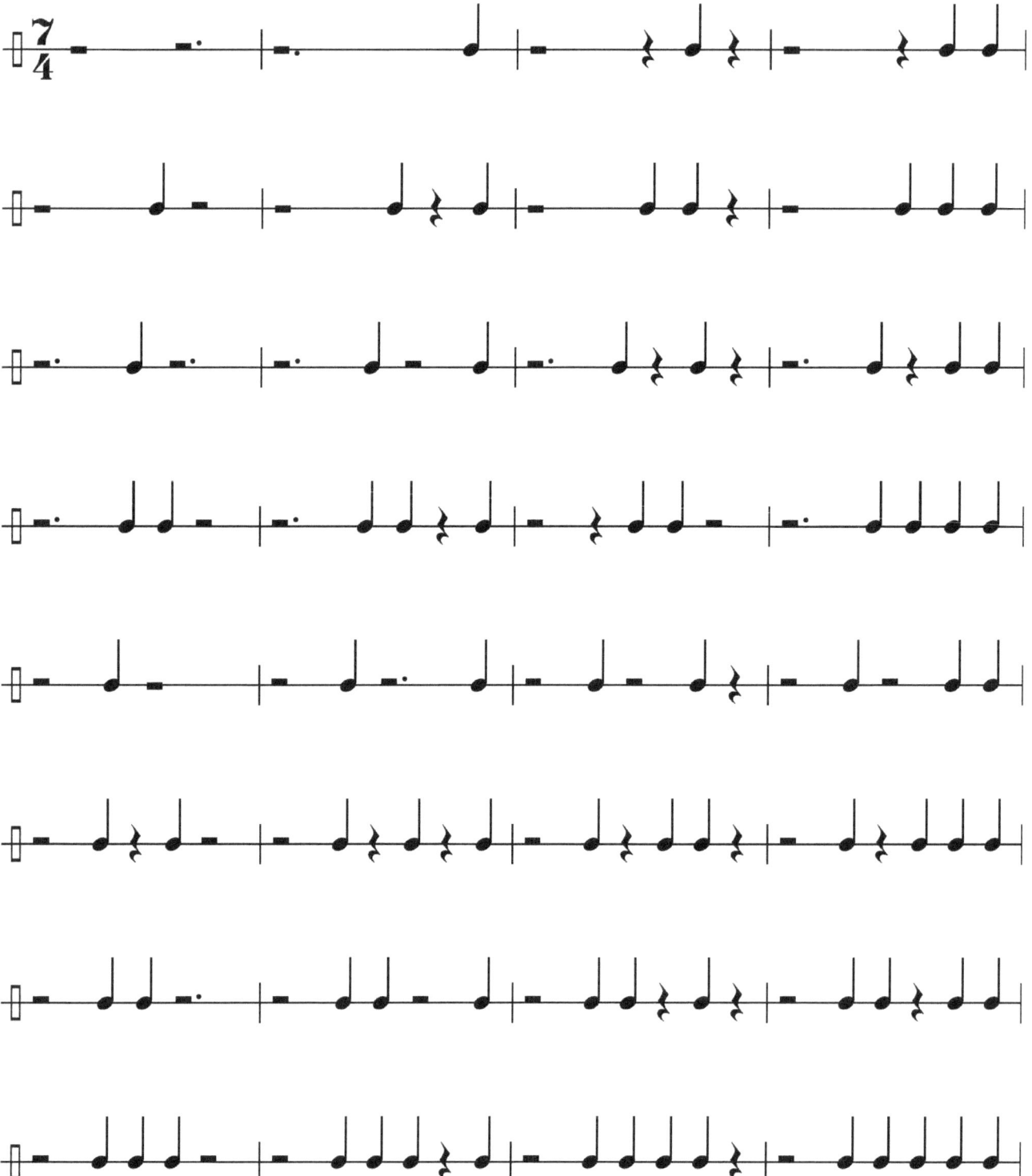

Level 7 Event Point Patterns
7/4 - Beat (cont'd)

Level 7 Event Point Patterns
7/4 - Beat (cont'd)

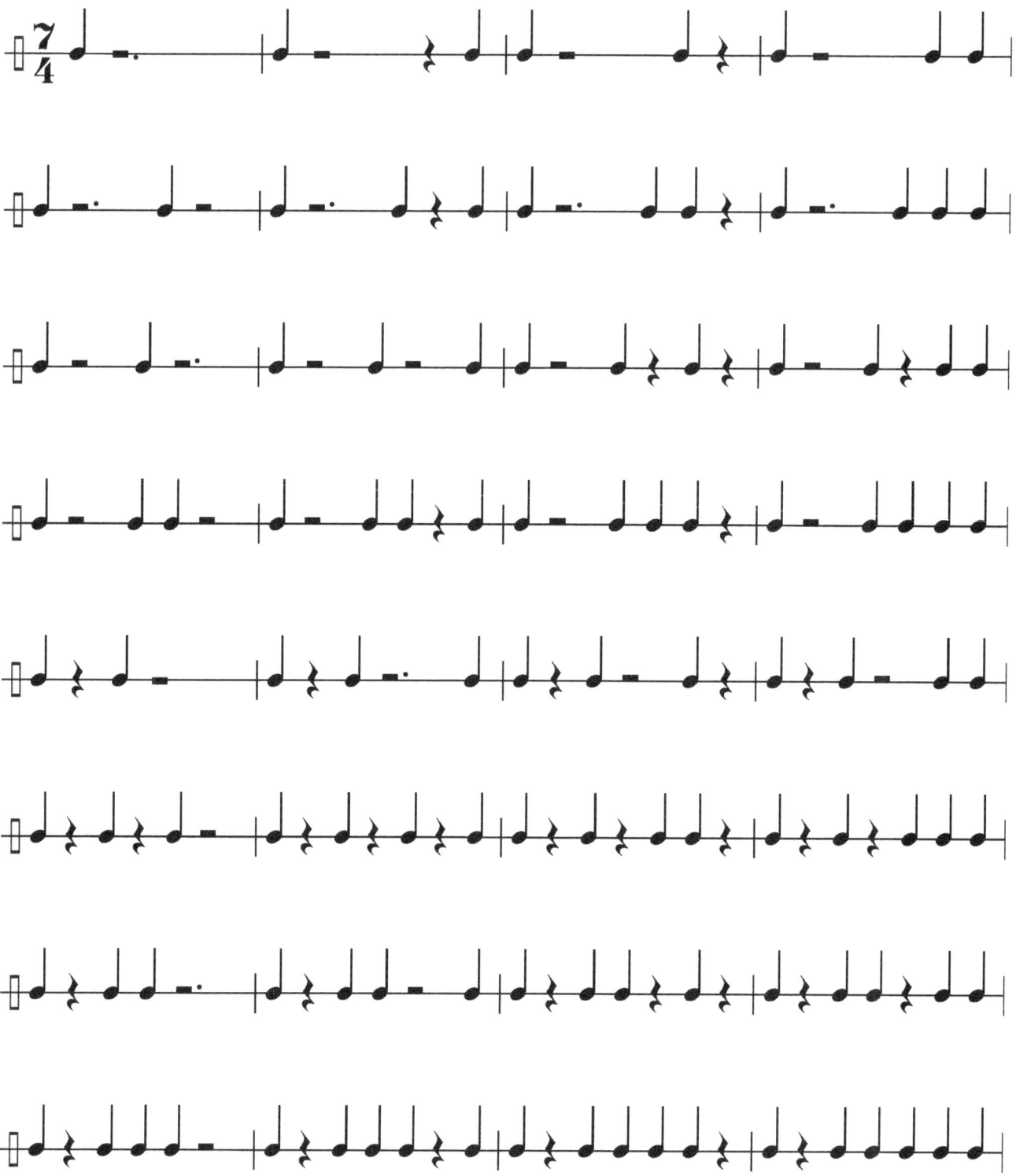

Level 7 Event Point Patterns
7/4 - Beat (cont'd)

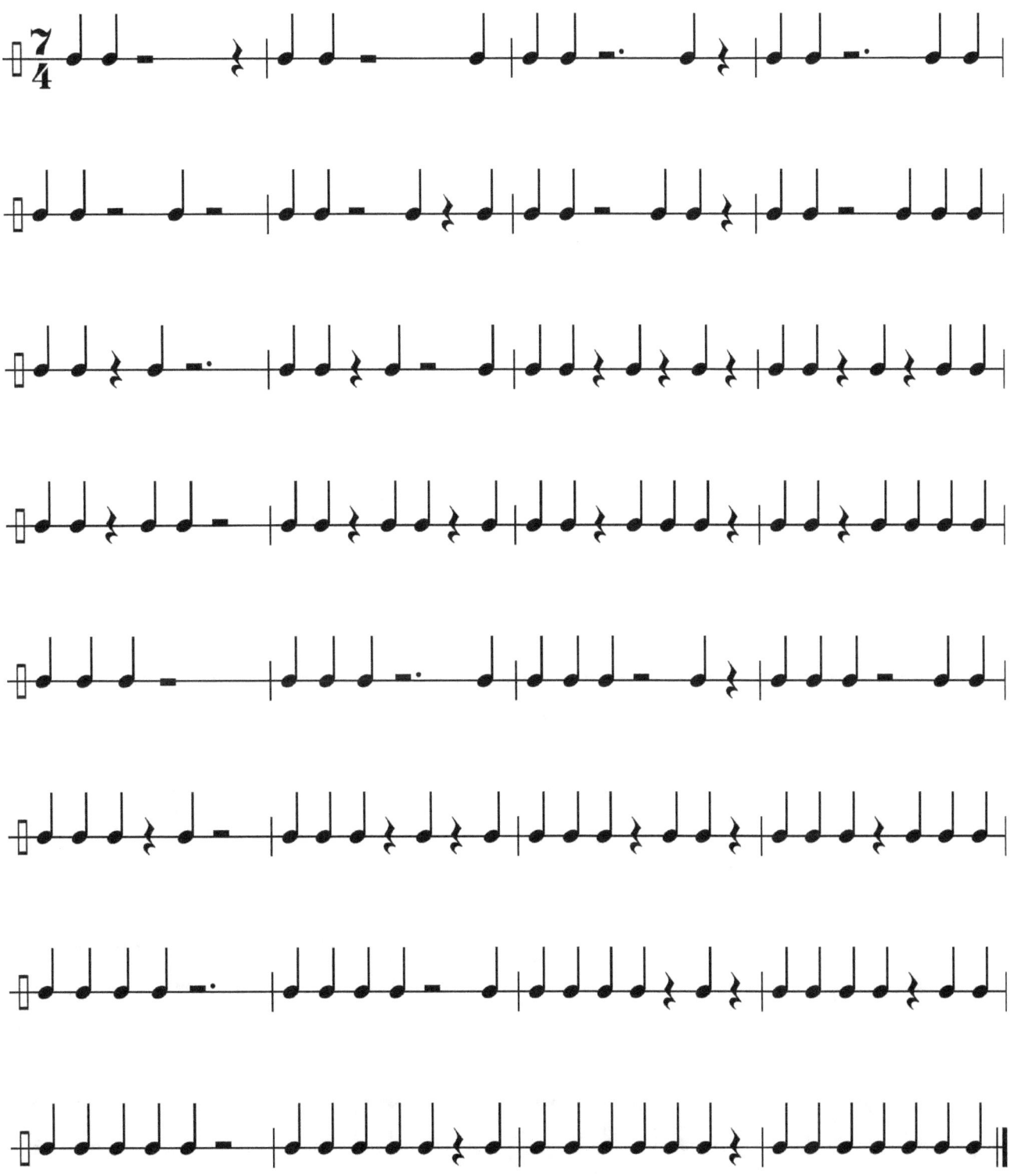

Level 7 Event Point Patterns
7/8 - Beat

Level 7 Event Point Patterns
7/8 - Beat (cont'd)

Level 7 Event Point Patterns
7/8 Beat (cont'd)

Level 7 Event Point Patterns
7/8 Beat (cont'd)

Level 7 Event Point Patterns
7/16 - Beat

Level 7 Event Point Patterns
7/16 - Beat (cont'd)

Level 7 Event Point Patterns
7/16 - Beat (cont'd)

Level 7 Event Point Patterns
7/16 - Beat (cont'd)

Level 7 Event Point Patterns
7/32 - Beat

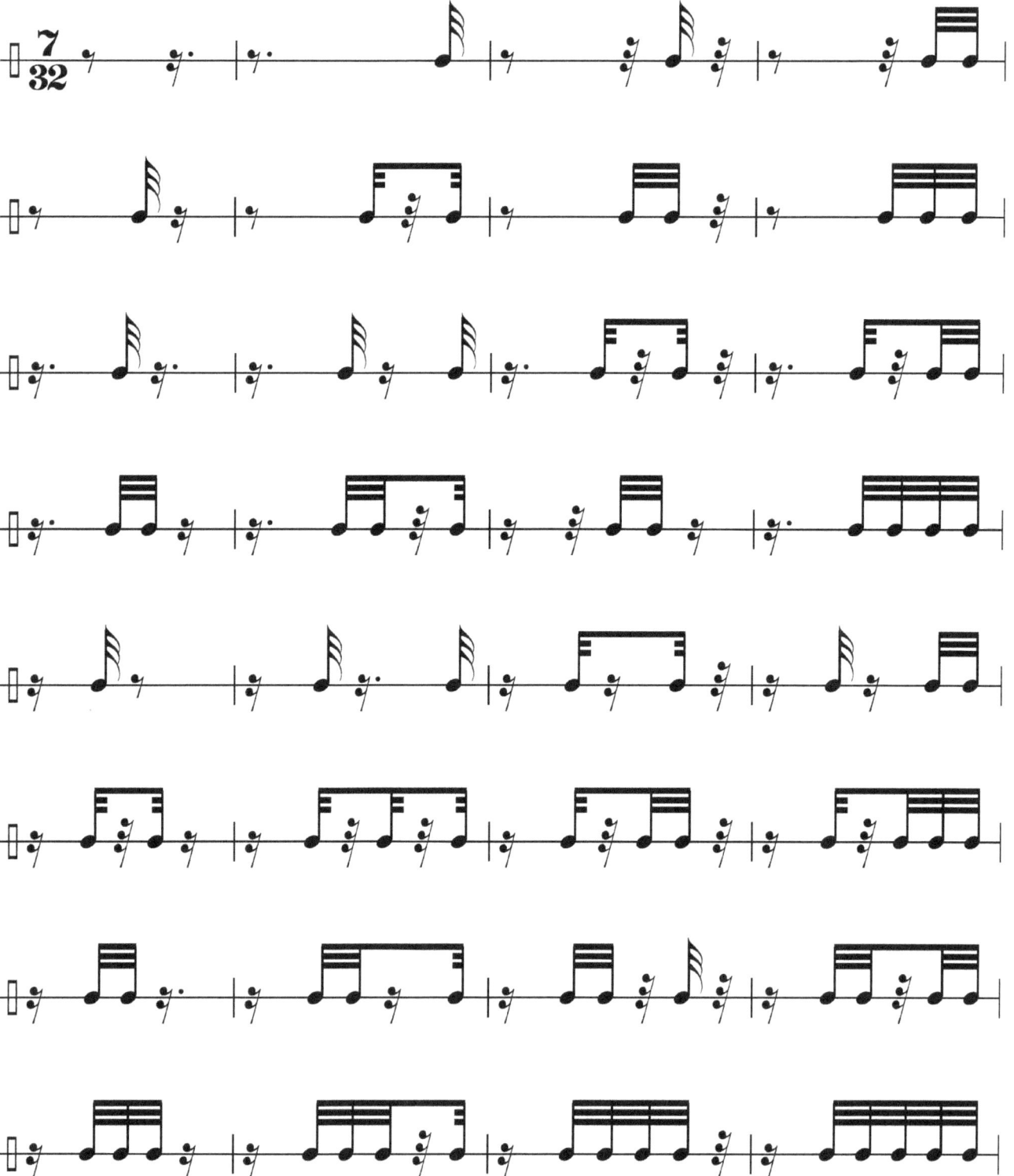

Level 7 Event Point Patterns
7/32 - Beat (cont'd)

170

Level 7 Event Point Patterns
7/32 - Beat (cont'd)

Level 7 Event Point Patterns
7/32 - Beat (cont'd)

Level 8
Event Point Patterns

In this section, we will:

- create the event point possibilities for Level 8 by systematically pairing 0's and 1's in eight combination tables with the Level 7 possibilities

- substitute the 0/1 combinations with five beat note values (half, quarter, eighth, sixteenth, and thirty-second) to create **Beat Division** levels in 4/2, 4/4, 4/8, 4/16 and 4/32

- substitute the 0/1 combinations with four beat rest/note values (half, quarter, eighth, and sixteenth) to create **Beat Subdivision** levels in 2/2, 2/4, 2/8 and 2/16

- place both groups of these re-written patterns in their respective music measure formats for reading/practice

There are **256** Level 8 Event Point Patterns.

```
1  *
2  * *
3  * * *
4  * * * *
5  * * * * *
6  * * * * * *
7  * * * * * * *
8  1 0 1 1 0 1 0 1
```

Level 8 Event Point Patterns - Discussion

We've now arrived at the last phase of our fundamental rhythm pattern generating process.

Beyond this level, the number of event point possibilities becomes too large for practical study. They would simply be repetitions of "elements" already seen in the Level 1 - 8 Event Point Pattern binary combination tables.

With this final section, we will be addressing how the Level 8 Event Point Patterns may be applied to two groups of metric contexts:

- **Beat Division** levels of 4/2, 4/4, 4/8, 4/16 and 4/32

- **Beat Subdivision** levels of 2/2, 2/4, 2/8 and 2/16

[*Author's note: We are excluding the 4/2 - 4/32 Beat Subdivision levels, because 2^{16} produces 65,536 event point possibilities. The 2/32 Beat Subdivision level has also been excluded from our examples, due to the relative obscurity of 128th rest/note values.*]

The Level 8 binary combination tables on pp. 182-221 do not reflect any specific time signatures, as they can be used for both the 4/2 - 4/32 Beat Division and 2/2 - 2/16 Beat Subdivision levels.

Phrasing varies slightly to emphasize the patterns' relationships to the beat note, but the ***number*** of combination possibilities at the 4/4 **division** level in **Figure 47**, for example, are **identical** to the number of combination possibilities at the 2/4 **subdivision** level: **256**.

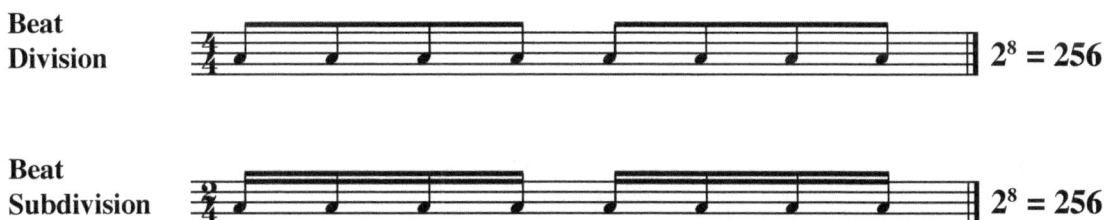

Figure 47. *Beat Division vs Beat Subdivision Equivalence*

This relationship applies equally to the 4/2 - 2/2, 4/8 - 2/8, and 4/16 - 2/16 beat division/beat subdivision levels.

Our final section contains over one hundred pages of rhythm pattern possibilities and variations, but it's likely that the 4/4 and 2/4 patterns will hold the most practical value. That's because they comprise a significant portion of most musicians' basic rhythm vocabularies. Mastery of these fundamental building blocks will greatly expand your rhythm comprehension and performance abilities.

Level 8 Event Point Patterns
0/1

	0	1
0 0 0 0 0 0 0	$0 0 0 0 0 0 0 0_{8.1}$	$0 0 0 0 0 0 0 1_{8.2}$
0 0 0 0 0 0 1	$0 0 0 0 0 0 1 0_{8.3}$	$0 0 0 0 0 0 1 1_{8.4}$
0 0 0 0 0 1 0	$0 0 0 0 0 1 0 0_{8.5}$	$0 0 0 0 0 1 0 1_{8.6}$
0 0 0 0 0 1 1	$0 0 0 0 0 1 1 0_{8.7}$	$0 0 0 0 0 1 1 1_{8.8}$
0 0 0 0 1 0 0	$0 0 0 0 1 0 0 0_{8.9}$	$0 0 0 0 1 0 0 1_{8.10}$
0 0 0 0 1 0 1	$0 0 0 0 1 0 1 0_{8.11}$	$0 0 0 0 1 0 1 1_{8.12}$
0 0 0 0 1 1 0	$0 0 0 0 1 1 0 0_{8.13}$	$0 0 0 0 1 1 0 1_{8.14}$
0 0 0 0 1 1 1	$0 0 0 0 1 1 1 0_{8.15}$	$0 0 0 0 1 1 1 1_{8.16}$
0 0 0 1 0 0 0	$0 0 0 1 0 0 0 0_{8.17}$	$0 0 0 1 0 0 0 1_{8.18}$
0 0 0 1 0 0 1	$0 0 0 1 0 0 1 0_{8.19}$	$0 0 0 1 0 0 1 1_{8.20}$
0 0 0 1 0 1 0	$0 0 0 1 0 1 0 0_{8.21}$	$0 0 0 1 0 1 0 1_{8.22}$
0 0 0 1 0 1 1	$0 0 0 1 0 1 1 0_{8.23}$	$0 0 0 1 0 1 1 1_{8.24}$
0 0 0 1 1 0 0	$0 0 0 1 1 0 0 0_{8.25}$	$0 0 0 1 1 0 0 1_{8.26}$
0 0 0 1 1 0 1	$0 0 0 1 1 0 1 0_{8.27}$	$0 0 0 1 1 0 1 1_{8.28}$
0 0 0 1 1 1 0	$0 0 0 1 1 1 0 0_{8.29}$	$0 0 0 1 1 1 0 1_{8.30}$
0 0 0 1 1 1 1	$0 0 0 1 1 1 1 0_{8.31}$	$0 0 0 1 1 1 1 1_{8.32}$

Level 8 Event Point Patterns
0/1 (cont'd)

	0	1
0 0 1 0 0 0 0	$00100000_{8.33}$	$00100001_{8.34}$
0 0 1 0 0 0 1	$00100010_{8.35}$	$00100011_{8.36}$
0 0 1 0 0 1 0	$00100100_{8.37}$	$00100101_{8.38}$
0 0 1 0 0 1 1	$00100110_{8.39}$	$00100111_{8.40}$
0 0 1 0 1 0 0	$00101000_{8.41}$	$00101001_{8.42}$
0 0 1 0 1 0 1	$00101010_{8.43}$	$00101011_{8.44}$
0 0 1 0 1 1 0	$00101100_{8.45}$	$00101101_{8.46}$
0 0 1 0 1 1 1	$00101110_{8.47}$	$00101111_{8.48}$
0 0 1 1 0 0 0	$00110000_{8.49}$	$00110001_{8.50}$
0 0 1 1 0 0 1	$00110010_{8.51}$	$00110011_{8.52}$
0 0 1 1 0 1 0	$00110100_{8.53}$	$00110101_{8.54}$
0 0 1 1 0 1 1	$00110110_{8.55}$	$00110111_{8.56}$
0 0 1 1 1 0 0	$00111000_{8.57}$	$00111001_{8.58}$
0 0 1 1 1 0 1	$00111010_{8.59}$	$00111011_{8.60}$
0 0 1 1 1 1 0	$00111100_{8.61}$	$00111101_{8.62}$
0 0 1 1 1 1 1	$00111110_{8.63}$	$00111111_{8.64}$

Level 8 Event Point Patterns
0/1 (cont'd)

	0	1
0 1 0 0 0 0 0	$0100000_{8.65}$	$0100001_{8.66}$
0 1 0 0 0 0 1	$0100010_{8.67}$	$0100011_{8.68}$
0 1 0 0 0 1 0	$0100100_{8.69}$	$0100101_{8.70}$
0 1 0 0 0 1 1	$0100110_{8.71}$	$0100111_{8.72}$
0 1 0 0 1 0 0	$0101000_{8.73}$	$0101001_{8.74}$
0 1 0 0 1 0 1	$0101010_{8.75}$	$0101011_{8.76}$
0 1 0 0 1 1 0	$0101100_{8.77}$	$0101101_{8.78}$
0 1 0 0 1 1 1	$0101110_{8.79}$	$0101111_{8.80}$
0 1 0 1 0 0 0	$0110000_{8.81}$	$0110001_{8.82}$
0 1 0 1 0 0 1	$0110010_{8.83}$	$0110011_{8.84}$
0 1 0 1 0 1 0	$0110100_{8.85}$	$0110101_{8.86}$
0 1 0 1 0 1 1	$0110110_{8.87}$	$0110111_{8.88}$
0 1 0 1 1 0 0	$0111000_{8.89}$	$0111001_{8.90}$
0 1 0 1 1 0 1	$0111010_{8.91}$	$0111011_{8.92}$
0 1 0 1 1 1 0	$0111100_{8.93}$	$0111101_{8.94}$
0 1 0 1 1 1 1	$0111110_{8.95}$	$0111111_{8.96}$

Level 8 Event Point Patterns
0/1 (cont'd)

	0	1
0 1 1 0 0 0 0	$0110 0000_{8.97}$	$01100001_{8.98}$
0 1 1 0 0 0 1	$01100010_{8.99}$	$01100011_{8.100}$
0 1 1 0 0 1 0	$01100100_{8.101}$	$01100101_{8.102}$
0 1 1 0 0 1 1	$01100110_{8.103}$	$01100111_{8.104}$
0 1 1 0 1 0 0	$01101000_{8.105}$	$01101001_{8.106}$
0 1 1 0 1 0 1	$01101010_{8.107}$	$01101011_{8.108}$
0 1 1 0 1 1 0	$01101100_{8.109}$	$01101101_{8.110}$
0 1 1 0 1 1 1	$01101110_{8.111}$	$01101111_{8.112}$
0 1 1 1 0 0 0	$01110000_{8.113}$	$01110001_{8.114}$
0 1 1 1 0 0 1	$01110010_{8.115}$	$01110011_{8.116}$
0 1 1 1 0 1 0	$01110100_{8.117}$	$01110101_{8.118}$
0 1 1 1 0 1 1	$01110110_{8.119}$	$01110111_{8.120}$
0 1 1 1 1 0 0	$01111000_{8.121}$	$01111001_{8.122}$
0 1 1 1 1 0 1	$01111010_{8.123}$	$01111011_{8.124}$
0 1 1 1 1 1 0	$01111100_{8.125}$	$01111101_{8.126}$
0 1 1 1 1 1 1	$01111110_{8.127}$	$01111111_{8.128}$

Level 8 Event Point Patterns
0/1 (cont'd)

	0	1
1 0 0 0 0 0 0	$1 0 0 0 0 0 0 0_{8.129}$	$1 0 0 0 0 0 0 1_{8.130}$
1 0 0 0 0 0 1	$1 0 0 0 0 0 1 0_{8.131}$	$1 0 0 0 0 0 1 1_{8.132}$
1 0 0 0 0 1 0	$1 0 0 0 0 1 0 0_{8.133}$	$1 0 0 0 0 1 0 1_{8.134}$
1 0 0 0 0 1 1	$1 0 0 0 0 1 1 0_{8.135}$	$1 0 0 0 0 1 1 1_{8.136}$
1 0 0 0 1 0 0	$1 0 0 0 1 0 0 0_{8.137}$	$1 0 0 0 1 0 0 1_{8.138}$
1 0 0 0 1 0 1	$1 0 0 0 1 0 1 0_{8.139}$	$1 0 0 0 1 0 1 1_{8.140}$
1 0 0 0 1 1 0	$1 0 0 0 1 1 0 0_{8.141}$	$1 0 0 0 1 1 0 1_{8.142}$
1 0 0 0 1 1 1	$1 0 0 0 1 1 1 0_{8.143}$	$1 0 0 0 1 1 1 1_{8.144}$
1 0 0 1 0 0 0	$1 0 0 1 0 0 0 0_{8.145}$	$1 0 0 1 0 0 0 1_{8.146}$
1 0 0 1 0 0 1	$1 0 0 1 0 0 1 0_{8.147}$	$1 0 0 1 0 0 1 1_{8.148}$
1 0 0 1 0 1 0	$1 0 0 1 0 1 0 0_{8.149}$	$1 0 0 1 0 1 0 1_{8.150}$
1 0 0 1 0 1 1	$1 0 0 1 0 1 1 0_{8.151}$	$1 0 0 1 0 1 1 1_{8.152}$
1 0 0 1 1 0 0	$1 0 0 1 1 0 0 0_{8.153}$	$1 0 0 1 1 0 0 1_{8.154}$
1 0 0 1 1 0 1	$1 0 0 1 1 0 1 0_{8.155}$	$1 0 0 1 1 0 1 1_{8.156}$
1 0 0 1 1 1 0	$1 0 0 1 1 1 0 0_{8.157}$	$1 0 0 1 1 1 0 1_{8.158}$
1 0 0 1 1 1 1	$1 0 0 1 1 1 1 0_{8.159}$	$1 0 0 1 1 1 1 1_{8.160}$

Level 8 Event Point Patterns
0/1 (cont'd)

	0	1
1 0 1 0 0 0 0	$1 0 1 0 0 0 0 0_{8.161}$	$1 0 1 0 0 0 0 1_{8.162}$
1 0 1 0 0 0 1	$1 0 1 0 0 0 1 0_{8.163}$	$1 0 1 0 0 0 1 1_{8.164}$
1 0 1 0 0 1 0	$1 0 1 0 0 1 0 0_{8.165}$	$1 0 1 0 0 1 0 1_{8.166}$
1 0 1 0 0 1 1	$1 0 1 0 0 1 1 0_{8.167}$	$1 0 1 0 0 1 1 1_{8.168}$
1 0 1 0 1 0 0	$1 0 1 0 1 0 0 0_{8.169}$	$1 0 1 0 1 0 0 1_{8.170}$
1 0 1 0 1 0 1	$1 0 1 0 1 0 1 0_{8.171}$	$1 0 1 0 1 0 1 1_{8.172}$
1 0 1 0 1 1 0	$1 0 1 0 1 1 0 0_{8.173}$	$1 0 1 0 1 1 0 1_{8.174}$
1 0 1 0 1 1 1	$1 0 1 0 1 1 1 0_{8.175}$	$1 0 1 0 1 1 1 1_{8.176}$
1 0 1 1 0 0 0	$1 0 1 1 0 0 0 0_{8.177}$	$1 0 1 1 0 0 0 1_{8.178}$
1 0 1 1 0 0 1	$1 0 1 1 0 0 1 0_{8.179}$	$1 0 1 1 0 0 1 1_{8.180}$
1 0 1 1 0 1 0	$1 0 1 1 0 1 0 0_{8.181}$	$1 0 1 1 0 1 0 1_{8.182}$
1 0 1 1 0 1 1	$1 0 1 1 0 1 1 0_{8.183}$	$1 0 1 1 0 1 1 1_{8.184}$
1 0 1 1 1 0 0	$1 0 1 1 1 0 0 0_{8.185}$	$1 0 1 1 1 0 0 1_{8.186}$
1 0 1 1 1 0 1	$1 0 1 1 1 0 1 0_{8.187}$	$1 0 1 1 1 0 1 1_{8.188}$
1 0 1 1 1 1 0	$1 0 1 1 1 1 0 0_{8.189}$	$1 0 1 1 1 1 0 1_{8.190}$
1 0 1 1 1 1 1	$1 0 1 1 1 1 1 0_{8.191}$	$1 0 1 1 1 1 1 1_{8.192}$

Level 8 Event Point Patterns
0/1 (cont'd)

	0	1
1 1 0 0 0 0 0	$1 1 0 0 0 0 0 0_{8.193}$	$1 1 0 0 0 0 0 1_{8.194}$
1 1 0 0 0 0 1	$1 1 0 0 0 0 1 0_{8.195}$	$1 1 0 0 0 0 1 1_{8.196}$
1 1 0 0 0 1 0	$1 1 0 0 0 1 0 0_{8.197}$	$1 1 0 0 0 1 0 1_{8.198}$
1 1 0 0 0 1 1	$1 1 0 0 0 1 1 0_{8.199}$	$1 1 0 0 0 1 1 1_{8.200}$
1 1 0 0 1 0 0	$1 1 0 0 1 0 0 0_{8.201}$	$1 1 0 0 1 0 0 1_{8.202}$
1 1 0 0 1 0 1	$1 1 0 0 1 0 1 0_{8.203}$	$1 1 0 0 1 0 1 1_{8.204}$
1 1 0 0 1 1 0	$1 1 0 0 1 1 0 0_{8.205}$	$1 1 0 0 1 1 0 1_{8.206}$
1 1 0 0 1 1 1	$1 1 0 0 1 1 1 0_{8.207}$	$1 1 0 0 1 1 1 1_{8.208}$
1 1 0 1 0 0 0	$1 1 0 1 0 0 0 0_{8.209}$	$1 1 0 1 0 0 0 1_{8.210}$
1 1 0 1 0 0 1	$1 1 0 1 0 0 1 0_{8.211}$	$1 1 0 1 0 0 1 1_{8.212}$
1 1 0 1 0 1 0	$1 1 0 1 0 1 0 0_{8.213}$	$1 1 0 1 0 1 0 1_{8.214}$
1 1 0 1 0 1 1	$1 1 0 1 0 1 1 0_{8.215}$	$1 1 0 1 0 1 1 1_{8.216}$
1 1 0 1 1 0 0	$1 1 0 1 1 0 0 0_{8.217}$	$1 1 0 1 1 0 0 1_{8.218}$
1 1 0 1 1 0 1	$1 1 0 1 1 0 1 0_{8.219}$	$1 1 0 1 1 0 1 1_{8.220}$
1 1 0 1 1 1 0	$1 1 0 1 1 1 0 0_{8.221}$	$1 1 0 1 1 1 0 1_{8.222}$
1 1 0 1 1 1 1	$1 1 0 1 1 1 1 0_{8.223}$	$1 1 0 1 1 1 1 1_{8.224}$

Level 8 Event Point Patterns
0/1 (cont'd)

	0	1
1110000	$11100000_{8.225}$	$11100001_{8.226}$
1110001	$11100010_{8.227}$	$11100011_{8.228}$
1110010	$11100100_{8.229}$	$11100101_{8.230}$
1110011	$11100110_{8.231}$	$11100111_{8.232}$
1110100	$11101000_{8.233}$	$11101001_{8.234}$
1110101	$11101010_{8.235}$	$11101011_{8.236}$
1110110	$11101100_{8.237}$	$11101101_{8.238}$
1110111	$11101110_{8.239}$	$11101111_{8.240}$
1111000	$11110000_{8.241}$	$11110001_{8.242}$
1111001	$11110010_{8.243}$	$11110011_{8.244}$
1111010	$11110100_{8.245}$	$11110101_{8.246}$
1111011	$11110110_{8.247}$	$11110111_{8.248}$
1111100	$11111000_{8.249}$	$11111001_{8.250}$
1111101	$11111010_{8.251}$	$11111011_{8.252}$
1111110	$11111100_{8.253}$	$11111101_{8.254}$
1111111	$11111110_{8.255}$	$11111111_{8.256}$

Level 8 Event Point Patterns
Quarter Rest/Note

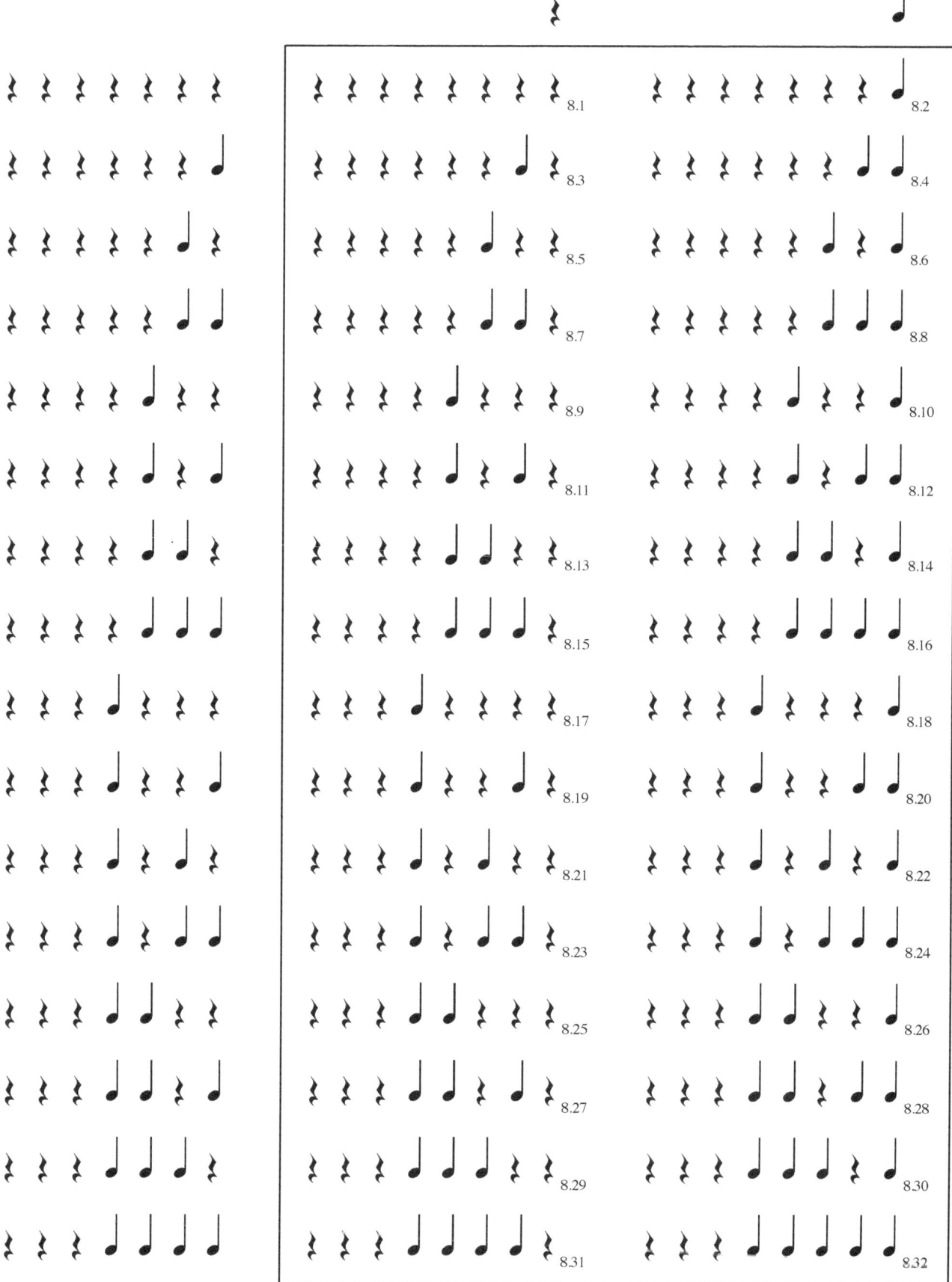

Level 8 Event Point Patterns
Quarter Rest/Note (cont'd)

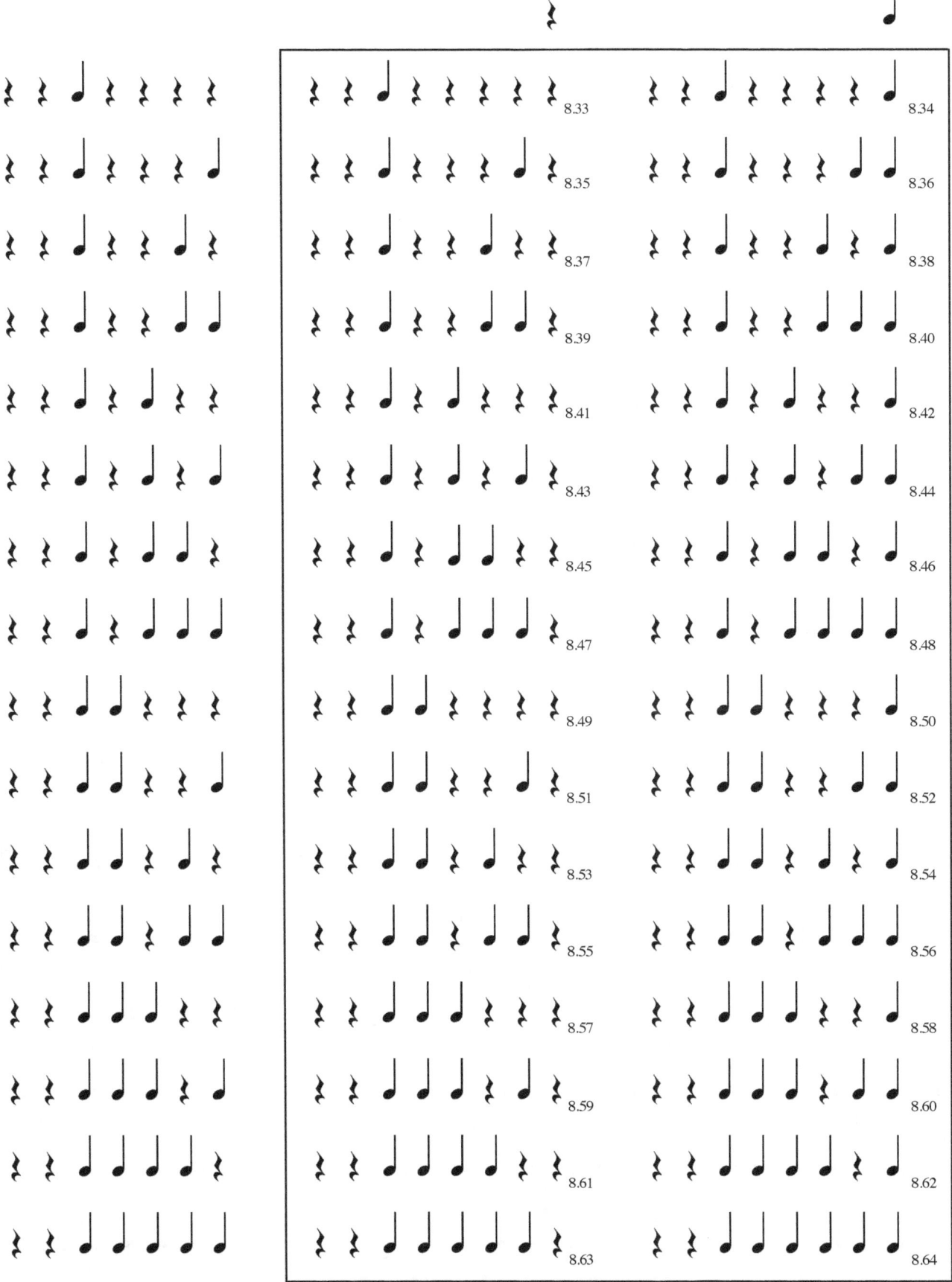

Level 8 Event Point Patterns
Quarter Rest/Note (cont'd)

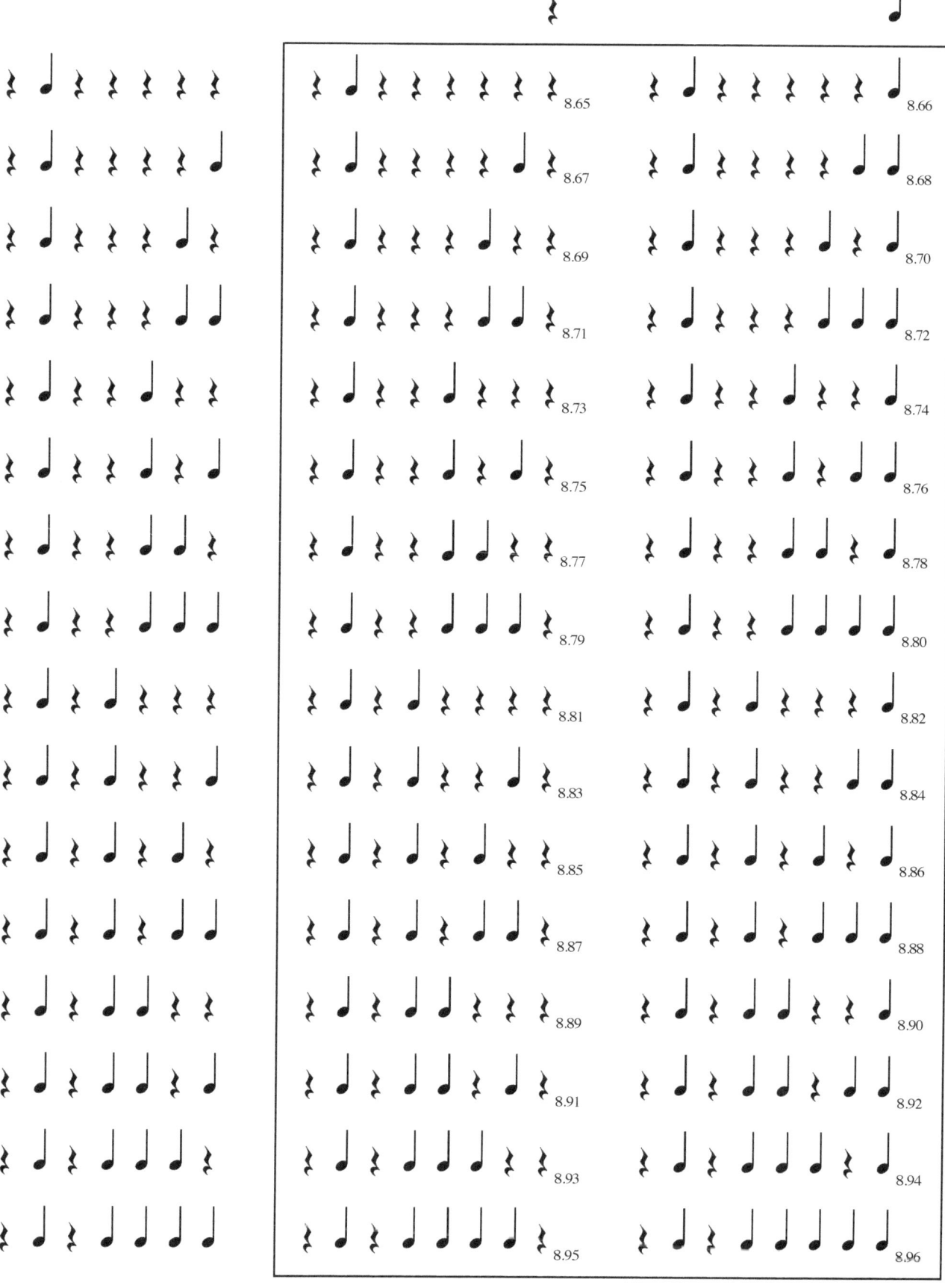

Level 8 Event Point Patterns
Quarter Rest/Note (cont'd)

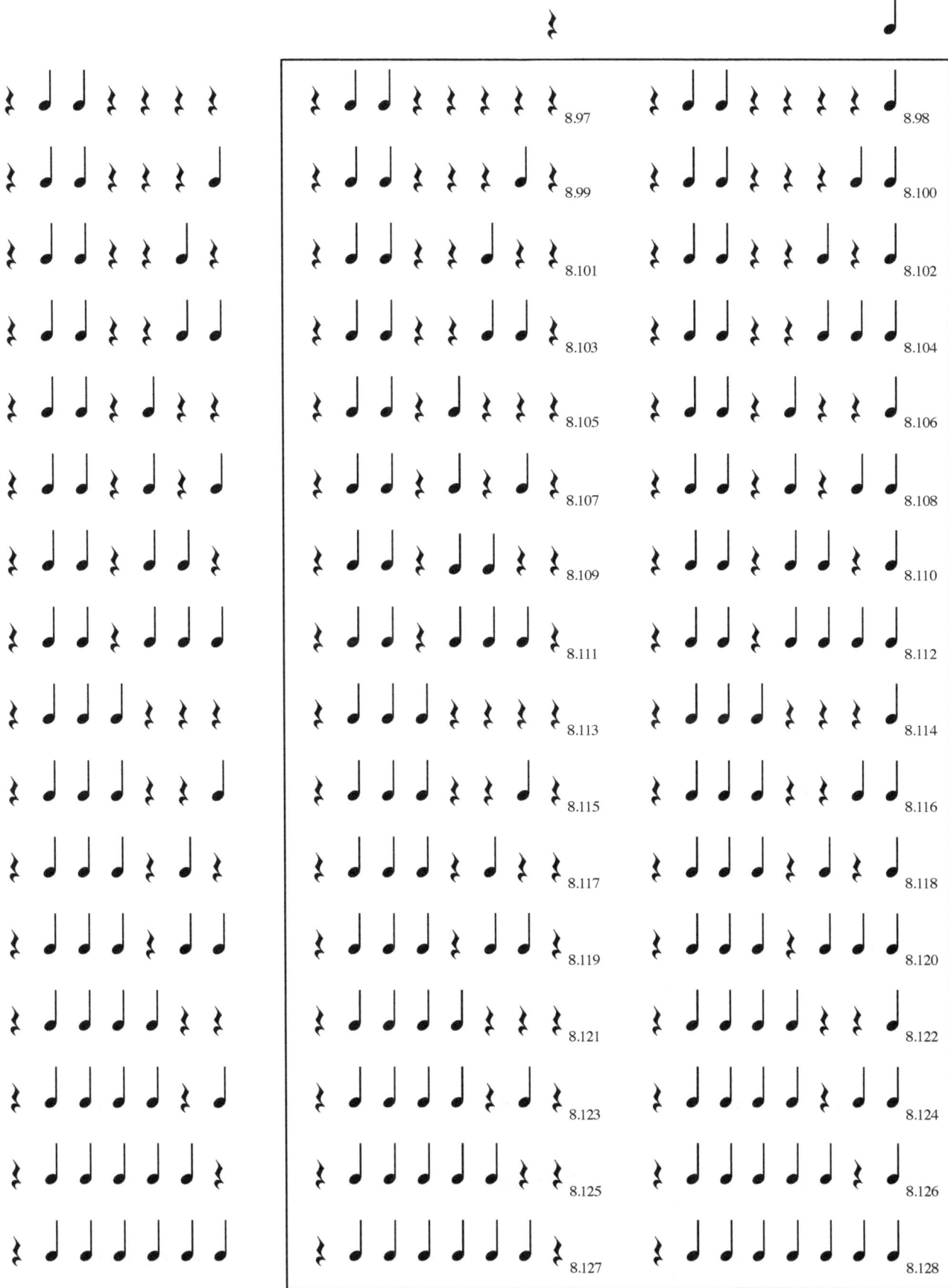

Level 8 Event Point Patterns
Quarter Rest/Note (cont'd)

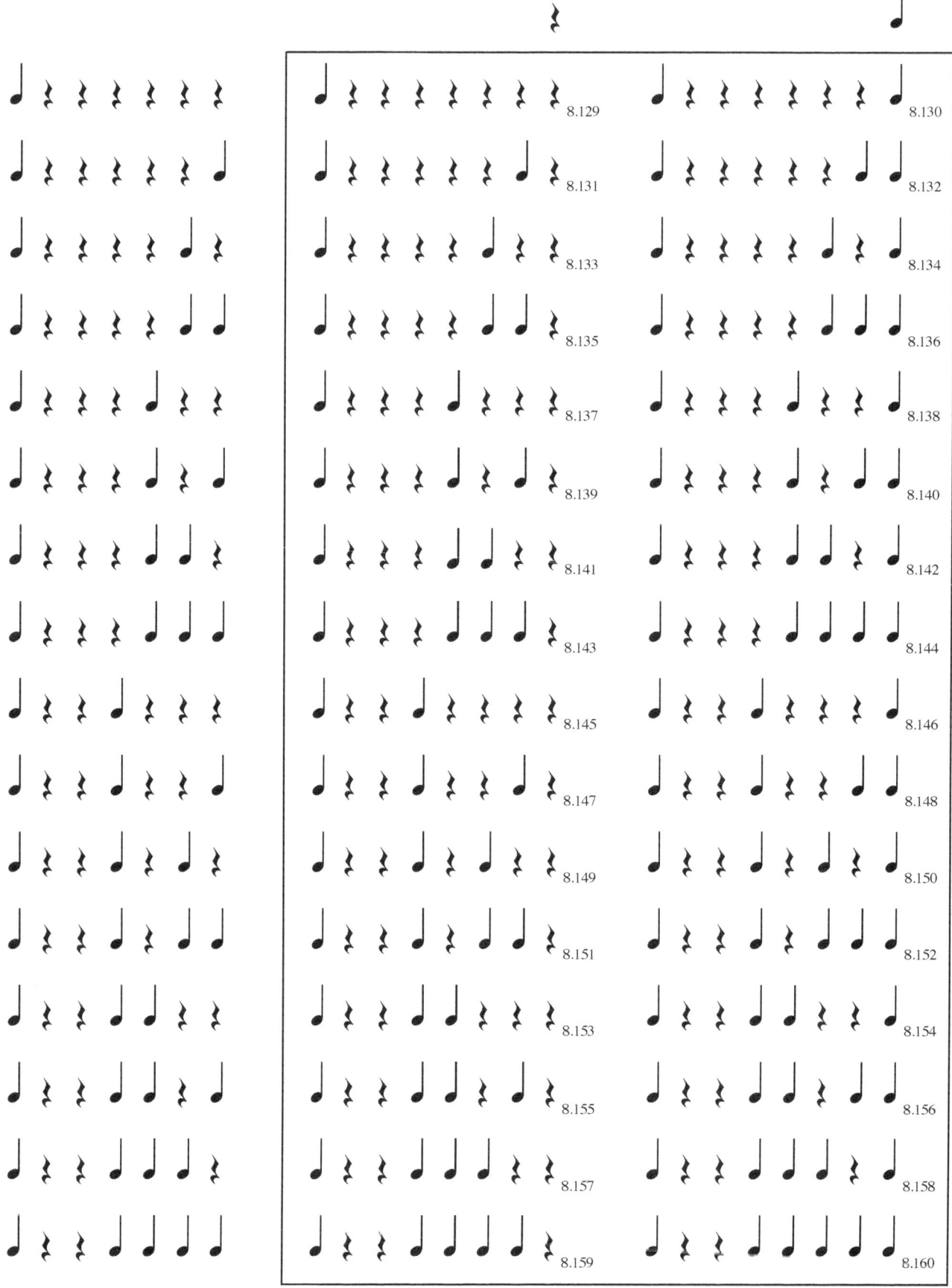

Level 8 Event Point Patterns
Quarter Rest/Note (cont'd)

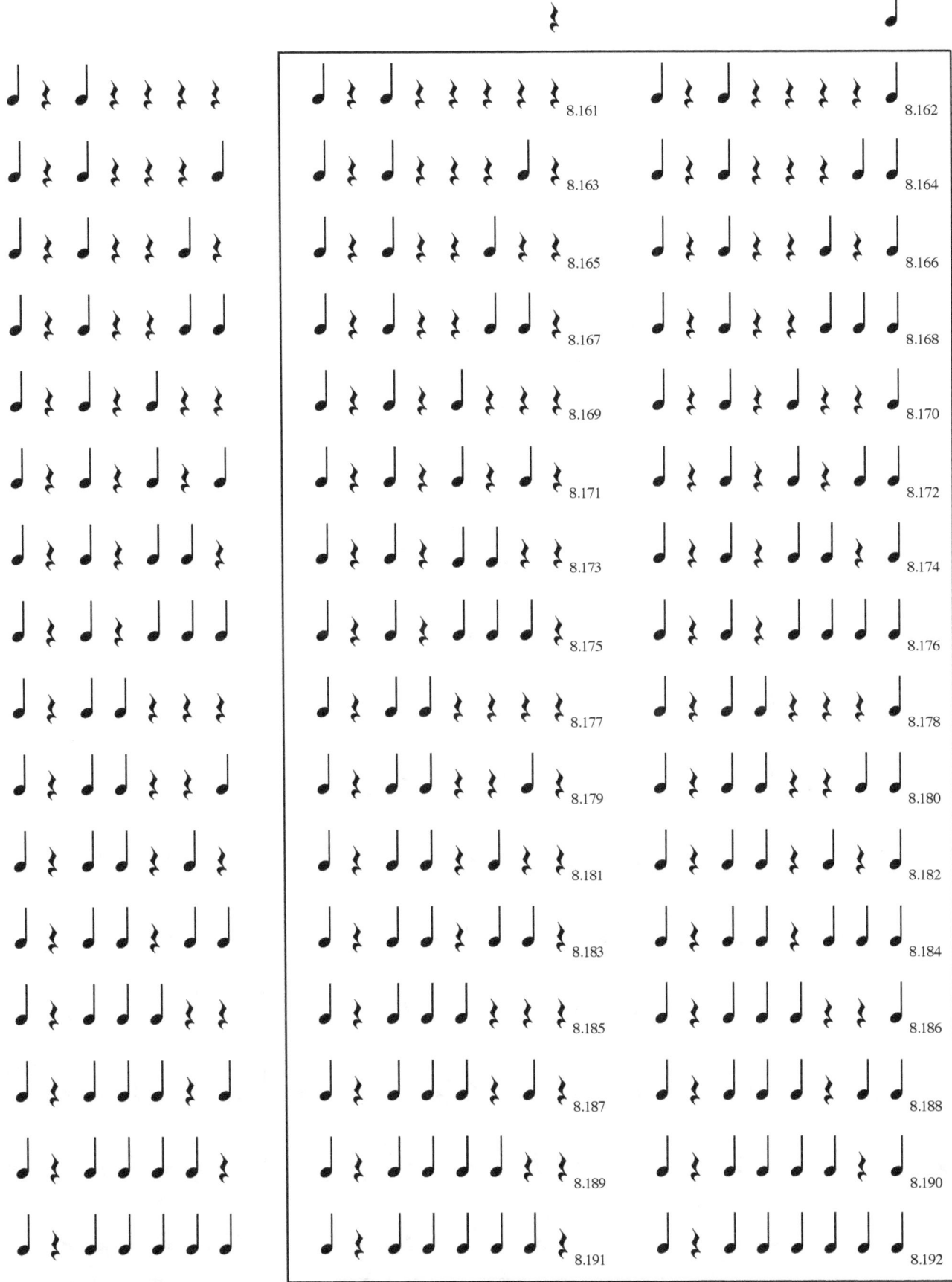

Level 8 Event Point Patterns
Quarter Rest/Note (cont'd)

Level 8 Event Point Patterns
Quarter Rest/Note (cont'd)

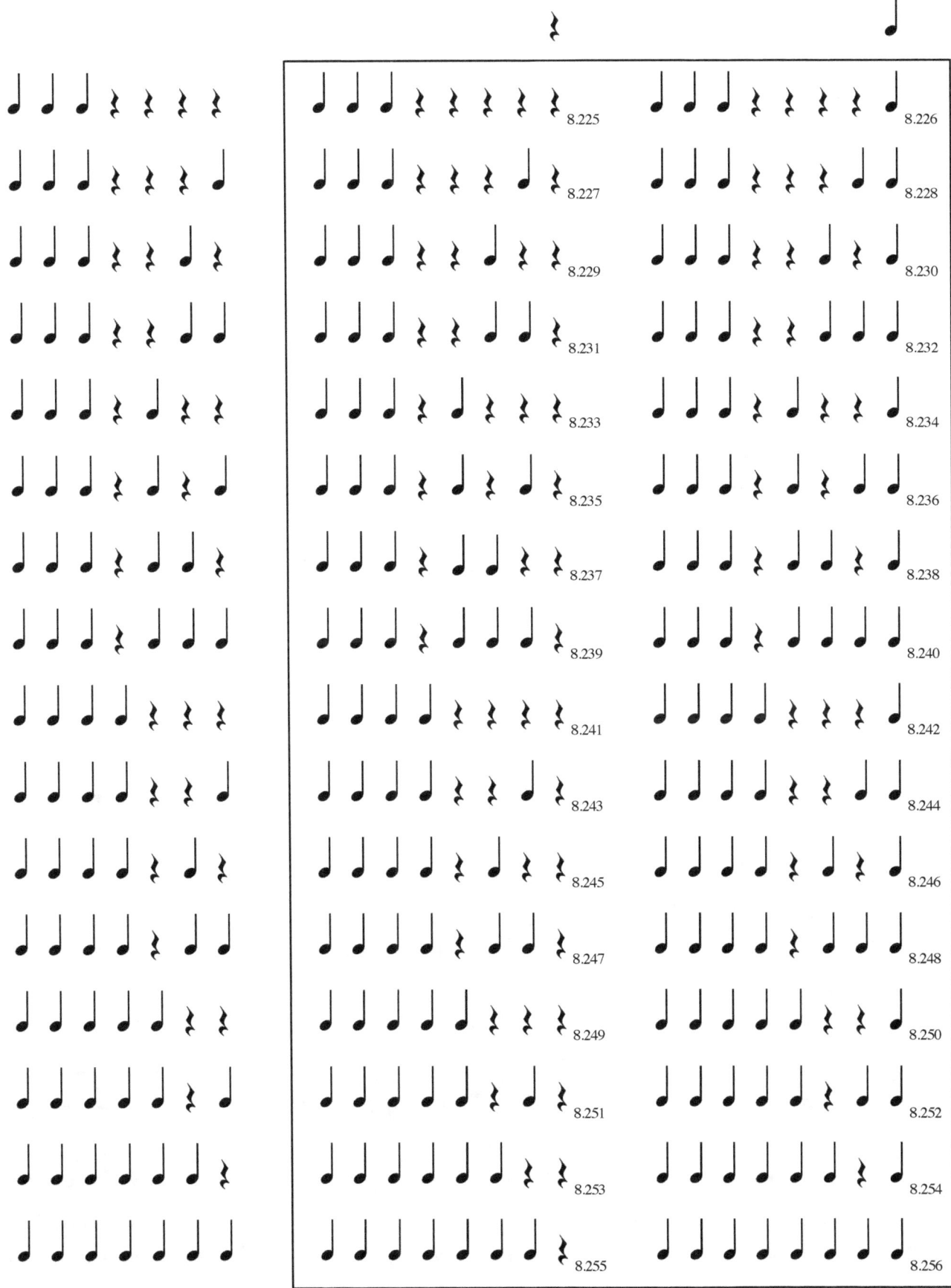

Level 8 Event Point Patterns
Eighth Rest/Note

Level 8 Event Point Patterns
Eighth Rest/Note (cont'd)

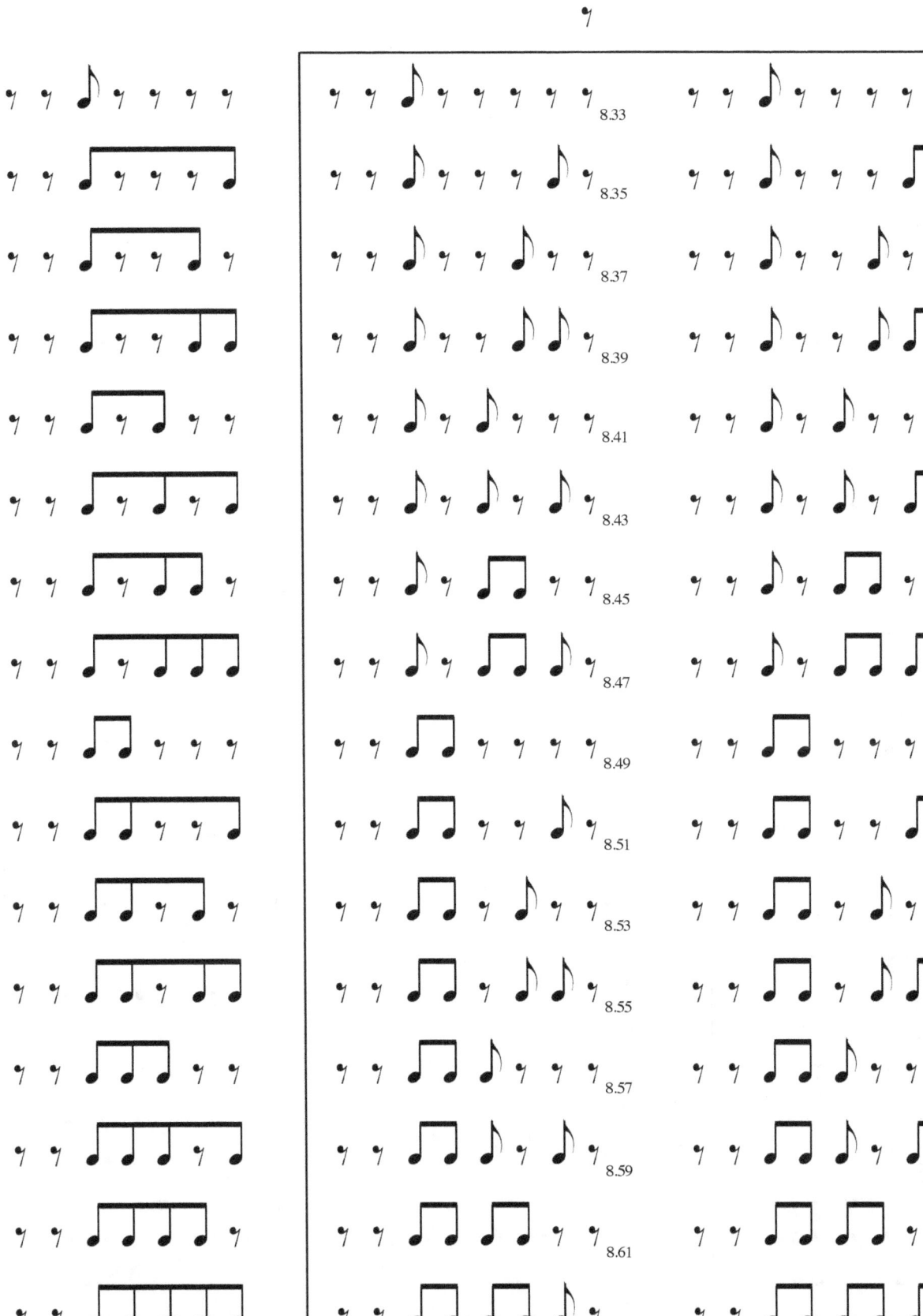

Level 8 Event Point Patterns
Eighth Rest/Note (cont'd)

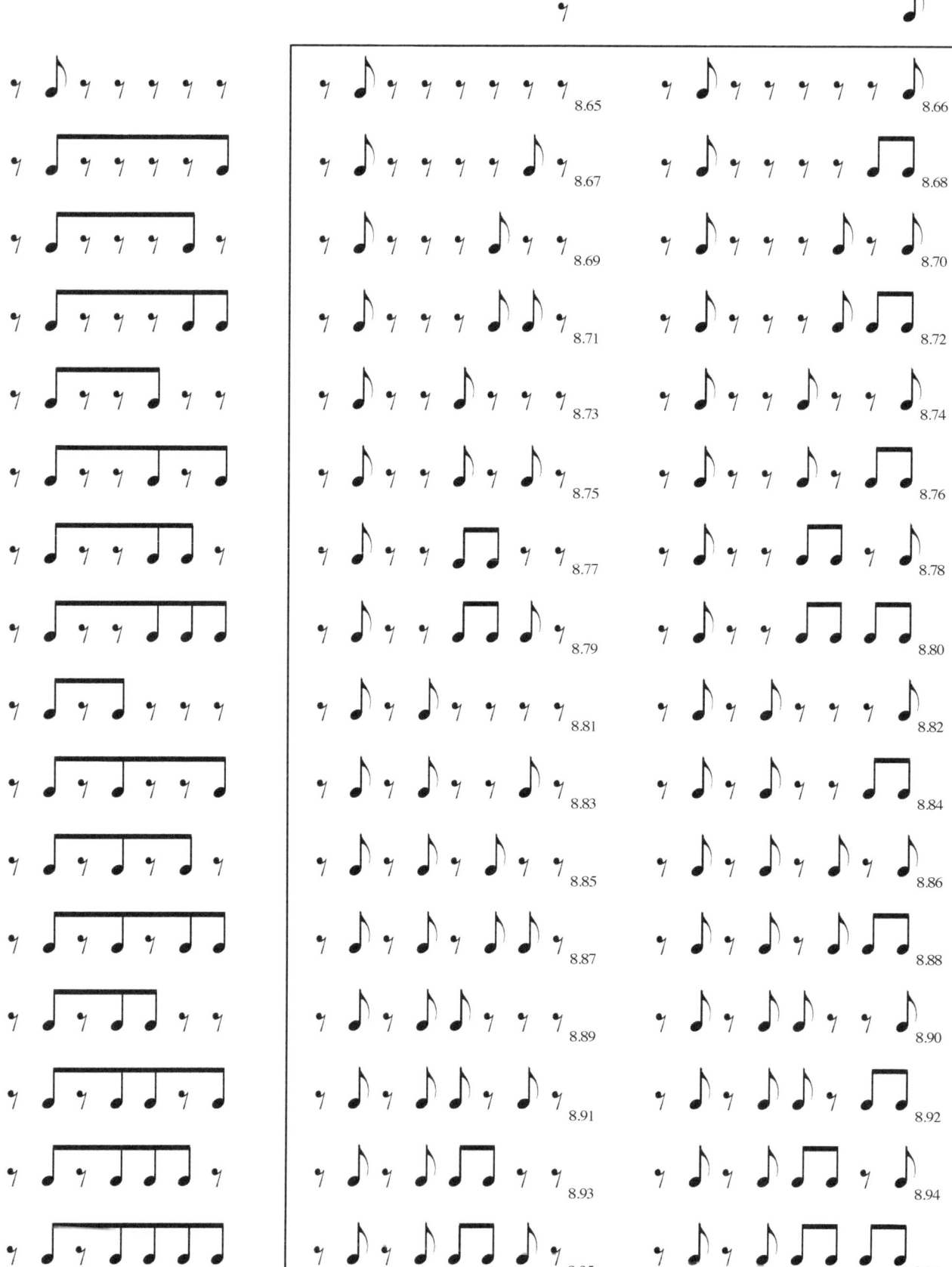

Level 8 Event Point Patterns
Eighth Rest/Note (cont'd)

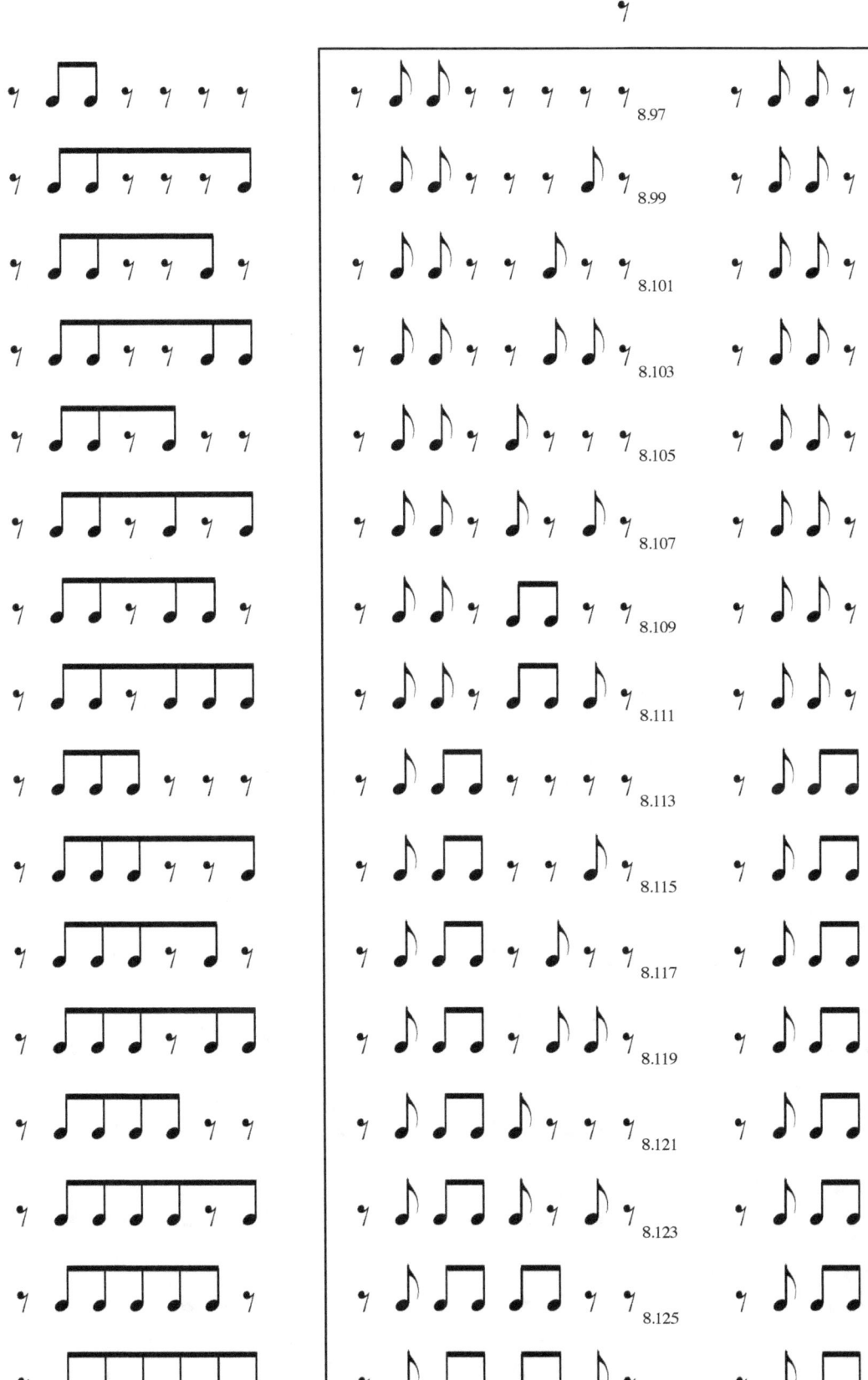

Level 8 Event Point Patterns
Eighth Rest/Note (cont'd)

Level 8 Event Point Patterns
Eighth Rest/Note (cont'd)

Level 8 Event Point Patterns
Eighth Rest/Note (cont'd)

Level 8 Event Point Patterns
Eighth Rest/Note (cont'd)

Level 8 Event Point Patterns
Sixteenth Rest/Note

Level 8 Event Point Patterns
Sixteenth Rest/Note (cont'd)

Level 8 Event Point Patterns
Sixteenth Rest/Note (cont'd)

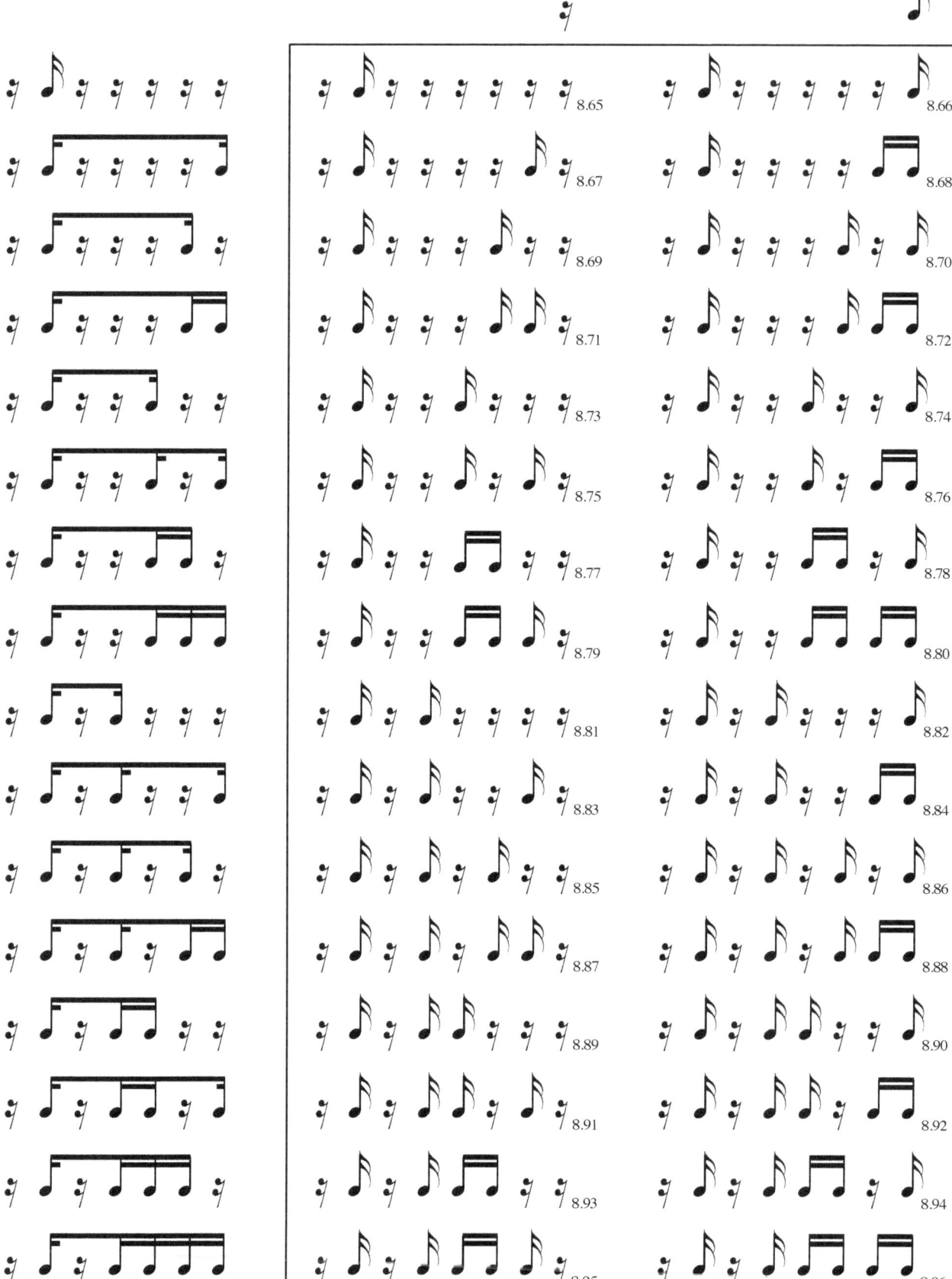

Level 8 Event Point Patterns
Sixteenth Rest/Note (cont'd)

Level 8 Event Point Patterns
Sixteenth Rest/Note (cont'd)

Level 8 Event Point Patterns
Sixteenth Rest/Note (cont'd)

204

Level 8 Event Point Patterns
Sixteenth Rest/Note (cont'd)

Level 8 Event Point Patterns
Sixteenth Rest/Note (cont'd)

Level 8 Event Point Patterns
Thirty-second Rest/Note

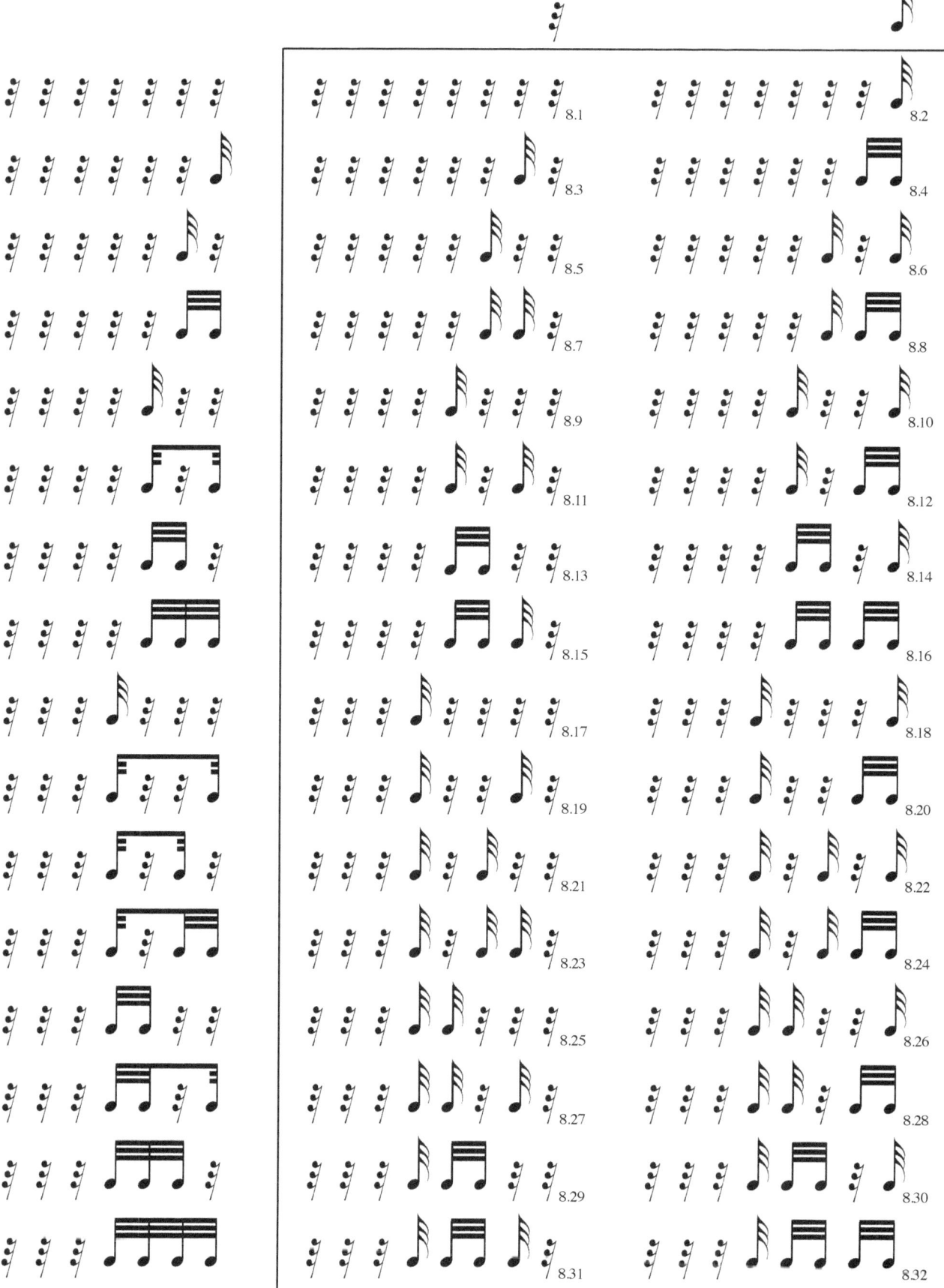

Level 8 Event Point Patterns
Thirty-second Rest/Note (cont'd)

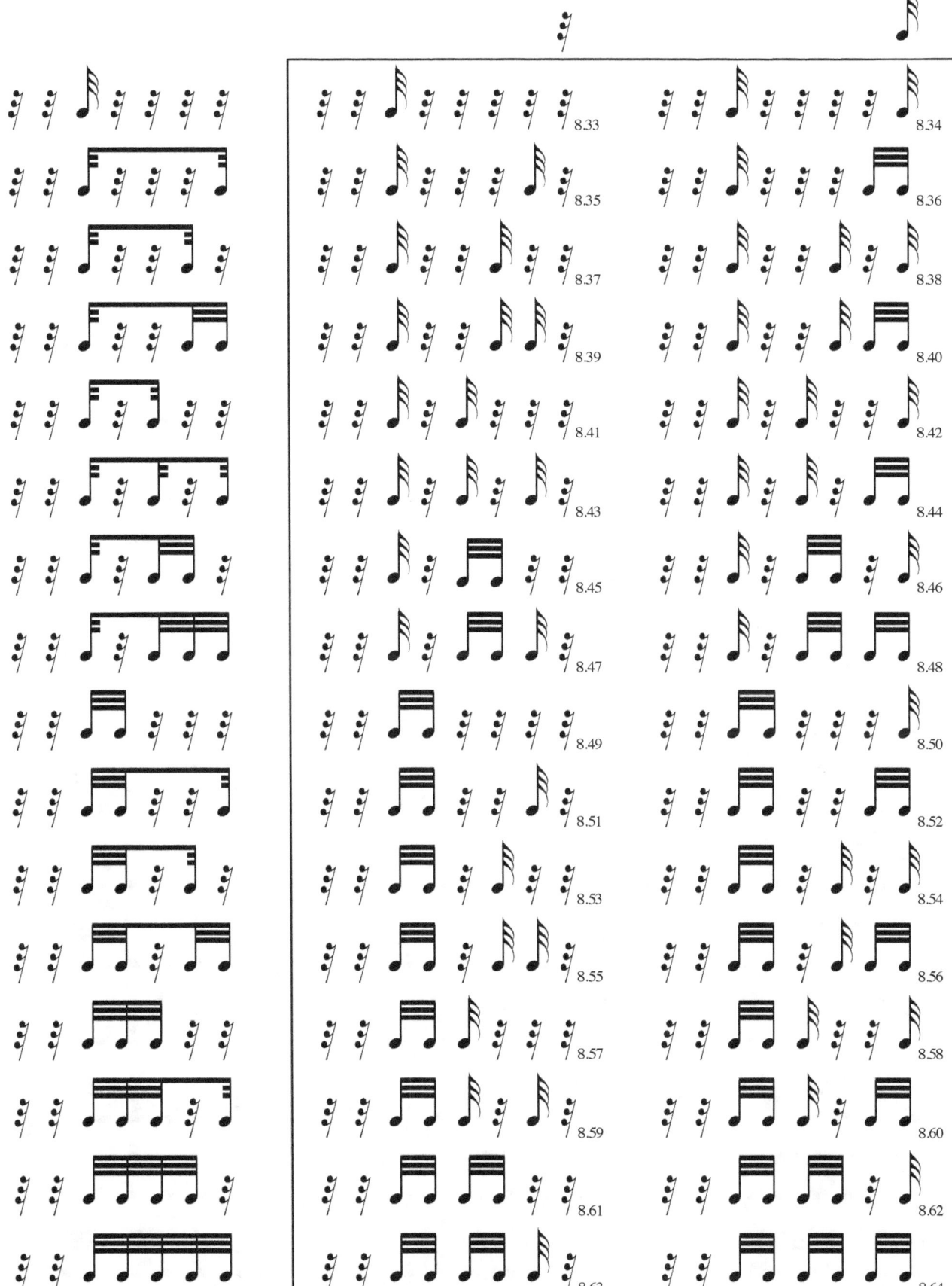

Level 8 Event Point Patterns
Thirty-second Rest/Note (cont'd)

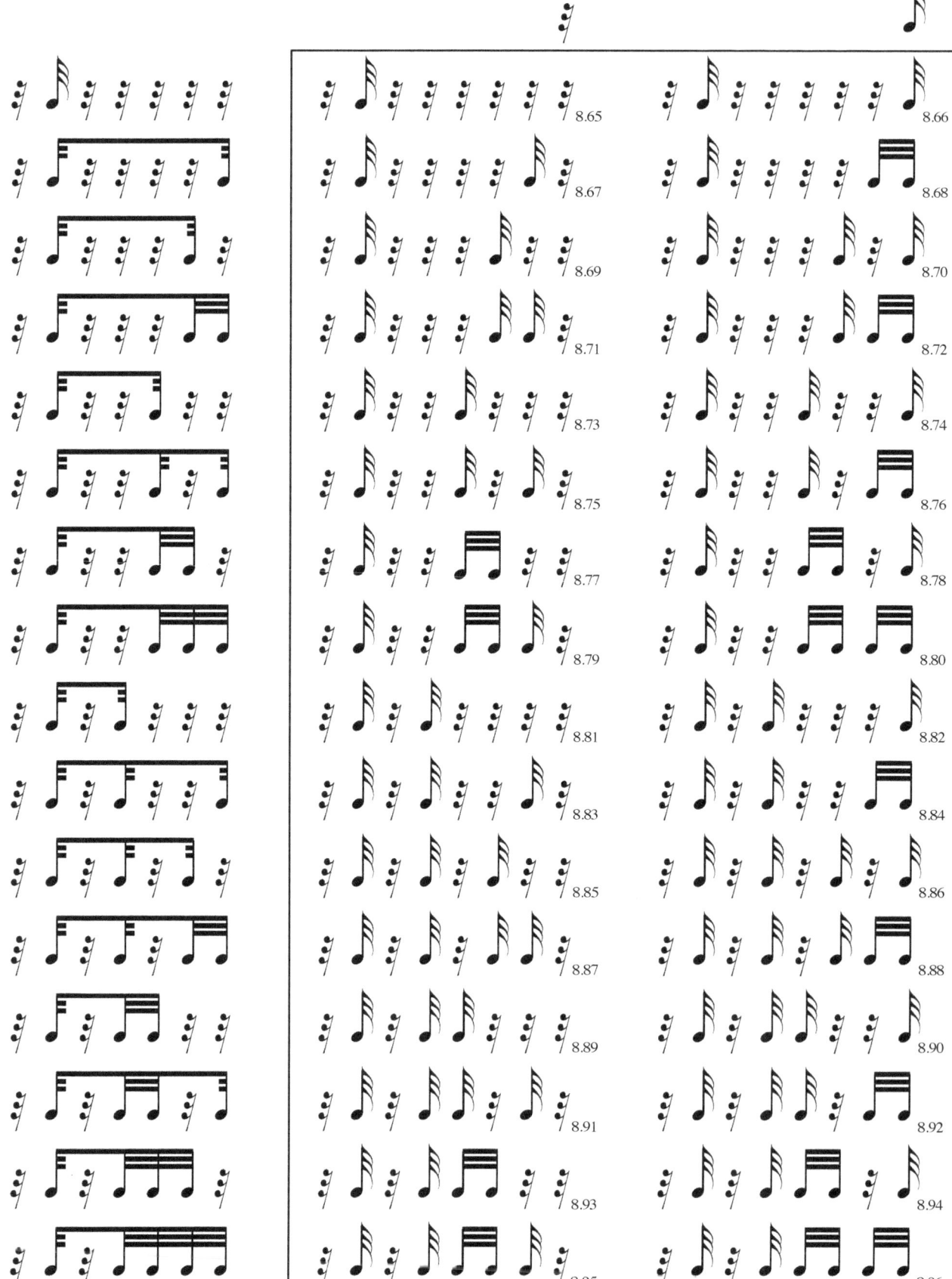

Level 8 Event Point Patterns
Thirty-second Rest/Note (cont'd)

Level 8 Event Point Patterns
Thirty-second Rest/Note (cont'd)

Level 8 Event Point Patterns
Thirty-second Rest/Note (cont'd)

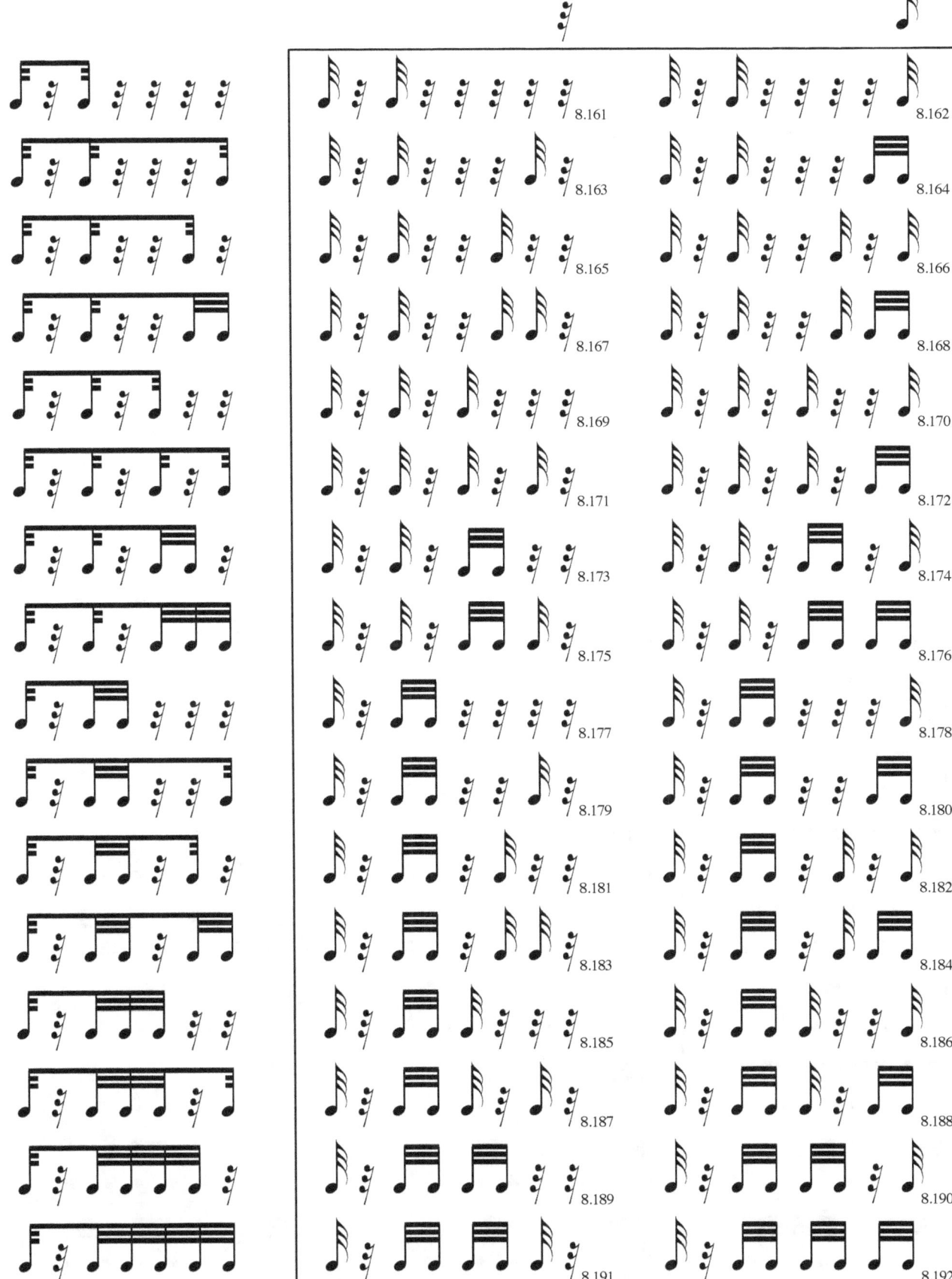

Level 8 Event Point Patterns
Thirty-second Rest/Note (cont'd)

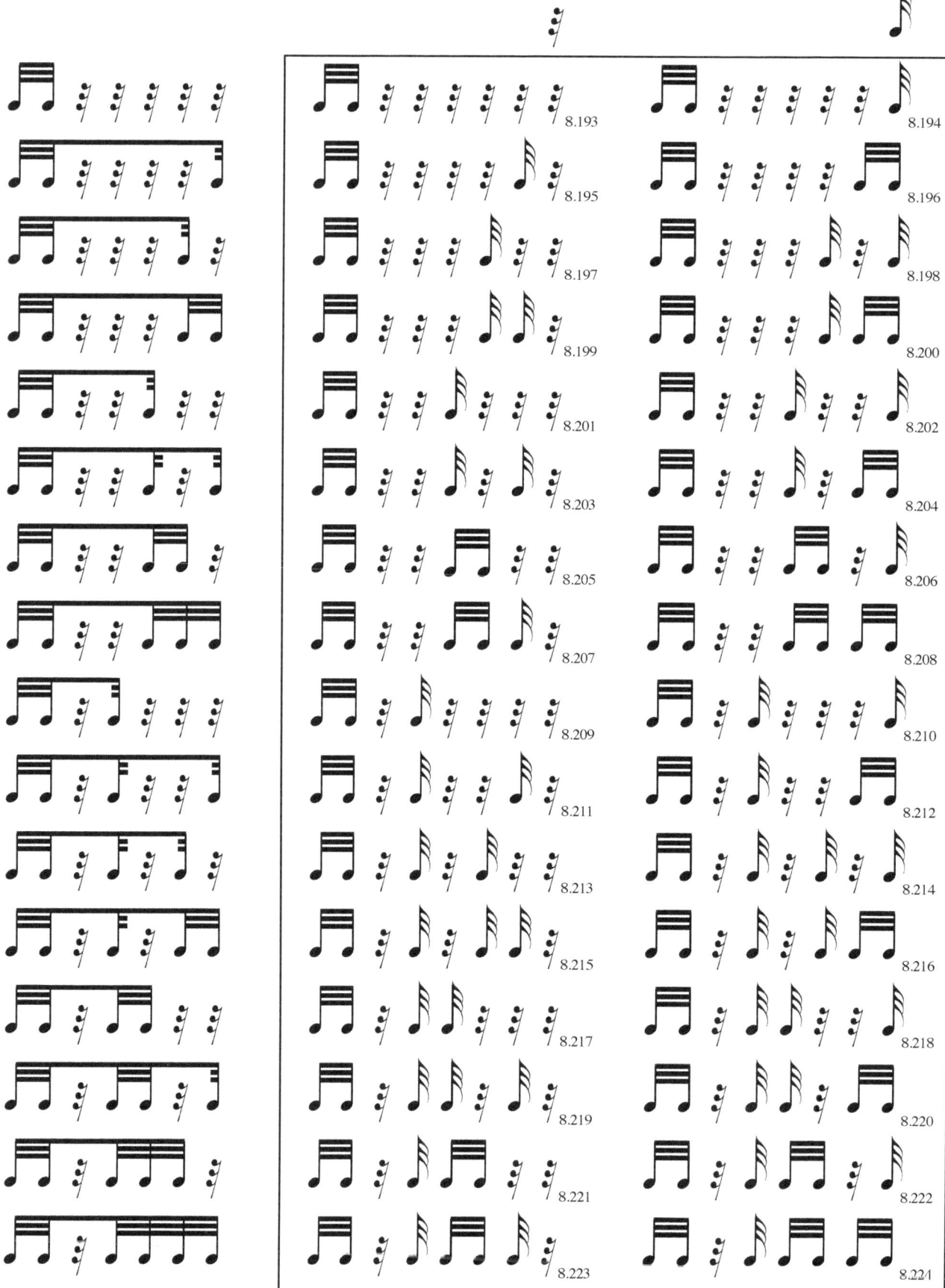

Level 8 Event Point Patterns
Thirty-second Rest/Note (cont'd)

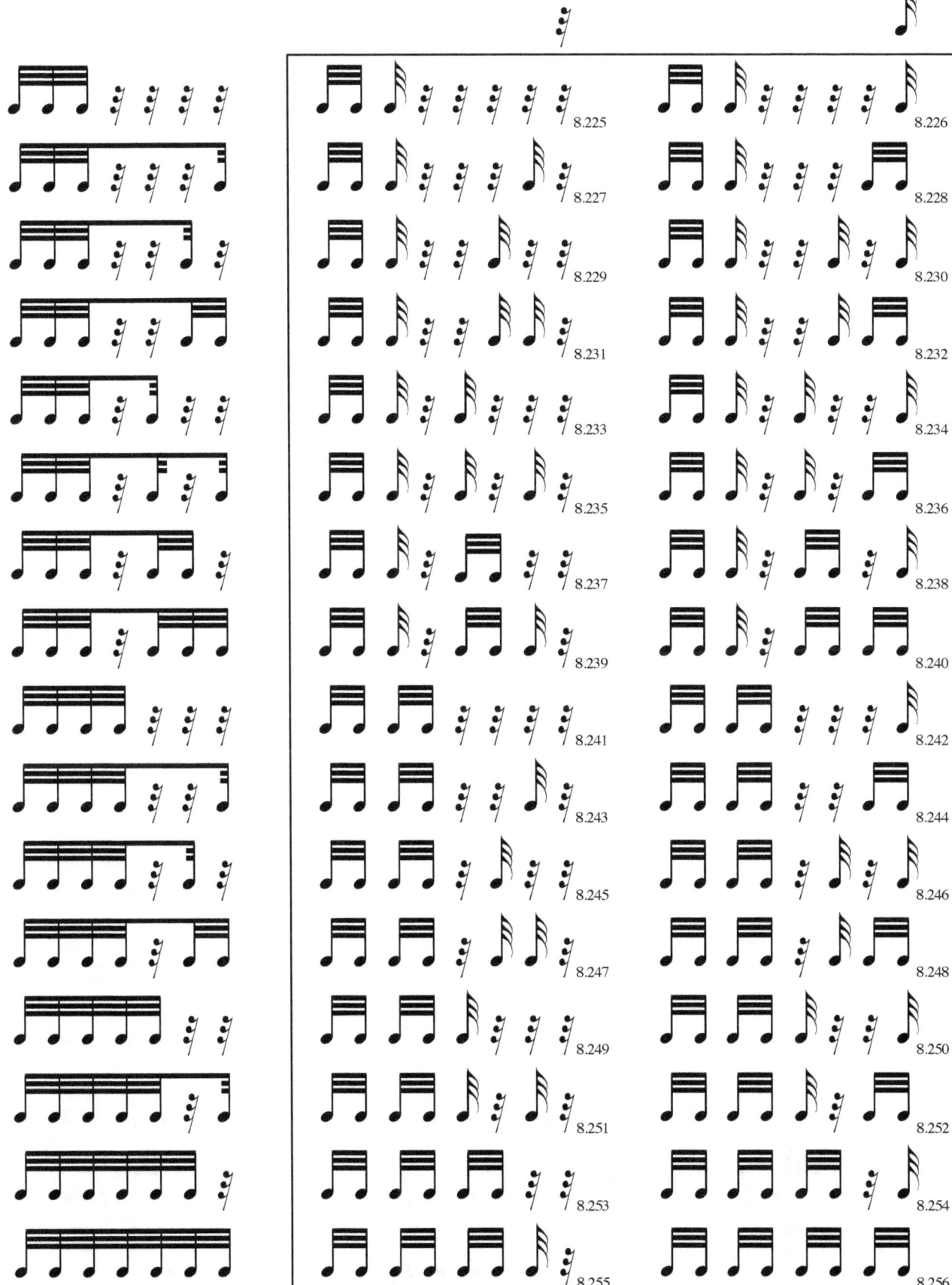

Level 8 Event Point Patterns
Sixty-fourth Rest/Note

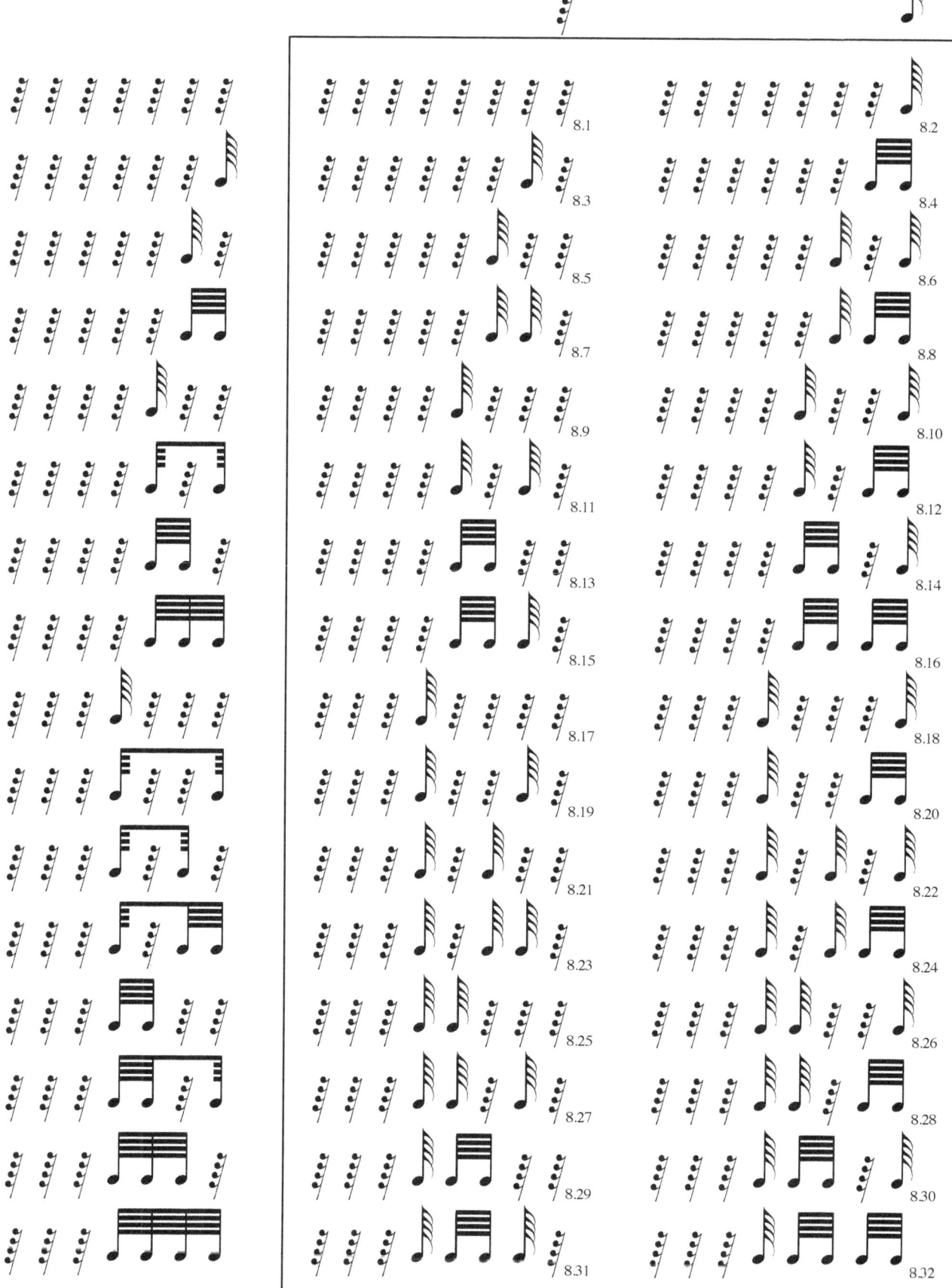

Level 8 Event Point Patterns
Sixty-fourth Rest/Note (cont'd)

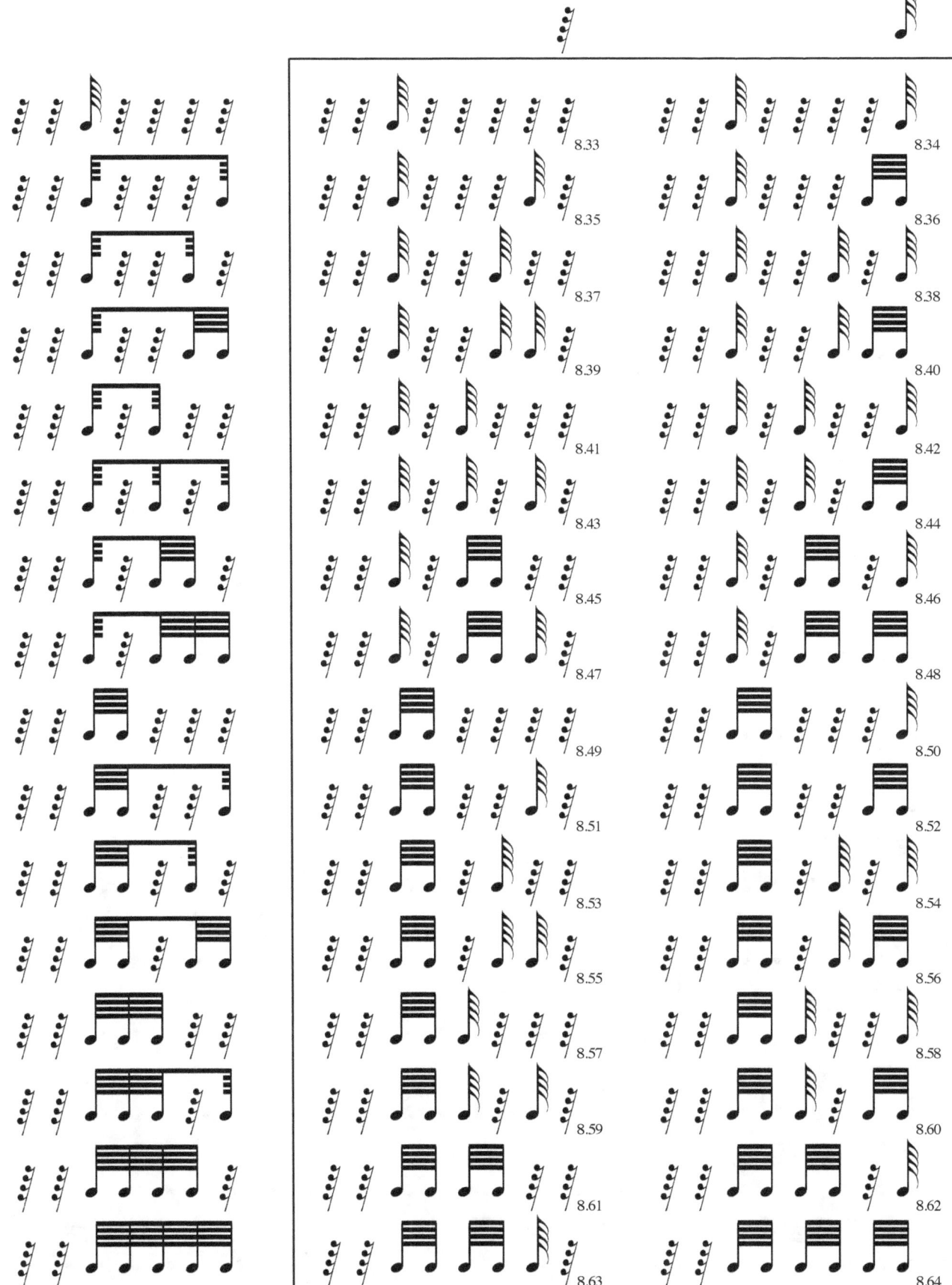

Level 8 Event Point Patterns
Sixty-fourth Rest/Note (cont'd)

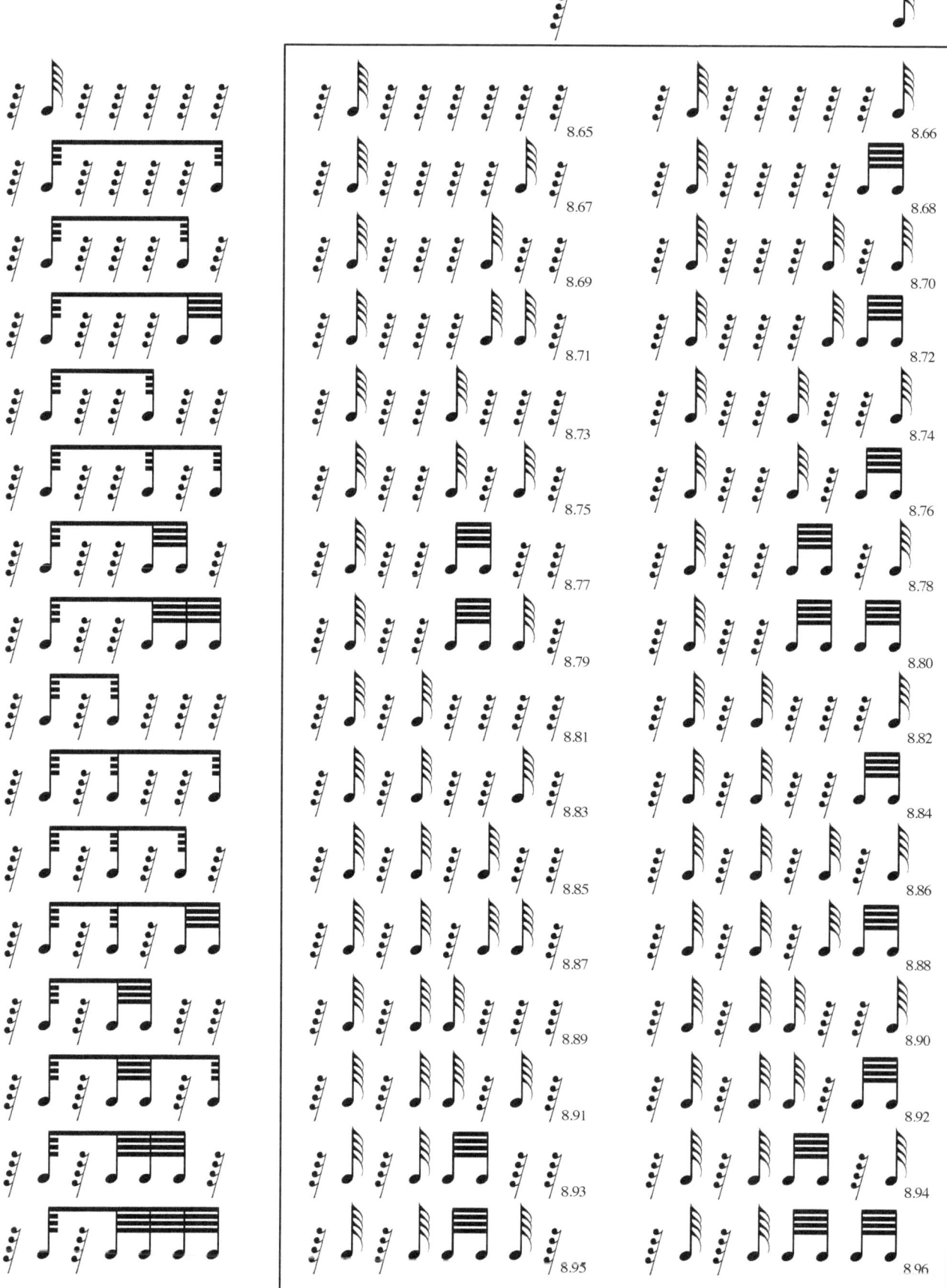

Level 8 Event Point Patterns
Sixty-fourth Rest/Note (cont'd)

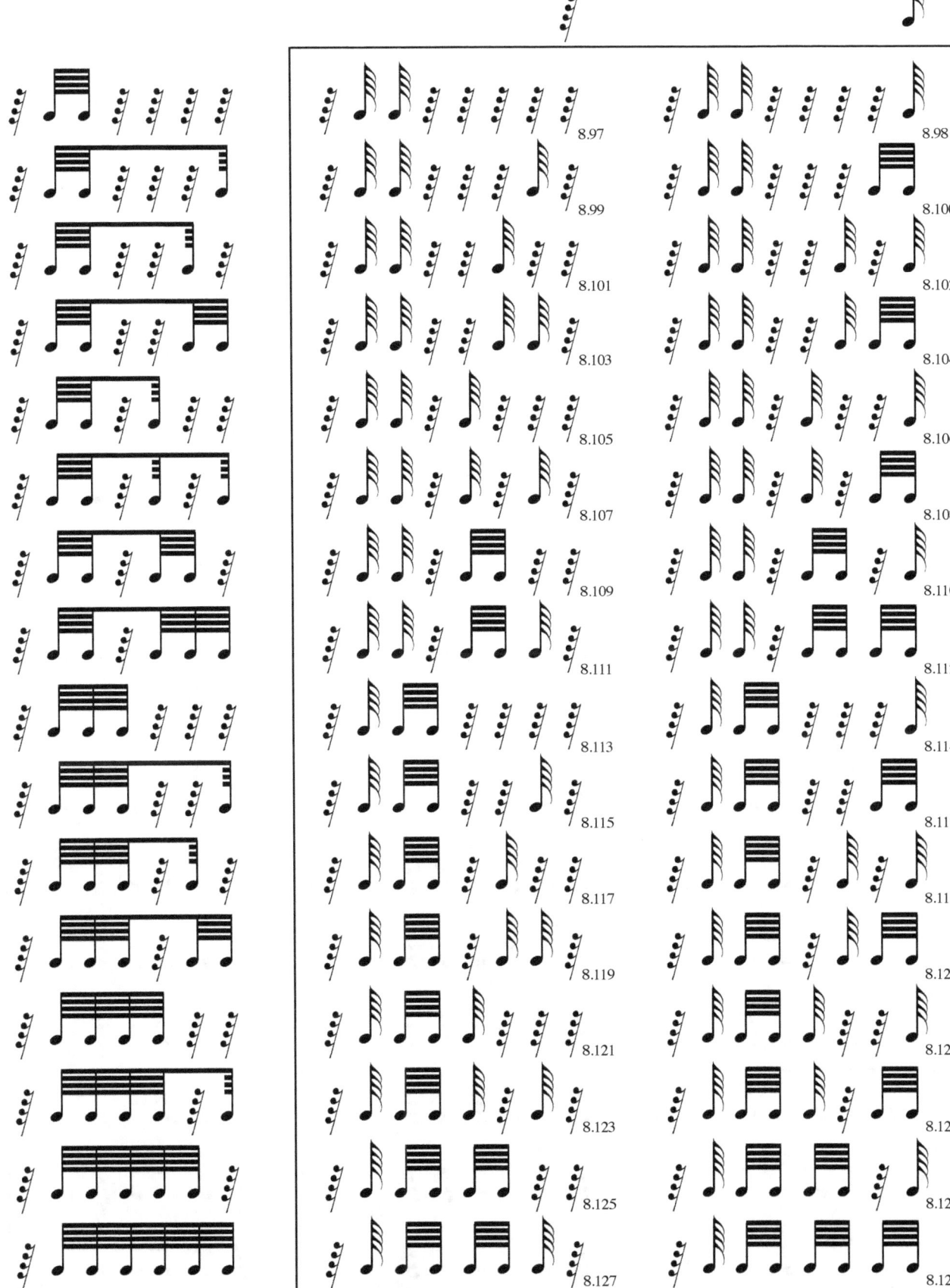

Level 8 Event Point Patterns
Sixty-fourth Rest/Note (cont'd)

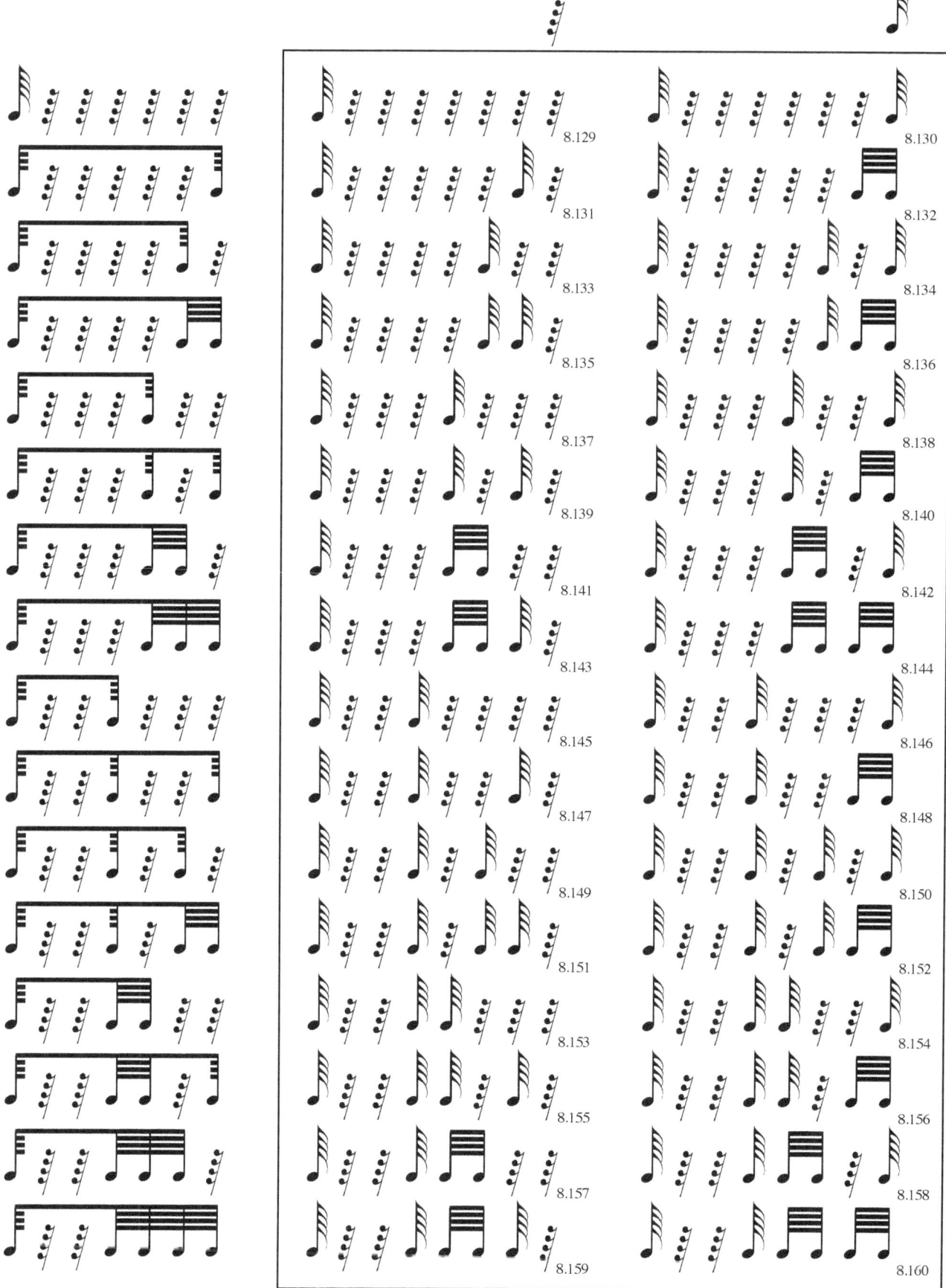

Level 8 Event Point Patterns
Sixty-fourth Rest/Note (cont'd)

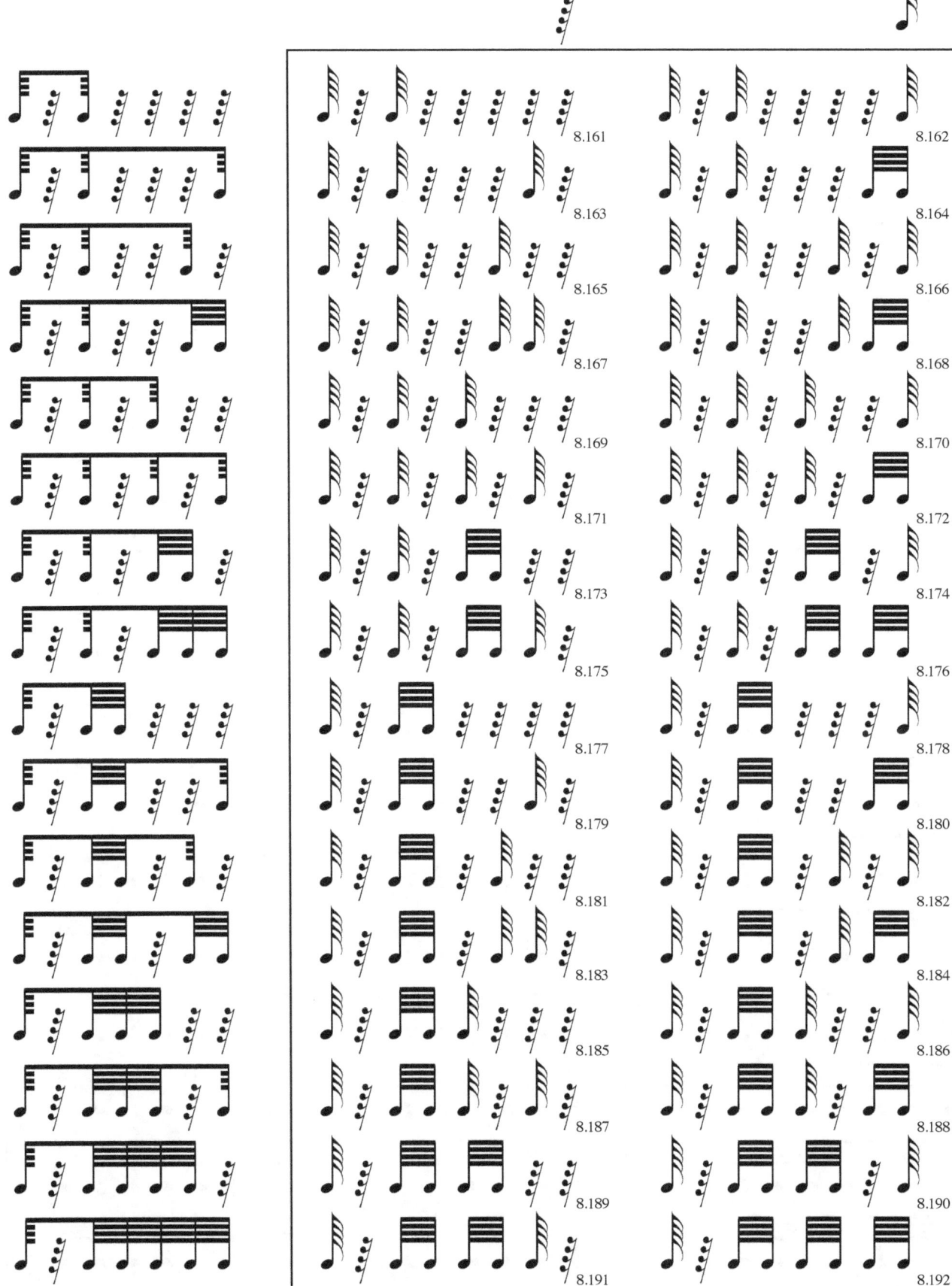

Level 8 Event Point Patterns
Sixty-fourth Rest/Note (cont'd)

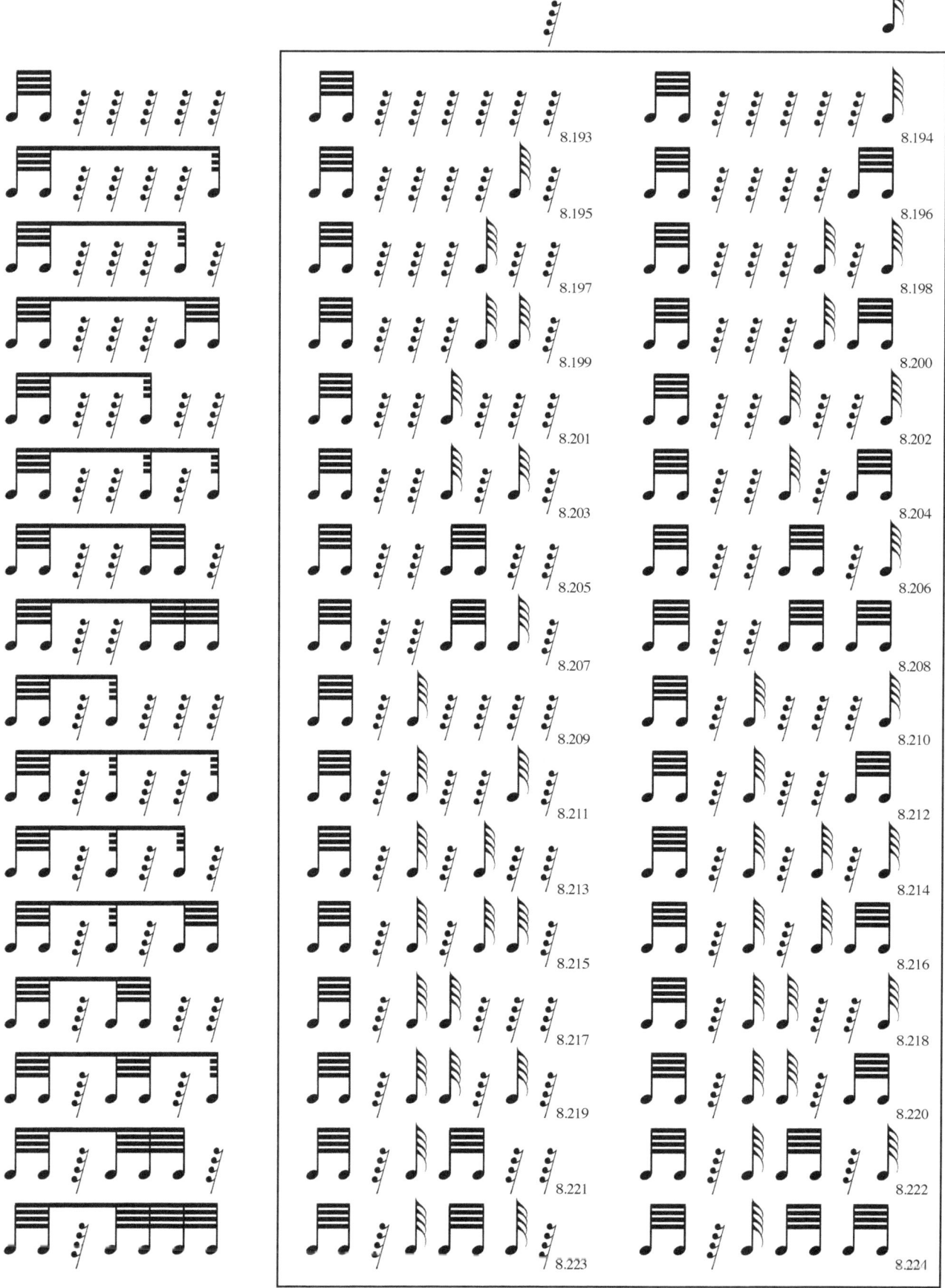

Level 8 Event Point Patterns
Sixty-fourth Rest/Note (cont'd)

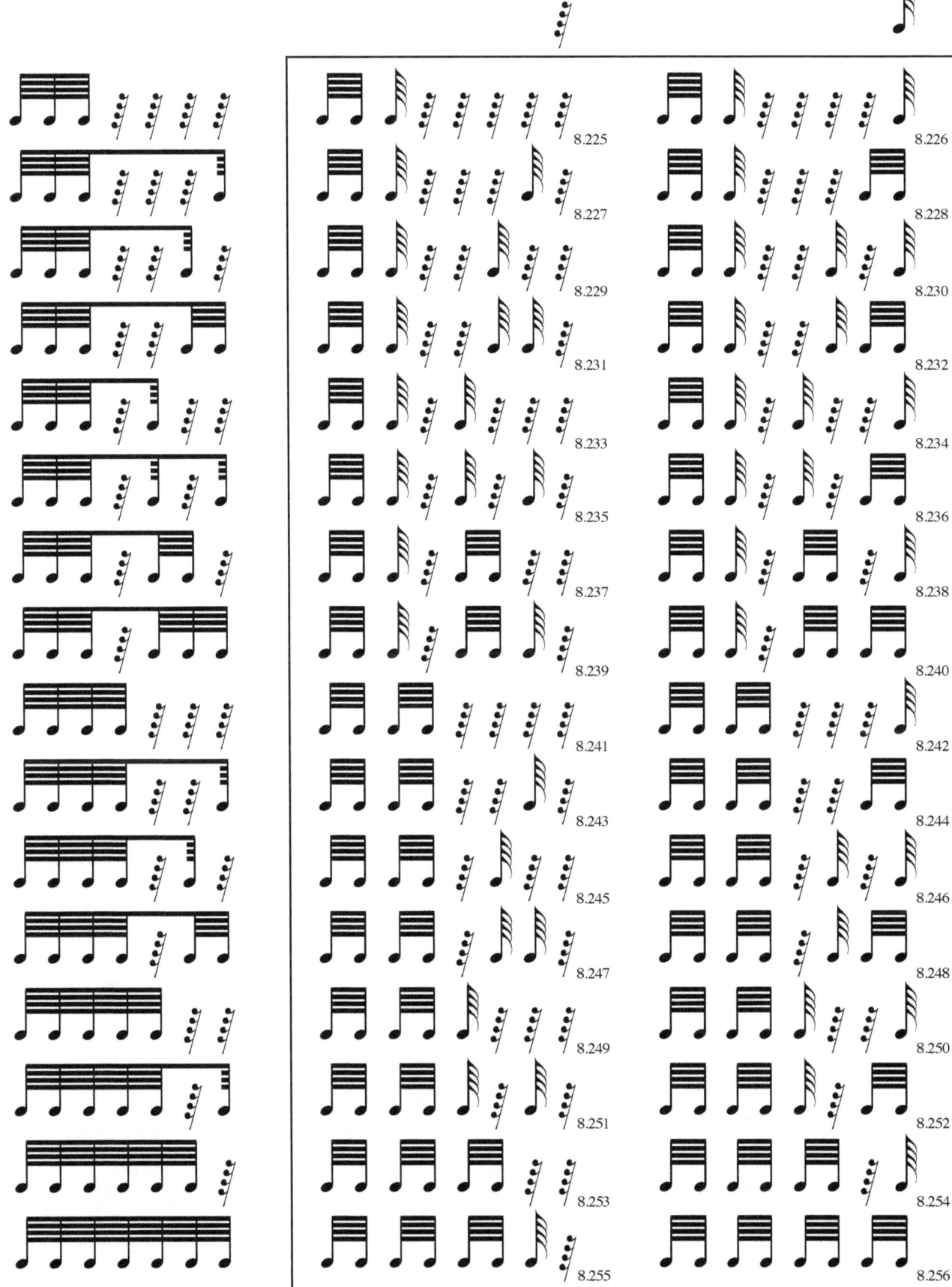

Music Measure Presentation of the Level 8 Event Point Patterns as Beat Division Notes

The following groups of patterns are presented in the beat division contexts of 4/2, 4/4, 4/8, 4/16, and 4/32.

To apply the practice methods discussed on page 35:

- **Read and Play** the patterns

- **Sing** the patterns

- **Audiate** (generate the sound in your mind) and **Visualize** performing the patterns

Level 8 Event Point Patterns

Beat Division

In this section, we present the Level 8 event point patterns in a practical and familiar context, that of measures containing four beats. As previously mentioned, we've limited the patterns to the beat division level (Level 4), due to there being 65,536 patterns at the beat subdivision level (Level 16).

The 4/4 patterns at the beat division level are an essential starting point for many rhythmic explorations. These same patterns, re-written in 4/2, 4/8, 4/16 and 4/32, will soon become much more recognizable through the course of any musician's advanced study, hopefully to the point where they will seem almost transparent. The only aspect inherently more complex about reading 4/32 as opposed to 4/4 is the density of the rests and notes.

Regarding notation formatting: We've beamed notes where applicable to emphasize the duple division. This is in keeping with traditional beaming convention, and it makes the patterns from the binary combination tables easier to read.

Additionally, readers will notice that the duration of the notes in the music measure format varies significantly from the durations found in the preceding binary combination tables. This is also done to make the patterns easier to read for study and practice purposes.

Level 8 Event Point Patterns
4/2 - Beat Division

Level 8 Event Point Patterns
4/2 - Beat Division (cont'd)

Level 8 Event Point Patterns
4/2 - Beat Division (cont'd)

Level 8 Event Point Patterns
4/2 - Beat Division (cont'd)

Level 8 Event Point Patterns
4/2 - Beat Division (cont'd)

Level 8 Event Point Patterns
4/2 - Beat Division (cont'd)

Level 8 Event Point Patterns
4/2 - Beat Division (cont'd

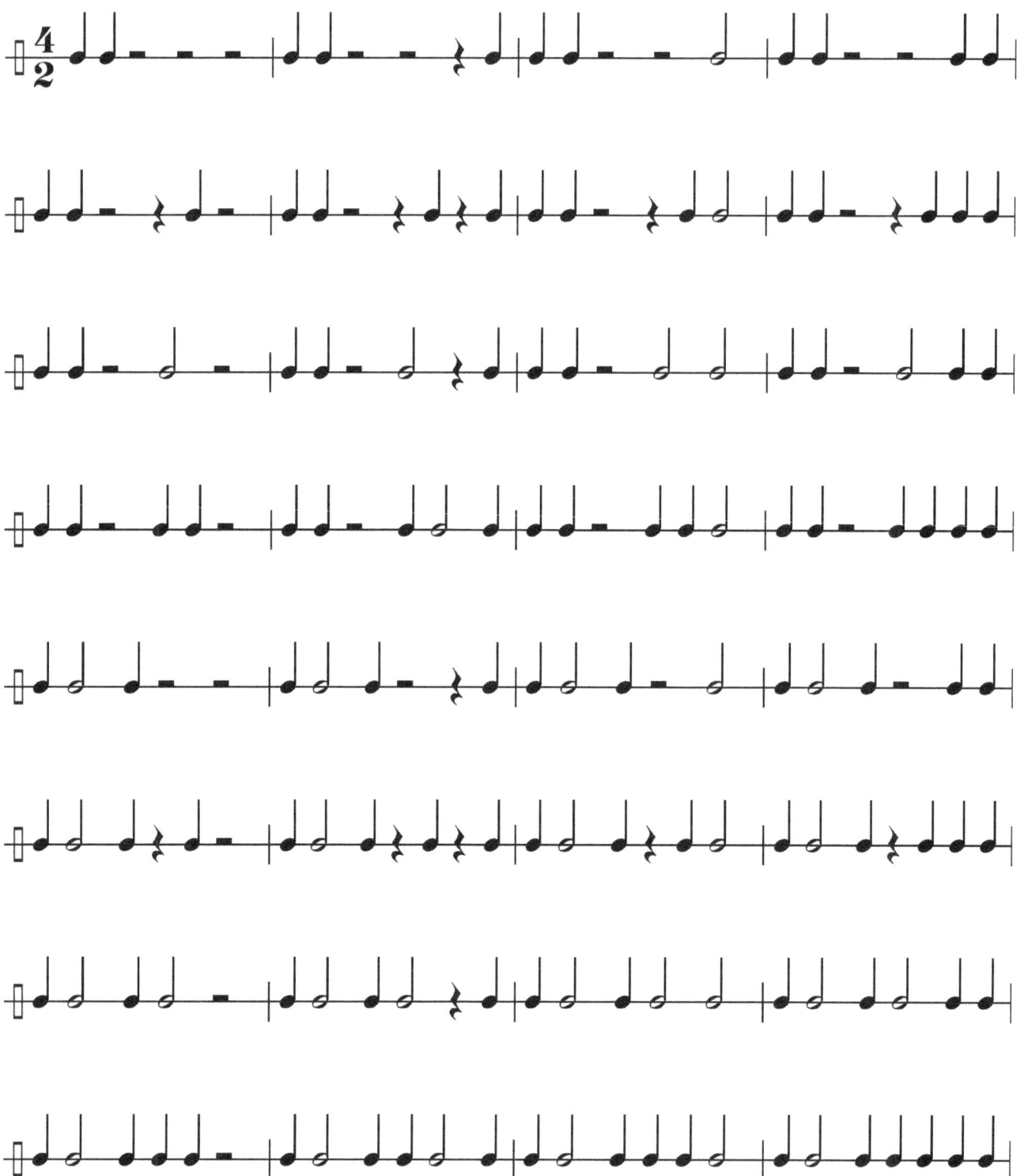

Level 8 Event Point Patterns
4/2 - Beat Division (cont'd

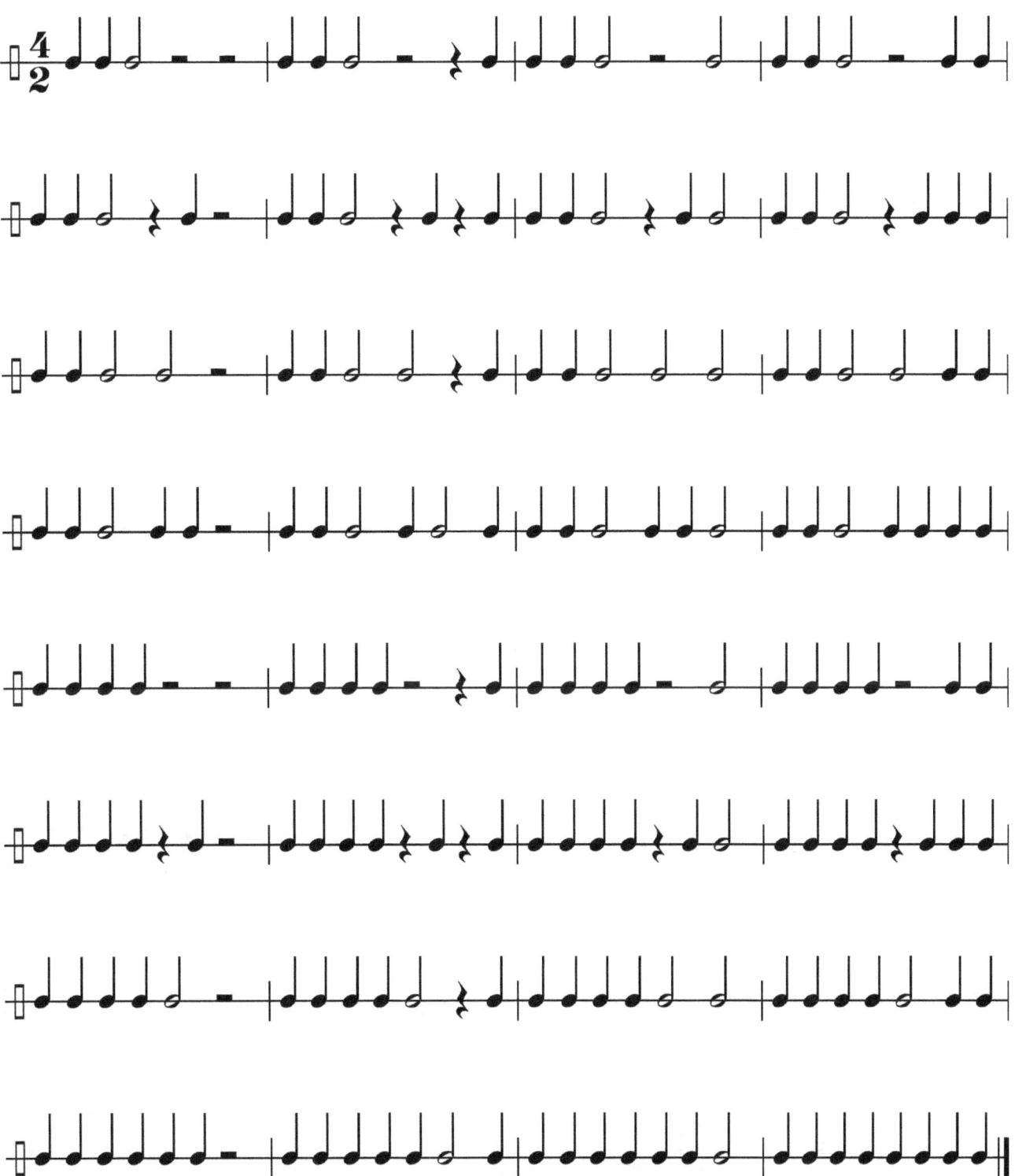

Level 8 Event Point Patterns
4/4 - Beat Division

Level 8 Event Point Patterns
4/4 - Beat Division (cont'd)

Level 8 Event Point Patterns
4/4 - Beat Division (cont'd)

Level 8 Event Point Patterns
4/4 - Beat Division (cont'd)

Level 8 Event Point Patterns
4/4 - Beat Division (cont'd)

Level 8 Event Point Patterns
4/4 - Beat Division (cont'd)

Level 8 Event Point Patterns
4/4 - Beat Division (cont'd)

Level 8 Event Point Patterns
4/4 - Beat Division (cont'd)

Level 8 Event Point Patterns
4/8 - Beat Division

Level 8 Event Point Patterns
4/8 - Beat Division (cont'd)

Level 8 Event Point Patterns
4/8 - Beat Division (cont'd)

Level 8 Event Point Patterns
4/8 - Beat Division (cont'd)

Level 8 Event Point Patterns
4/8 - Beat Division (cont'd)

Level 8 Event Point Patterns
4/8 - Beat Division (cont'd)

Level 8 Event Point Patterns
4/8 - Beat Division (cont'd)

Level 8 Event Point Patterns
4/8 - Beat Division (cont'd)

Level 8 Event Point Patterns
4/16 - Beat Division

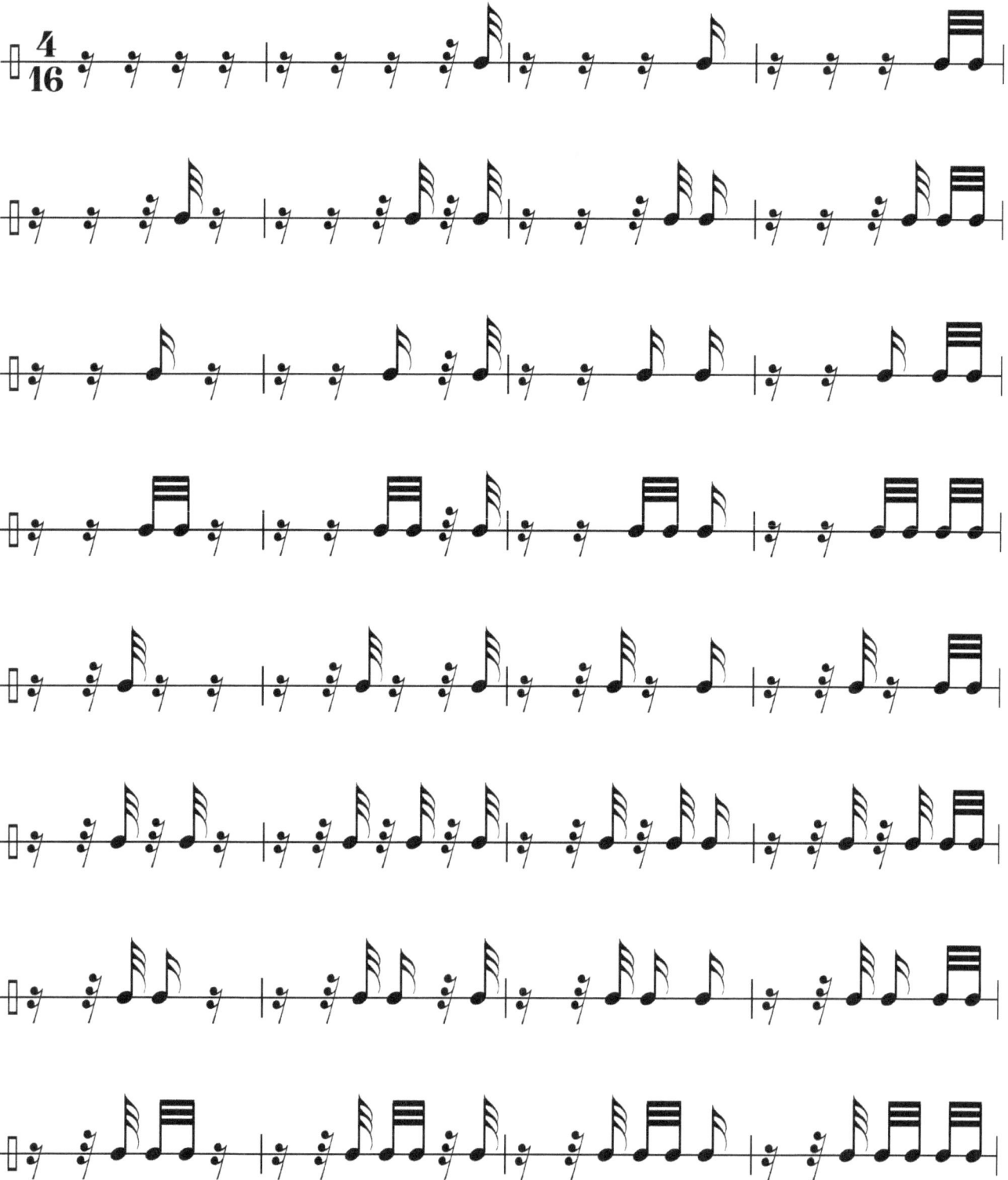

Level 8 Event Point Patterns
4/16 - Beat Division (cont'd)

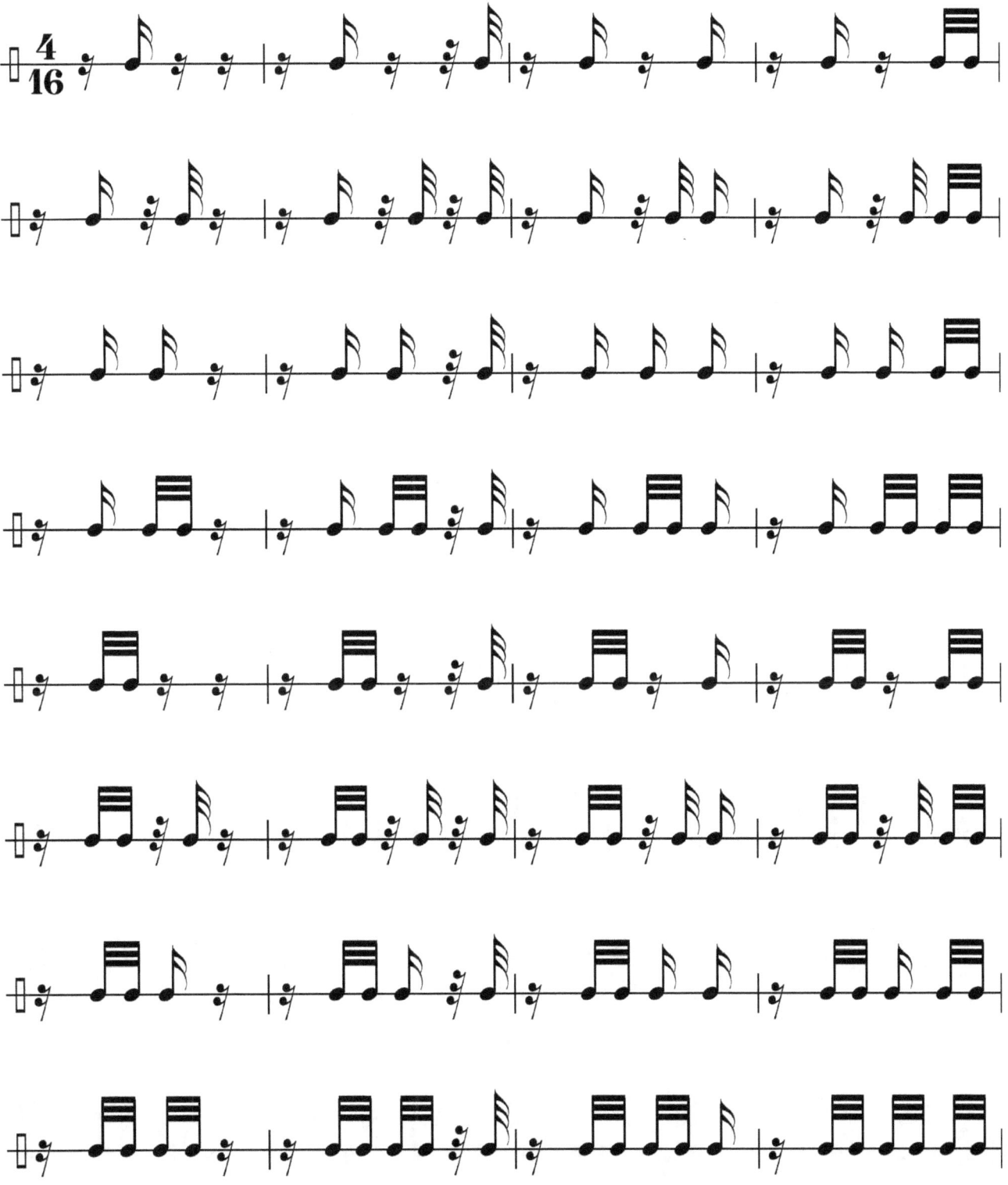

Level 8 Event Point Patterns
4/16 - Beat Division (cont'd)

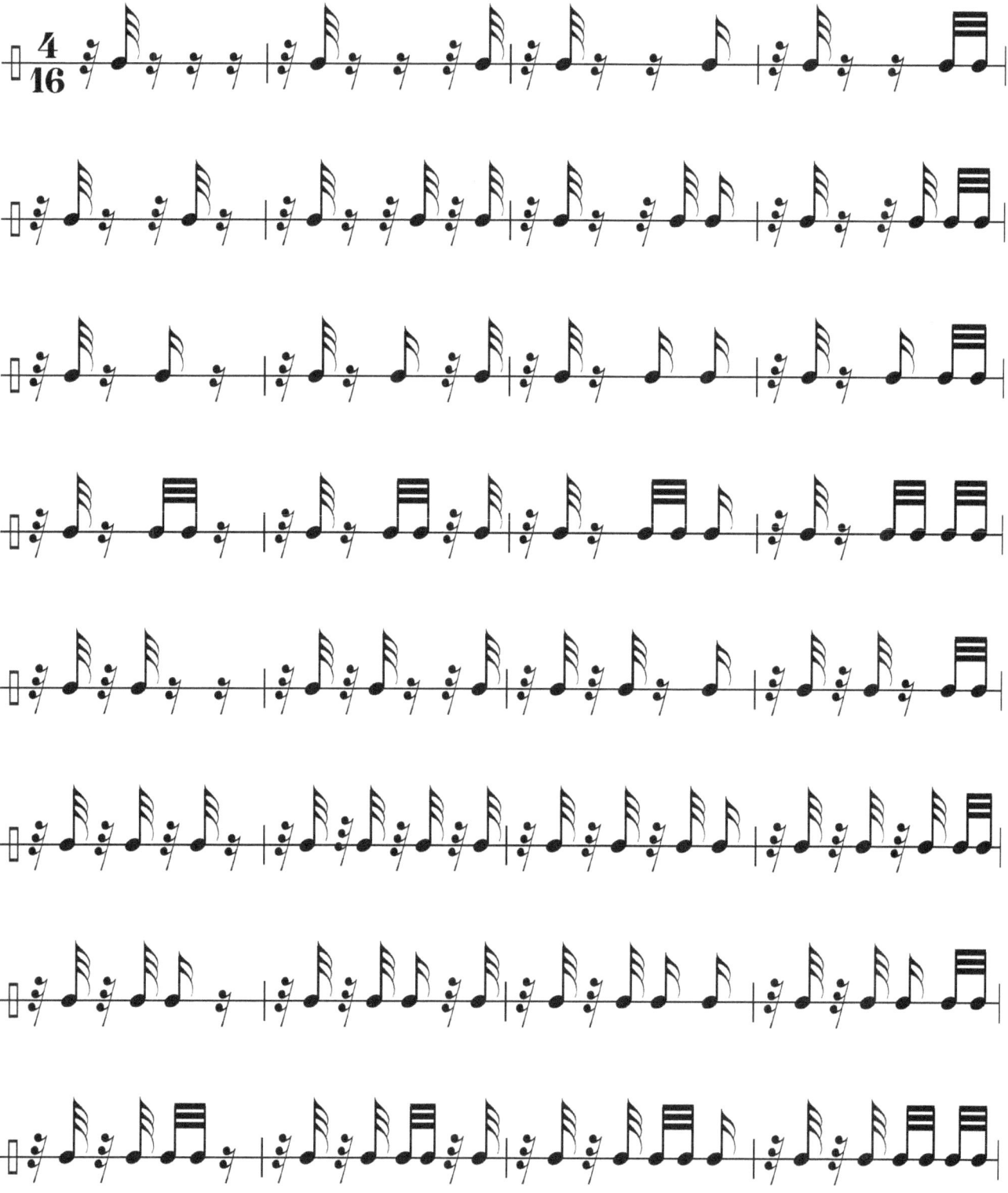

Level 8 Event Point Patterns
4/16 - Beat Division (cont'd)

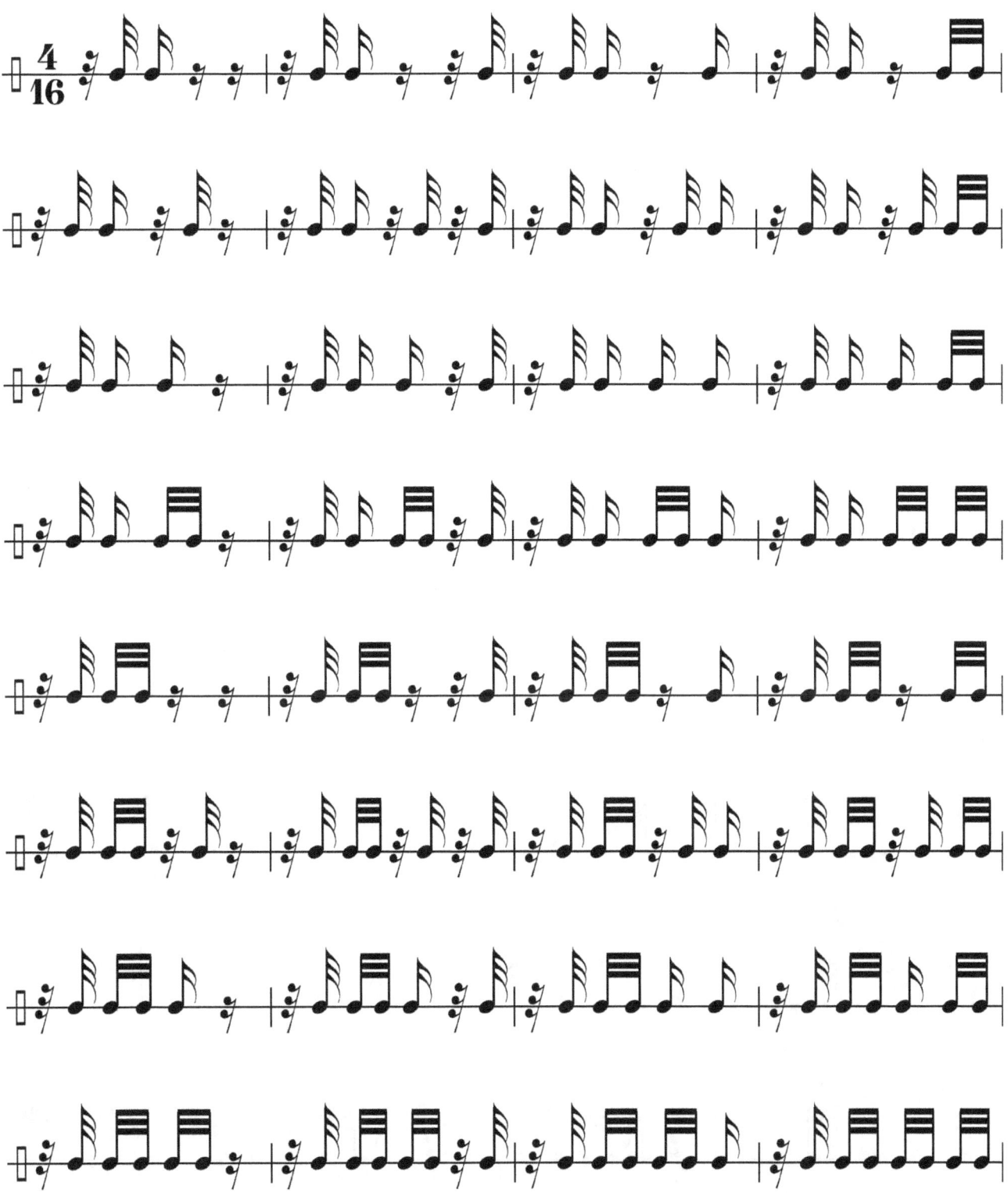

Level 8 Event Point Patterns
4/16 - Beat Division (cont'd)

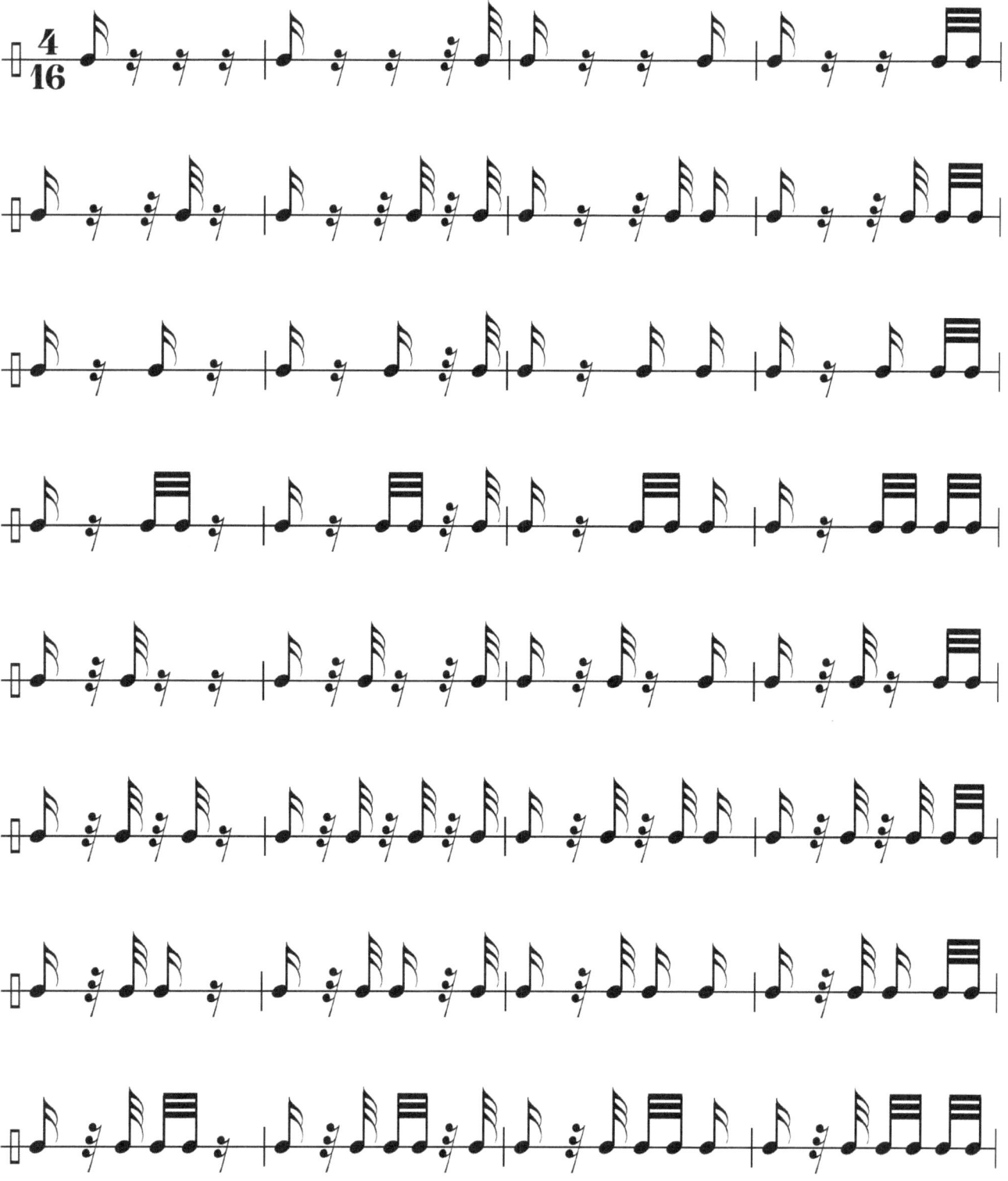

Level 8 Event Point Patterns
4/16 - Beat Division (cont'd)

Level 8 Event Point Patterns
4/16 - Beat Division (cont'd)

Level 8 Event Point Patterns
4/16 - Beat Division (cont'd)

Level 8 Event Point Patterns
4/32 - Beat Division

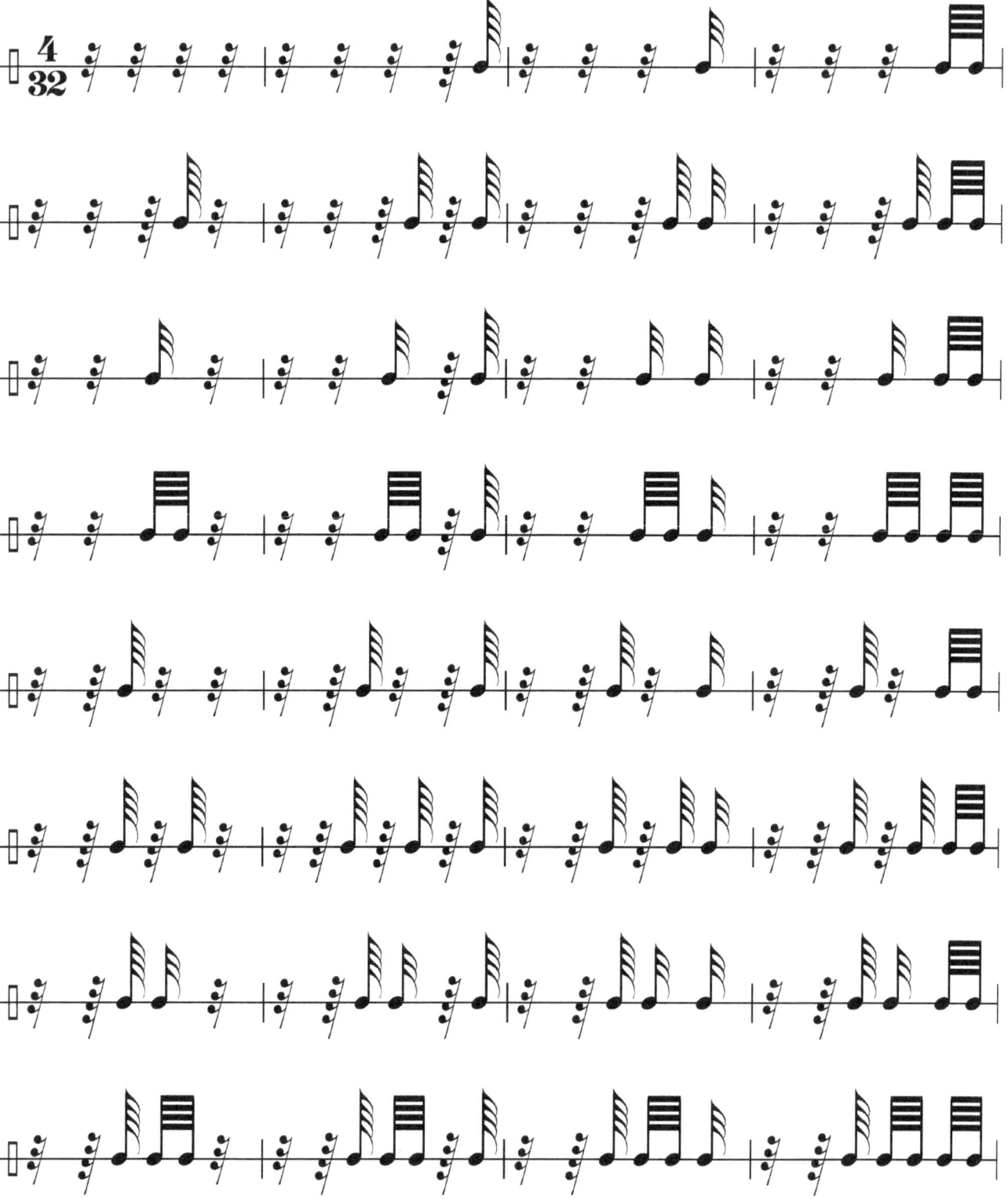

Level 8 Event Point Patterns
4/32 - Beat Division (cont'd)

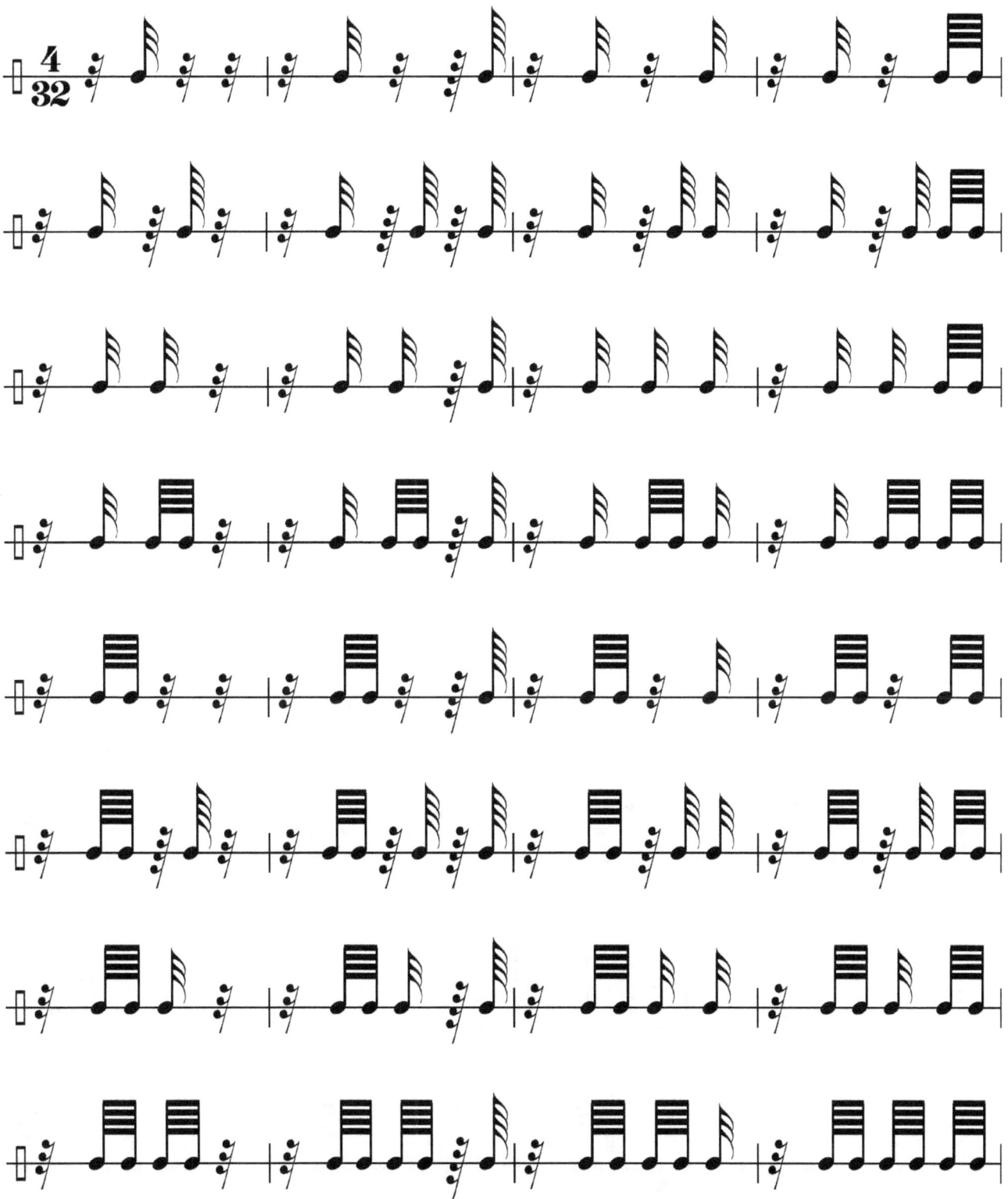

Level 8 Event Point Patterns
4/32 - Beat Division (cont'd)

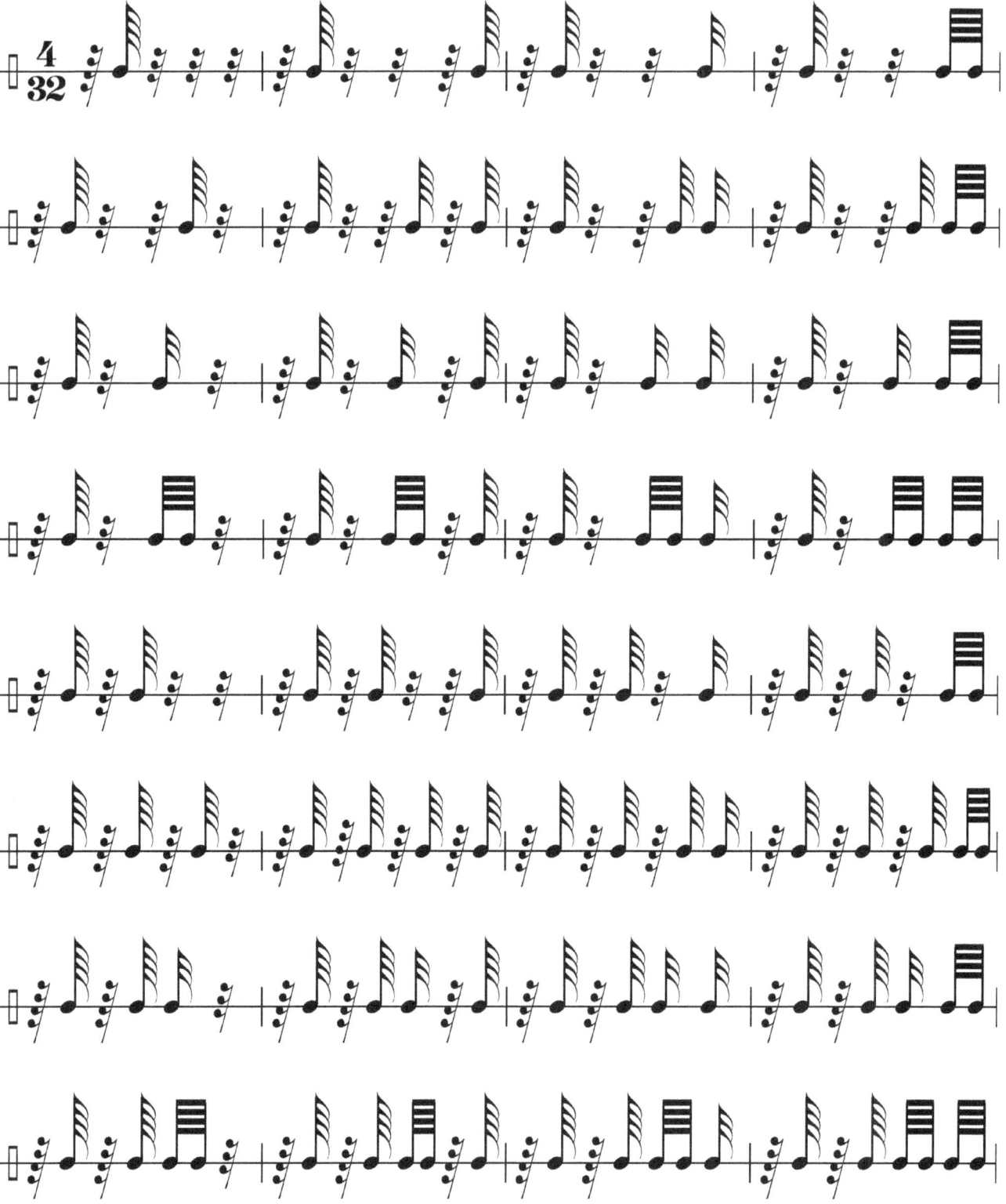

Level 8 Event Point Patterns
4/32 - Beat Division (cont'd)

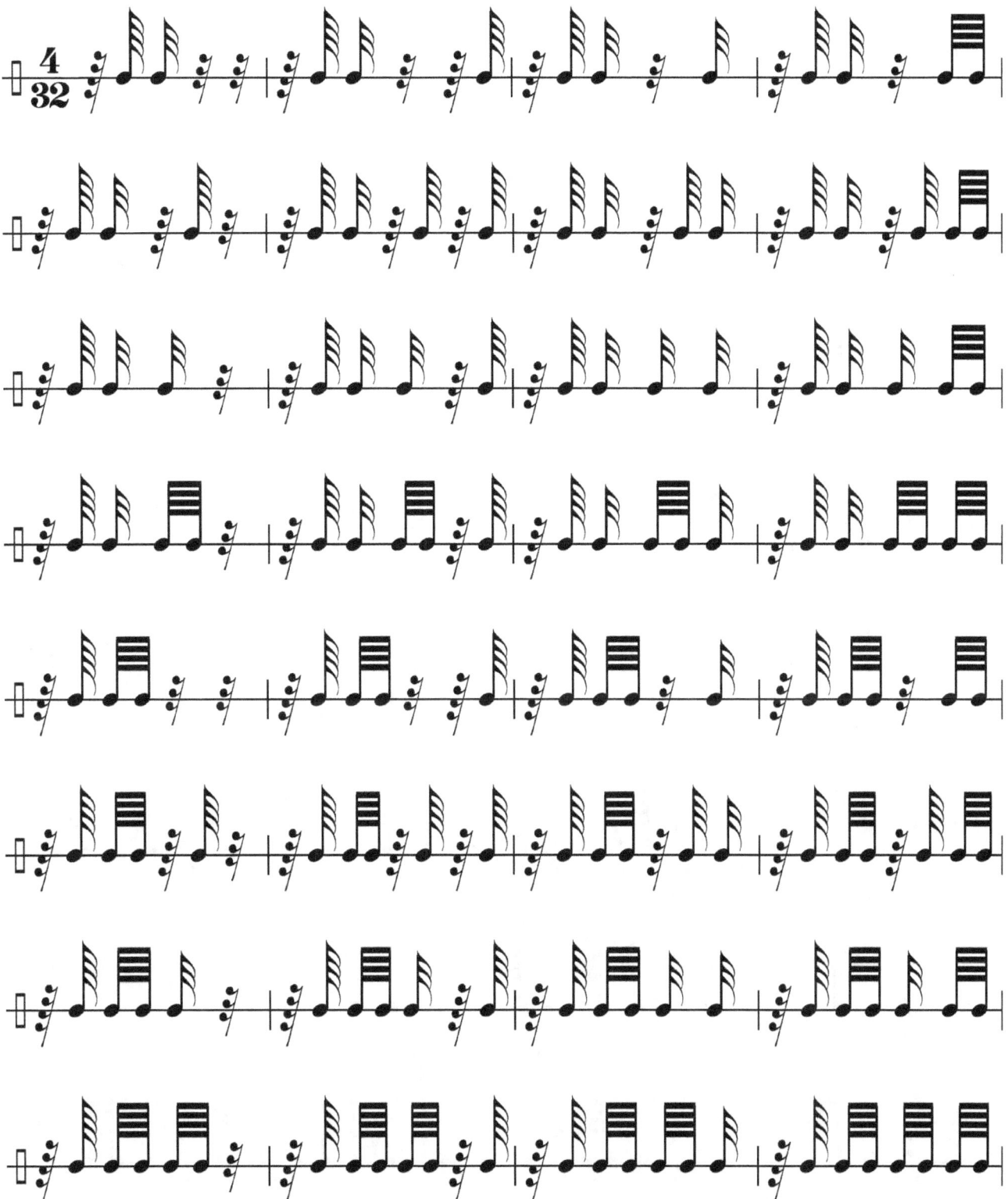

Level 8 Event Point Patterns
4/32 - Beat Division (cont'd)

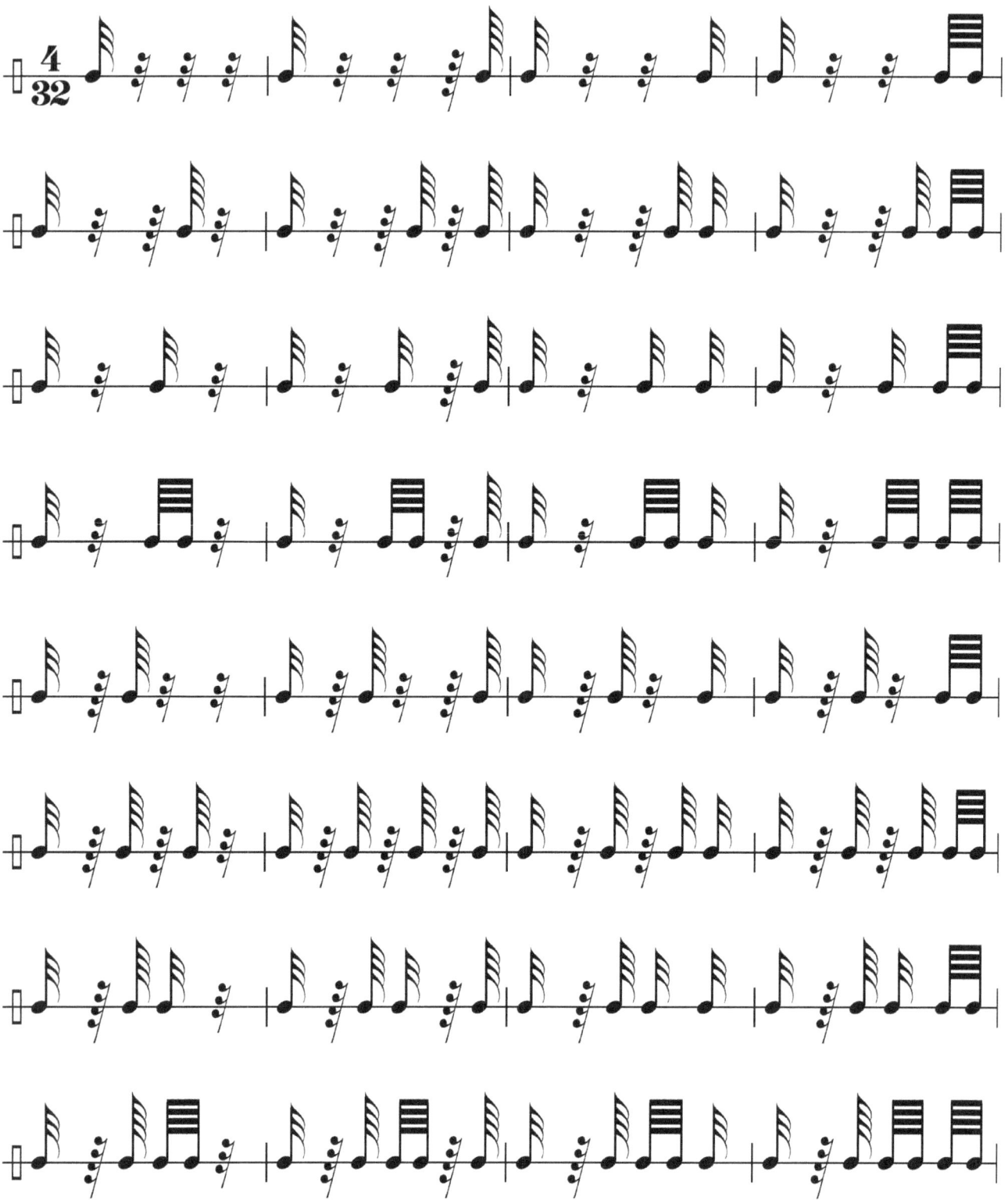

Level 8 Event Point Patterns
4/32 - Beat Division (cont'd)

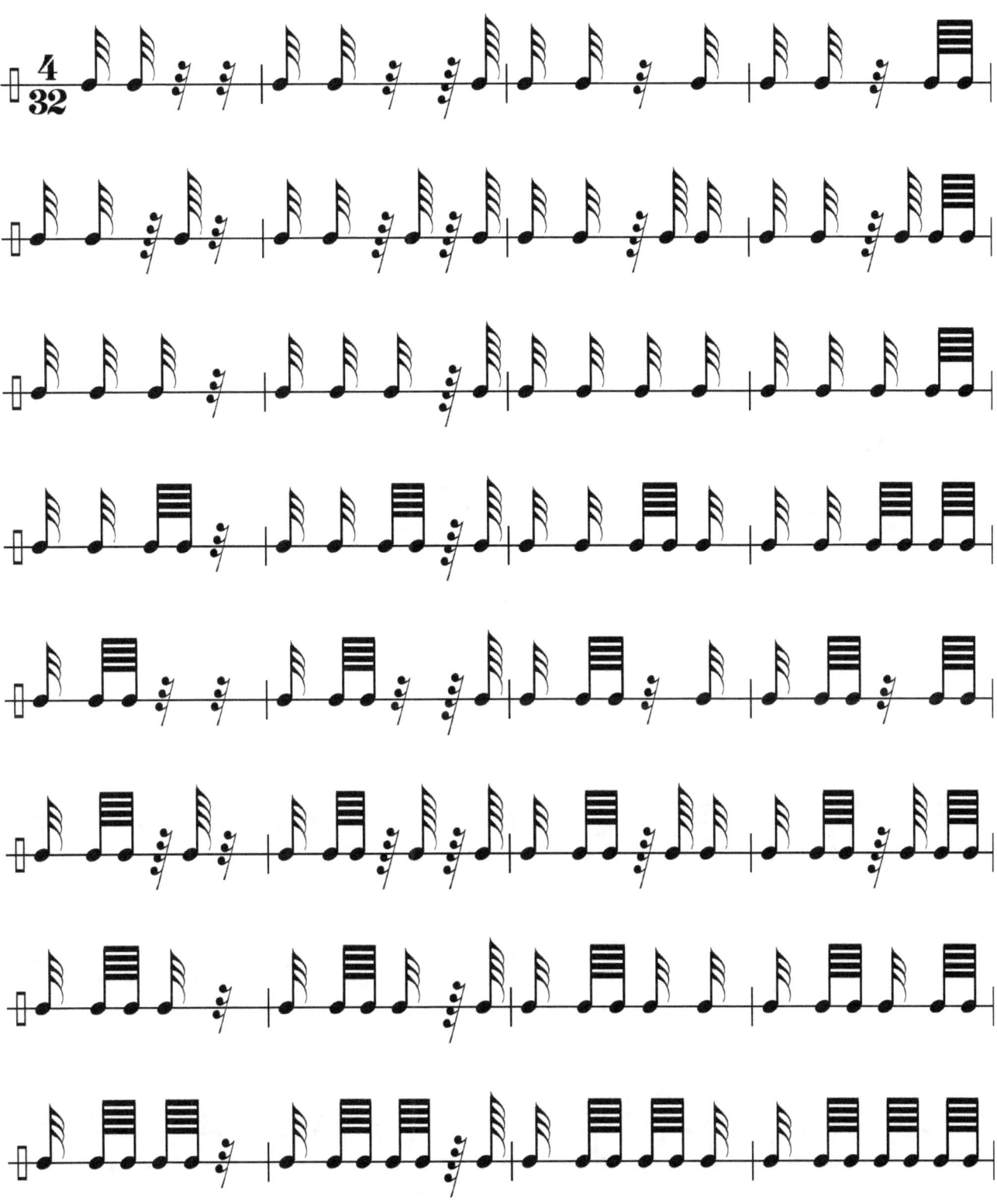

Level 8 Event Point Patterns
4/32 - Beat Division (cont'd)

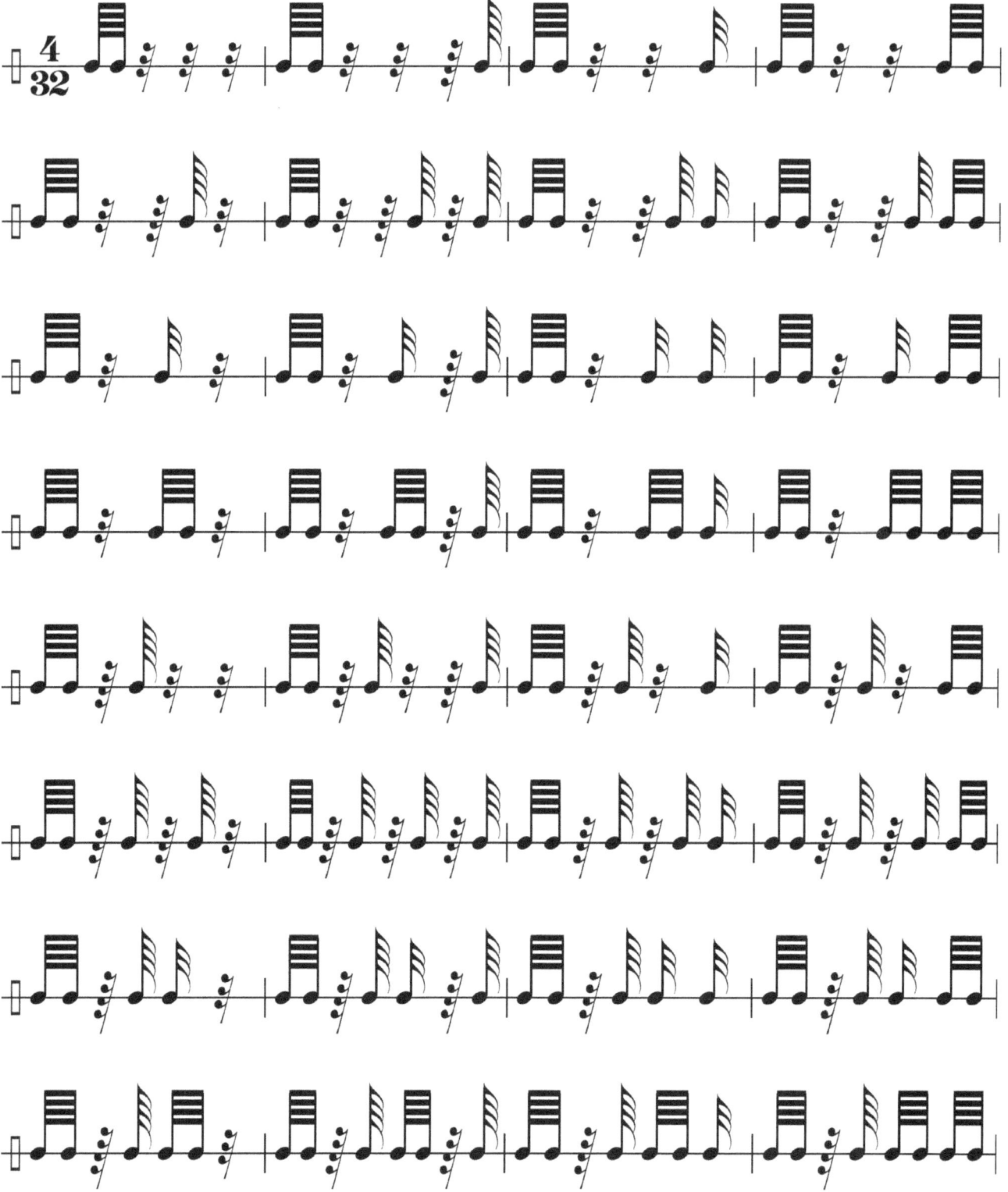

Level 8 Event Point Patterns
4/32 - Beat Division (cont'd)

Music Measure Presentation of the Level 8 Event Point Patterns as Beat Subdivision Notes

The following groups of patterns are presented in the context of the beat subdivision level for 2/2, 2/4, 2/8 and 2/16.

2/32 is not included in this section due to the relative obscurity of 128th rest/note use.

To apply the practice methods discussed on page 35:

- **Read and Play** the patterns

- **Sing** the patterns

- **Audiate** (generate the sound in your mind) and **Visualize** performing the patterns

Level 8 Event Point Patterns

Beat Subdivision

We have used as literal an approach as possible throughout this book to present the fundamental building blocks with few, if any, variables (e.g., dotted rests/notes, ties, etc.). By now the point has surely been made that a logical and absolute structure for rhythm pattern development exists underneath the relative notation used to represent it.

However, to make the subdivision patterns for 2/2, 2/4, 2/8 and 2/16 more readable and to be of more practical value, we are including the use of dotted notes. As with certain instances of dotted notes used in the Level 6 combinations, the spirit of our absolute sound shape intention remains intact.

We've also beamed notes where applicable to emphasize the duple division. This is in keeping with traditional beaming convention and makes the patterns from the binary combination tables easier to read and master.

Level 8 Event Point Patterns
2/2 - Beat Subdivision

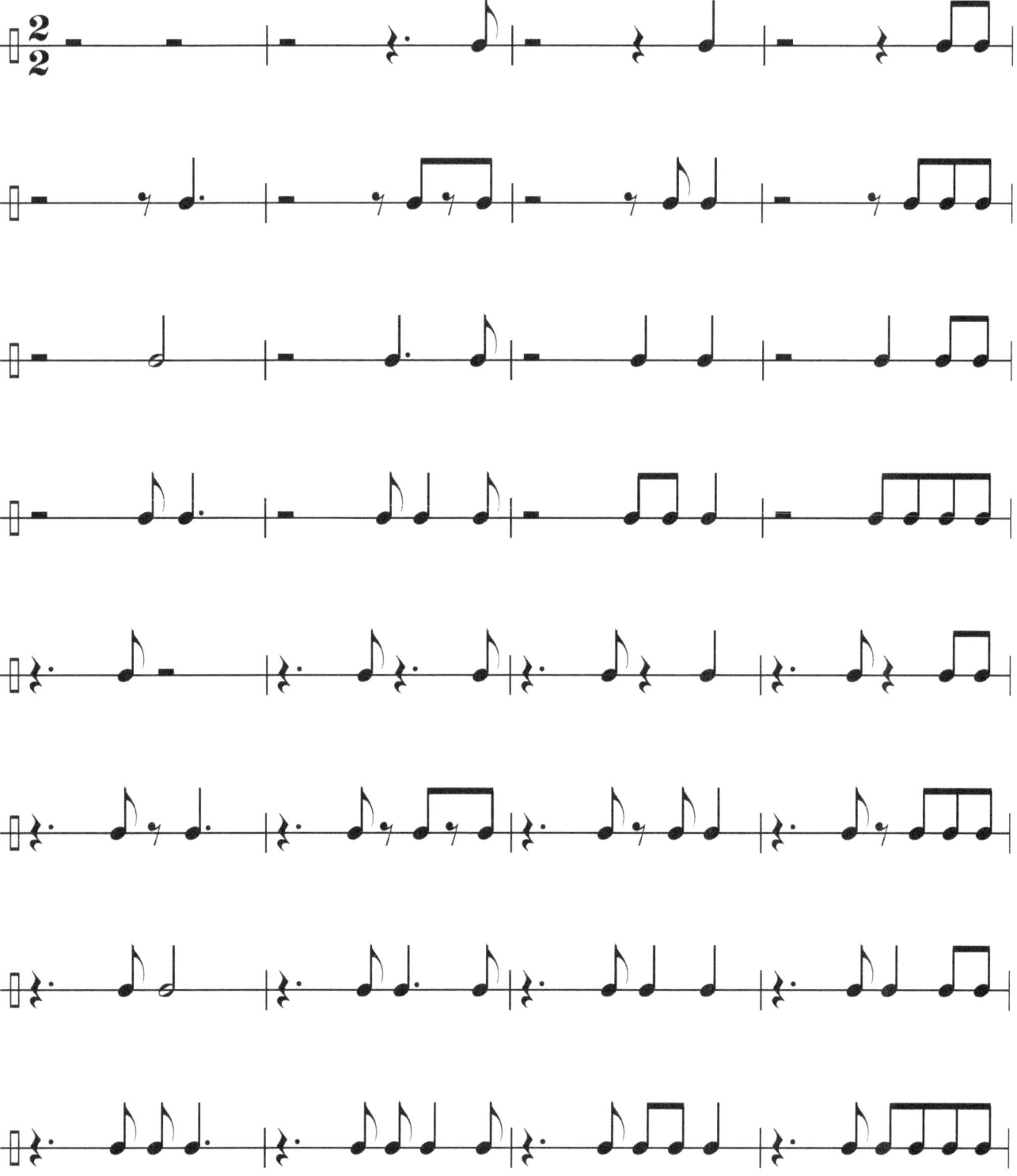

Level 8 Event Point Patterns
2/2 - Beat Subdivision (cont'd)

Level 8 Event Point Patterns
2/2 - Beat Subdivision (cont'd)

Level 8 Event Point Patterns
2/2 - Beat Subdivision (cont'd)

Level 8 Event Point Patterns
2/2 - Beat Subdivision (cont'd)

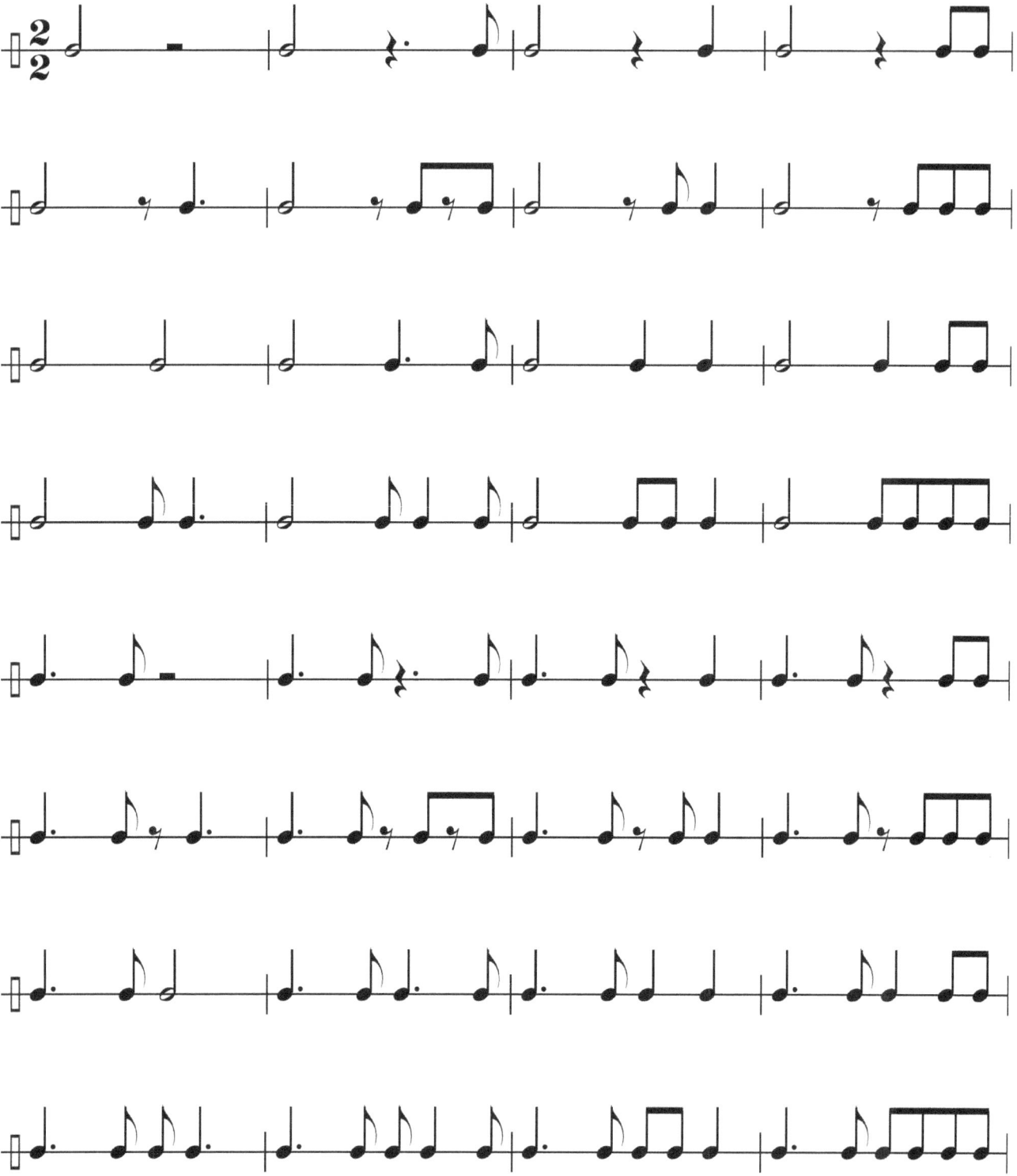

Level 8 Event Point Patterns
2/2 - Beat Subdivision (cont'd)

Level 8 Event Point Patterns
2/2 - Beat Subdivision (cont'd)

Level 8 Event Point Patterns
2/2 - Beat Subdivision (cont'd)

Level 8 Event Point Patterns
2/4 - Beat Subdivision

Level 8 Event Point Patterns
2/4 - Beat Subdivision (cont'd)

Level 8 Event Point Patterns
2/4 - Beat Subdivision (cont'd)

Level 8 Event Point Patterns
2/4 - Beat Subdivision (cont'd)

Level 8 Event Point Patterns
2/4 - Beat Subdivision (cont'd)

Level 8 Event Point Patterns
2/4 - Beat Subdivision (cont'd)

Level 8 Event Point Patterns
2/4 - Beat Subdivision (cont'd)

Level 8 Event Point Patterns
2/4 - Beat Subdivision (cont'd)

282

Level 8 Event Point Patterns
2/8 - Beat Subdivision

Level 8 Event Point Patterns
2/8 - Beat Subdivision (cont'd)

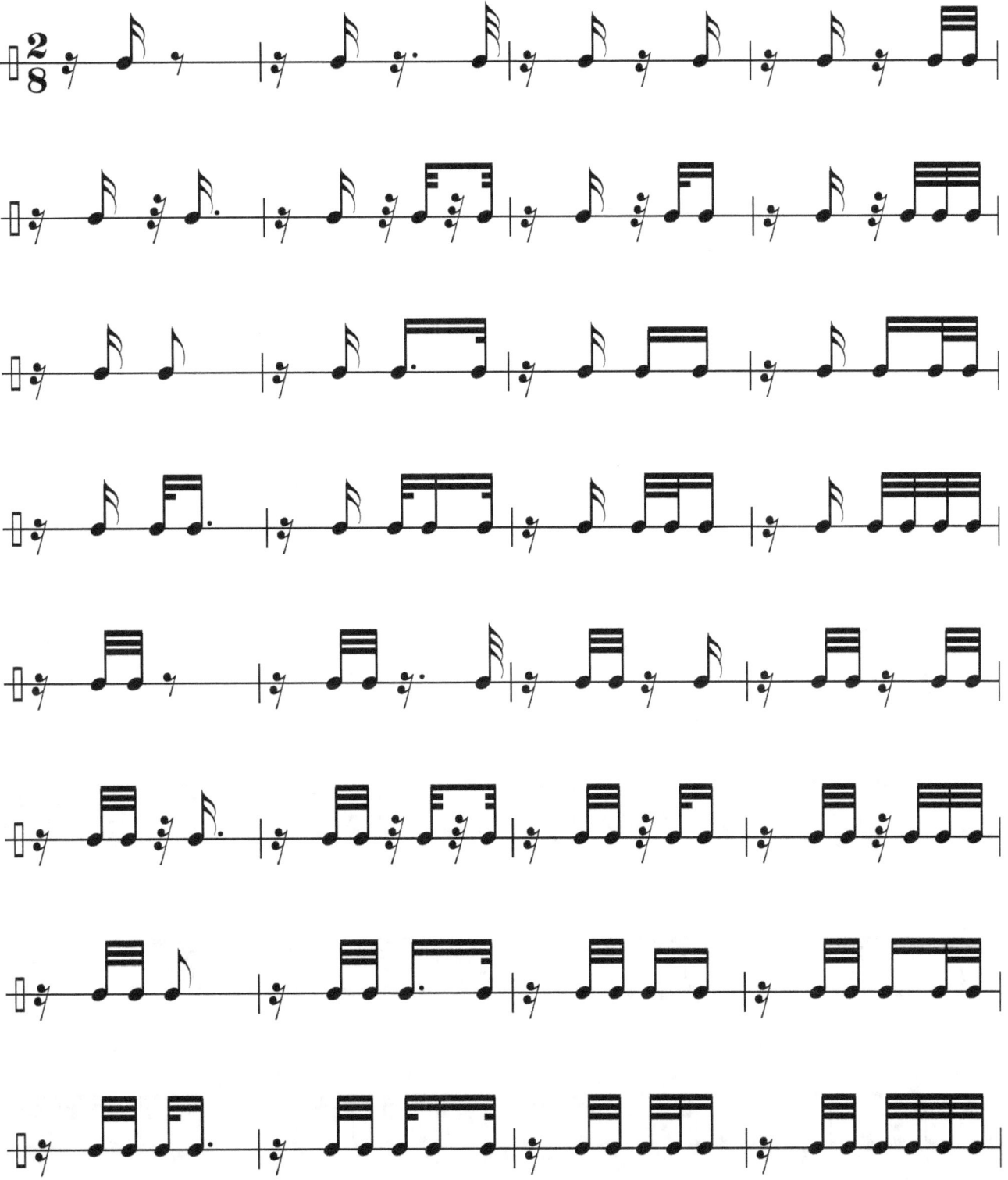

Level 8 Event Point Patterns
2/8 - Beat Subdivision (cont'd)

Level 8 Event Point Patterns
2/8 - Beat Subdivision (cont'd)

Level 8 Event Point Patterns
2/8 - Beat Subdivision (cont'd)

Level 8 Event Point Patterns
2/8 - Beat Subdivision (cont'd)

Level 8 Event Point Patterns
2/8 - Beat Subdivision (cont'd)

Level 8 Event Point Patterns
2/8 - Beat Subdivision (cont'd)

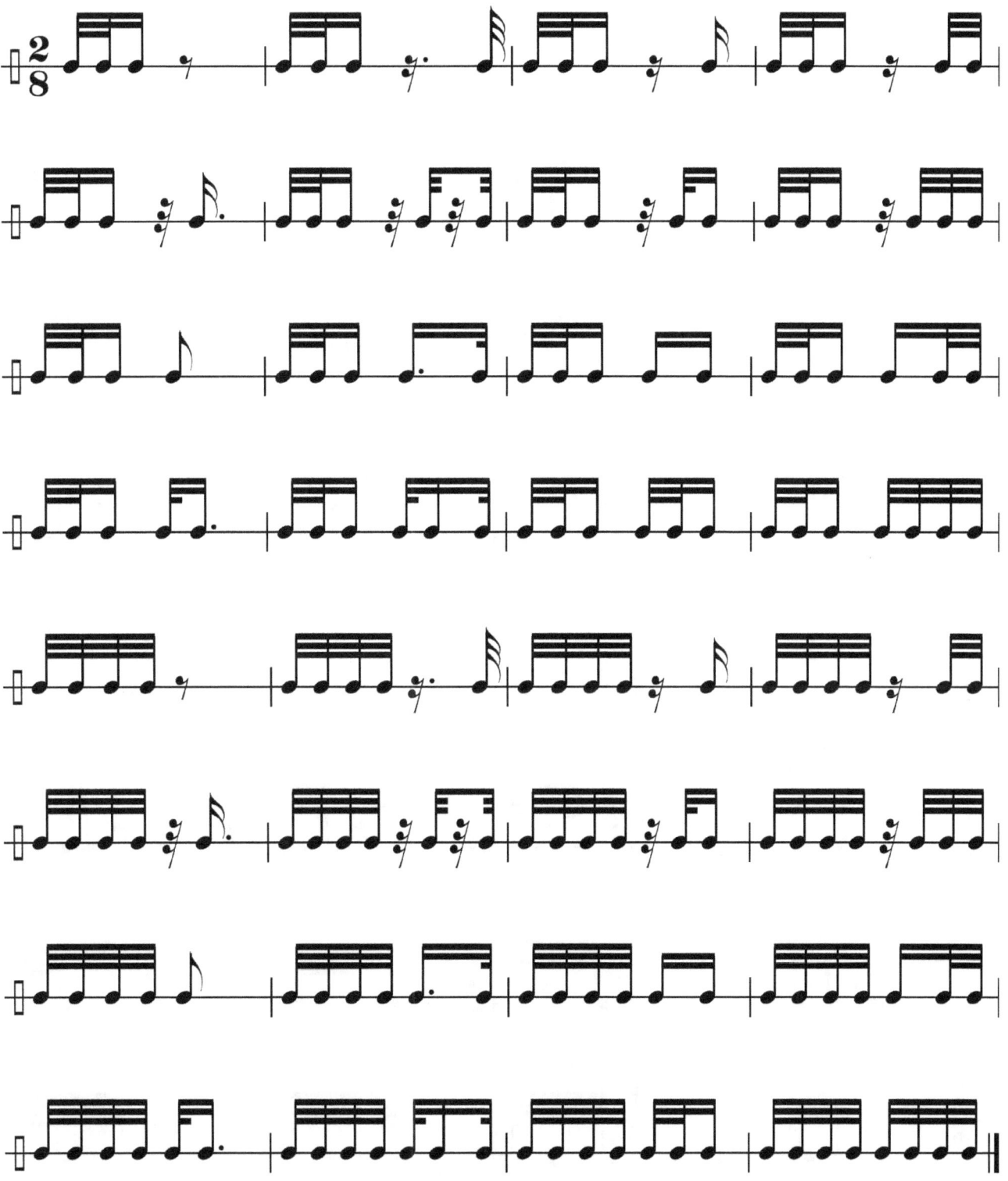

Level 8 Event Point Patterns
2/16 - Beat Subdivision

Level 8 Event Point Patterns
2/16 - Beat Subdivision (cont'd)

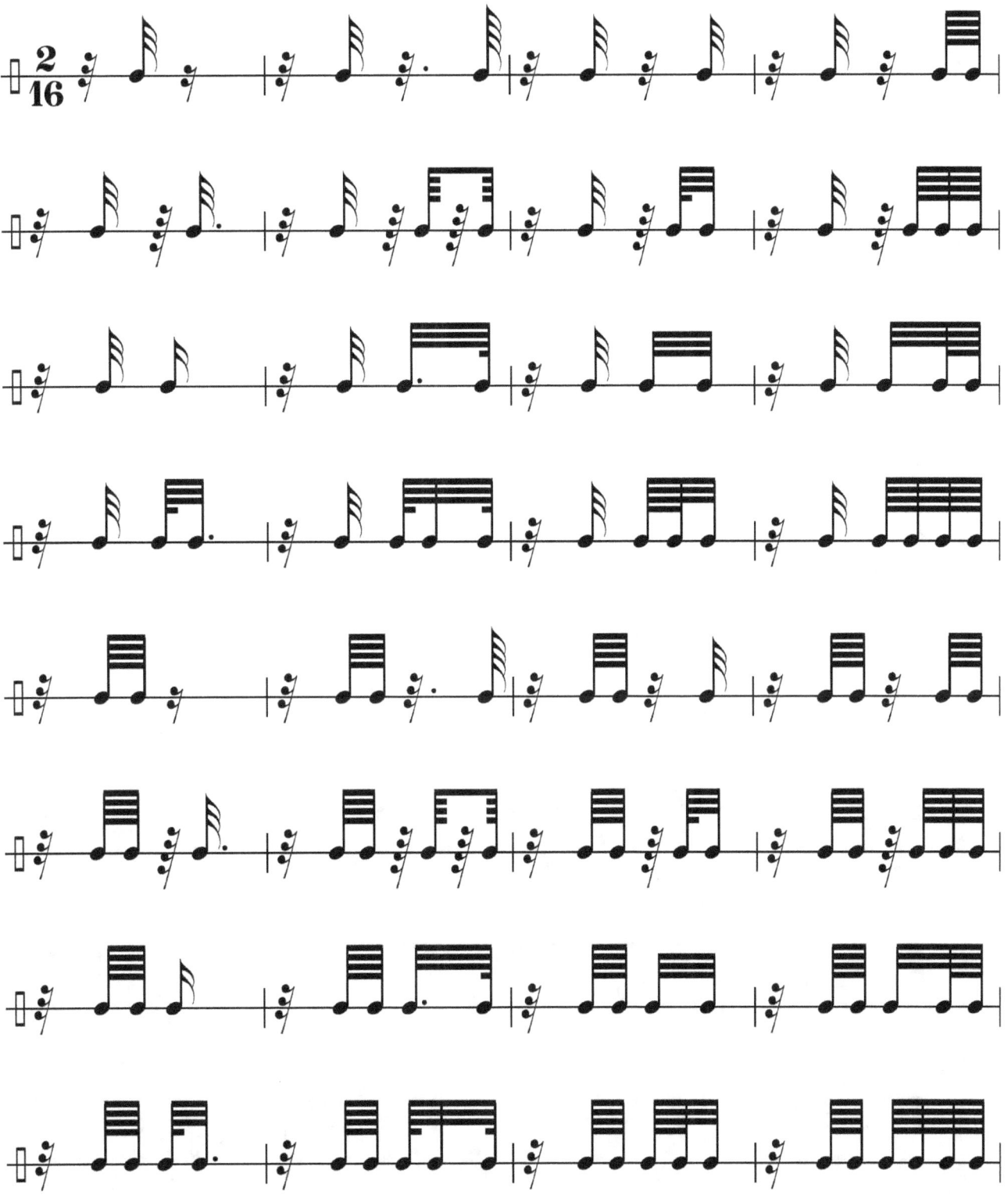

Level 8 Event Point Patterns
2/16 - Beat Subdivision (cont'd)

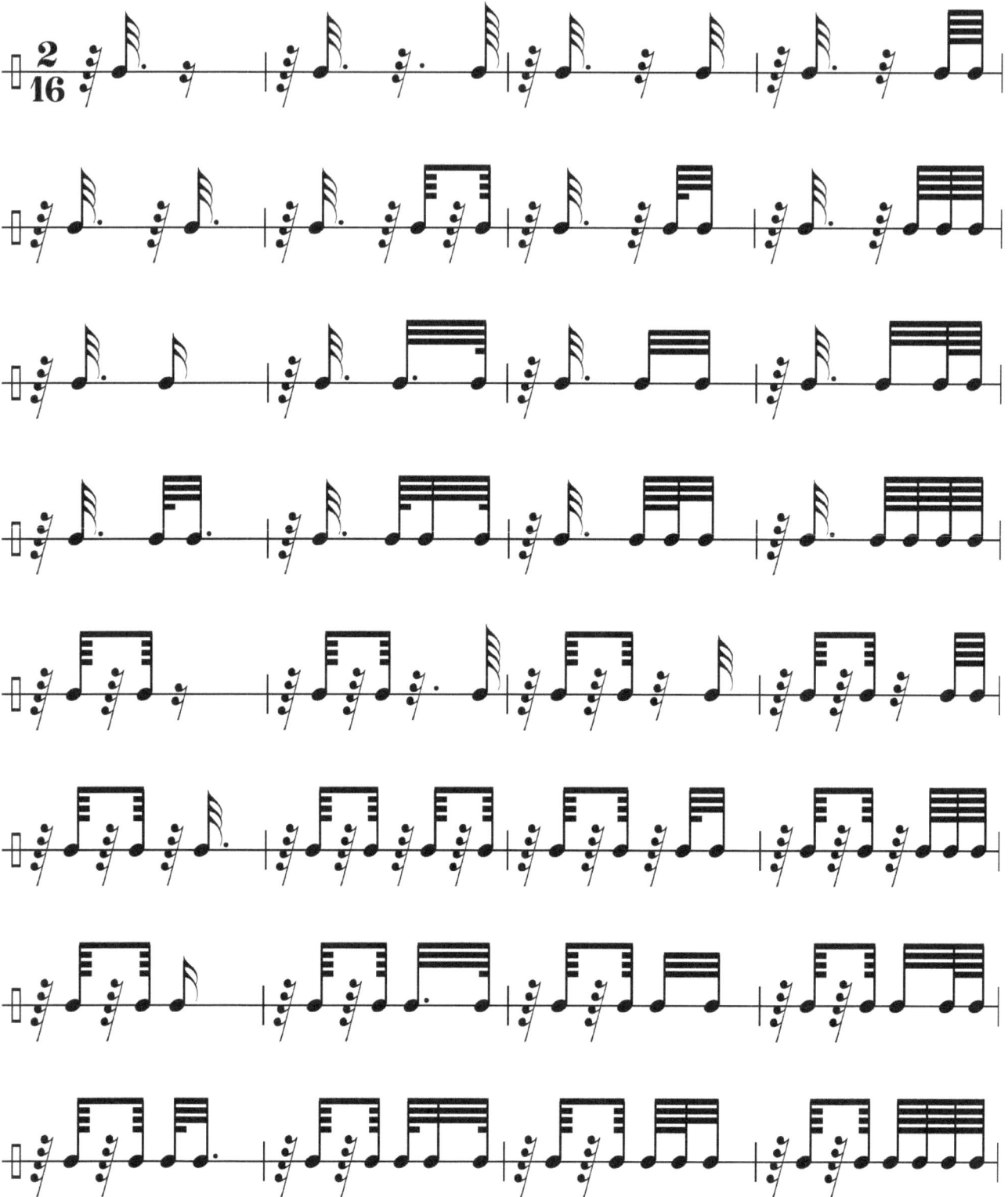

Level 8 Event Point Patterns
2/16 - Beat Subdivision (cont'd)

Level 8 Event Point Patterns
2/16 - Beat Subdivision (cont'd)

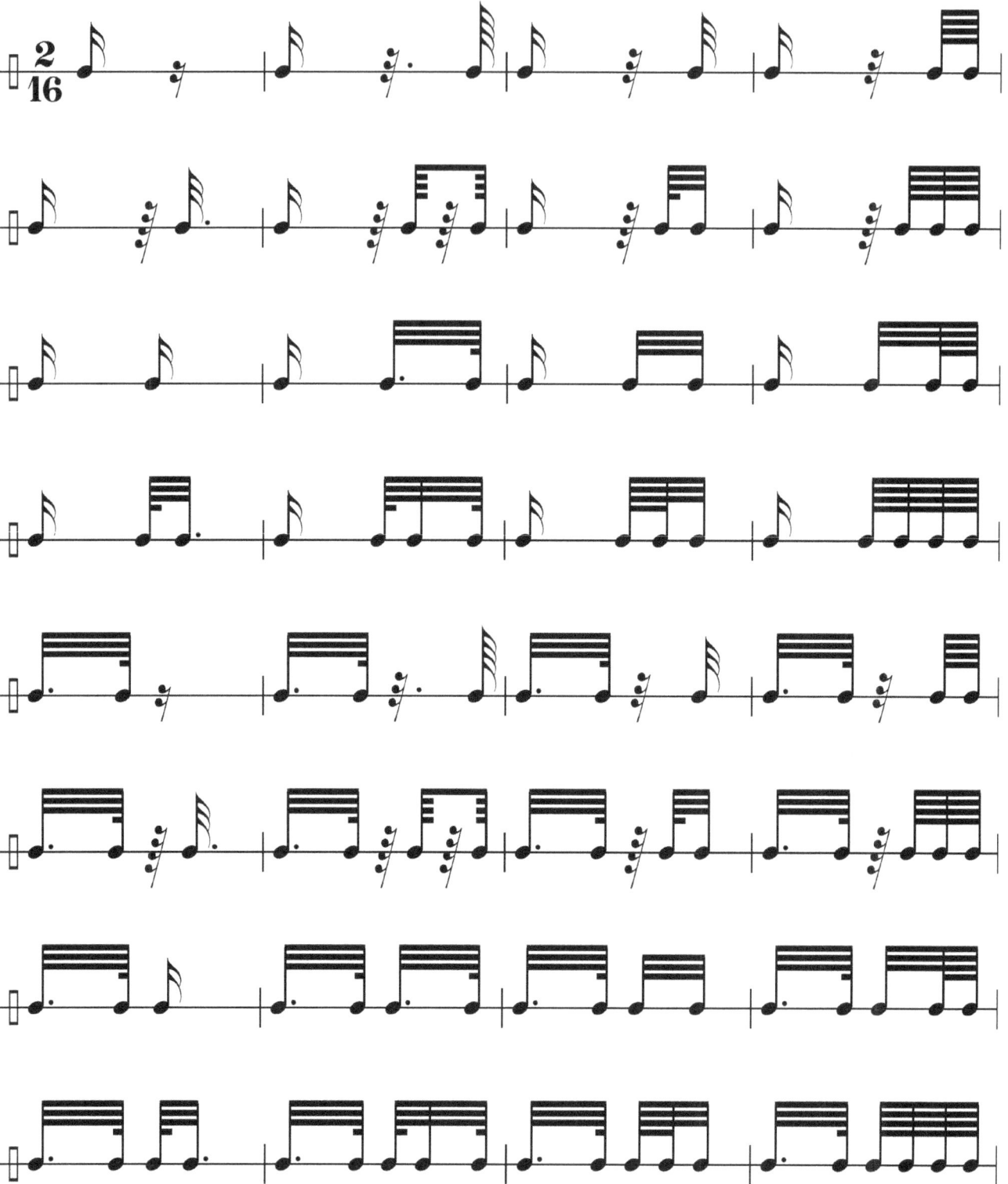

Level 8 Event Point Patterns
2/16 - Beat Subdivision (cont'd)

Level 8 Event Point Patterns
2/16 - Beat Subdivision (cont'd)

Level 8 Event Point Patterns
2/16 - Beat Subdivision (cont'd)

Epilogue

The Elements of Rhythm Volume I was introduced as a rhythm pattern resource. We applied basic math to produce the complete list of fundamental building block rhythm patterns, and in doing so, we replaced chance exploration with absolute understanding.

For readers willing to put forth the effort, this book offers many paths. Some may prove to be very challenging, but regardless of where they eventually lead, one outcome remains certain: While there are indeed an infinite number of rhythm pattern combinations, we can now study their finite elements, master them, and make them our own.

That's when the real playing begins.

* / / *

Appendices

Appendices A - E

- **Appendix A:** College Course Teaching Guidelines for Drum Set Players

- **Appendix B:** College Course Teaching Guidelines for Percussionists

- **Appendix C:** College Course Teaching Guidelines for Instrumentalists/Vocalists

- **Appendix D:** Course Teaching Guidelines for Middle School, High School and College Music Theory/Rhythm Theory Studies

- **Appendix E:** Presentation/Teaching Guidelines for Drum Circle Facilitators

Our approach to rhythm pattern theory is markedly different from traditional methods. It is therefore important to emphasize flexibility in adapting and modifying the guidelines for all the focus groups listed above.

Music teachers providing instruction for all levels of students (beginning with middle school) can also combine these guidelines with practice suggestions provided in *The Elements of Rhythm Volume II, Relative Notation and Counting Syllables*.

An example of this approach may be found on page 308 of this book, following the ***Appendices***.

Appendix A

College Course Teaching Guidelines for Drum Set Players

Objective: Present *The Elements of Rhythm Volume I* to drum set players, placing emphasis on the concept of absolute sound shapes.

Goals: Student will be able to discuss and explain the binary theory of rhythm pattern development and be able to perform all of the patterns for Event Point Levels 2 - 8 using alternating Hand-to-Hand, Hand-Foot, and Foot-to-Foot combinations at slow, medium and fast tempos and at varying volume levels.

Overview: Presentation of binary theory, construction of binary combination tables, re-writing of binary patterns using conventional notation, reproduction of notation in respective music measure formats, demonstration of patterns in Event Point Levels 2 - 8.

Integration: These guidelines may be modified as needed for integration into existing drum set course time frames.

Structure: Introduction to the system fundamentals can be presented in a 1- hour classs, using the recommended sequence of events:

- Present measures and basic beat division, using / as beat and * as division of beat parts

- Introduce new terms: event points, event point levels, event point patterns, and absolute sound shapes

- Assign 0's and 1's to event points as symbols for silence and sound

- Calculate the number of event point possibilities per event point level using the 2^n formula

- Introduce the binary combination tables

- Pair up the 0's and 1's in the binary combination tables

- Re-write the patterns using conventional notation

- Present the re-written patterns in their respective music measure formats

Discussion: Explain concepts of relative nature of notation and counting syllables, and absolute sound shapes; present various music scenarios for the patterns.

Appendix B

College Course Teaching Guidelines for Percussionists

Objectives: Present *The Elements of Rhythm Volume 1* to percussionists, placing emphasis on the concept of absolute sound shapes.

Goals: Student will be able to discuss and explain the binary theory of rhythm pattern development and be able to perform all of the patterns for Event Point Levels 2 - 8 using Hand-to-Hand technique on bongos and conga drums. Student will perform all the patterns at slow, medium and fast tempos, at varying volume levels.

Overview: Presentation of binary theory, construction of binary combination tables, re-writing of binary patterns using conventional notation, reproduction of notation in respective music measure formats, demonstration of patterns in Event Point Levels 2 - 8.

Integration: These guidelines may be modified as needed for integration into existing percussion course time frames.

Structure: Introduction to the system fundamentals can be presented in a 1- hour class, using the recommended sequence of events:

- Present measures and basic beat division, using / as beat and * as division of beat parts

- Introduce new terms: event points, event point levels, event point patterns, and absolute sound shapes

- Assign 0's and 1's to event points as symbols for silence and sound

- Calculate the number of event point possibilities per event point level using the 2^n formula

- Introduce the binary combination tables

- Pair up the 0's and 1's in the binary combination tables

- Re-write the patterns using conventional notation

- Present the re-written patterns in their respective music measure formats

Discussion: Explain concepts of relative nature of notation and counting syllables, and absolute sound shapes; present various music scenarios for the patterns.

Appendix C

College Course Teaching Guidelines for Instrumentalists/Vocalists

Objective: Present *The Elements of Rhythm Volume 1* to instrumentalists and vocalists, placing emphasis on the concept of absolute sound shapes.

Goals: Student will be able to discuss and explain the binary theory of rhythm pattern development and be able to perform all of the patterns for Event Point Levels 2 - 8 on their respective instruments.

Overview: Presentation of binary theory, construction of binary combination tables, re-writing of binary patterns using conventional notation, reproduction of notation in respective music measure formats, demonstration of patterns in Event Point Levels 2 - 8.

Integration: These guidelines may be modified as needed for integration into existing instrumental/vocal course time frames.

Structure: Introduction to the system fundamentals can be presented in a 1- hour class, using the recommended sequence of events:

- Present measures and basic beat division, using / as beat and * as division of beat parts

- Introduce new terms: event points, event point levels, event point patterns, and absolute sound shapes

- Assign 0's and 1's to event points as symbols for silence and sound

- Calculate the number of event point possibilities per event point level using the 2^n formula

- Introduce the binary combination tables

- Pair up the 0's and 1's in the binary combination tables

- Re-write the patterns using conventional notation

- Present the re-written patterns in their respective music measure formats

Discussion: Explain concepts of relative nature of notation and counting syllables, and absolute sound shapes; present various music scenarios for the patterns.

Appendix D

Course Teaching Guidelines for Middle School, High School and College Music Theory/Rhythm Theory Studies

Objectives: Present and integrate *The Elements of Rhythm Volume I* into existing music theory courses and/or establish a stand-alone rhythm pattern theory course.

Goals: Student will be able to explain the binary theory of rhythm pattern development and identify source rhythms from selected passages in compositions using the binary rhythm pattern indexing system.

Overview: Presentation of binary theory, construction of binary combination tables, re-writing of binary patterns using conventional notation, reproduction of notation in respective music measure formats, performance of patterns in music measure formats, introduction to the binary rhythm pattern indexing system.

Integration: The broad range of the patterns' possible applications into existing music theory courses suggests that such designs and course time frames are best left to individual instructors.

Structure: Introduction to the system fundamentals can be presented in a 1- hour class, using the recommended sequence of events:

- Present measures and basic beat division, using / as beat and * as division of beat parts

- Introduce new terms: event points, event point levels, event point patterns, and absolute sound shapes

- Assign 0's and 1's to event points as symbols for silence and sound

- Calculate the number of event point possibilities per event point level using the 2^n formula

- Introduce the binary combination tables

- Pair up the 0's and 1's in the binary combination tables

- Re-write the patterns using conventional notation

- Present the re-written patterns in their respective music measure formats

Discussion: Explain concepts of relative nature of notation and counting syllables, and absolute sound shapes; present various music scenarios for the patterns.

Appendix D (cont'd)

Target Audiences

Music and Math Courses: Classes from middle school through college may include the binary theory, sample generation of patterns in binary combination tables, and the Binary Rhythm Pattern Indexing System.

Middle School/High School Music Theory: For middle school, focus can be placed on the concept of fundamental patterns and pattern comprehension; for high school, include limited examples of composition analysis.

First Year College Introduction to Music Fundamentals Class: Introduce subject matter when presenting rhythm and meter principles.

First Year College Music Theory: Introduce subject matter at beginning of rhythm and meter review.

First Year College Rhythm Pattern Theory: Incorporate *Appendix C*, utilizing examples of composition analysis and binary rhythm pattern indexing system identification.

Rhythm Lab Use

For schools with dedicated rhythm and drumming labs, the theory portion can be introduced in a single 1- hour class (**Appendix D**, *Structure*, page 304), with group lab assignments addressing each individual Event Point Level. These assignments can be tailored to focus on select portions of the Event Point Level binary combination tables and music measure formats.

The list of fundamental patterns can be modified for use with rhythm pattern ear training modules in existing music theory coursework by also using select portions of the materials.

Individual study involving home-study rhythm training software may apply the patterns by focusing on whatever Event Point Levels are being reviewed. For example, if 5-note and 7-note polyrhythms are the focus, a student could study all of Event Point Level 5 to master the beat note versions of the patterns.

They could then practice and conceive of these patterns as polyrhythms, following the suggested exercises on pp. 53-57.

Next, they could proceed to Event Point Level 7 and follow the same steps with the suggested exercises on pp. 123-125 and p. 150.

This practice method of beat note mastery may be applied to any of the Event Point Levels.

Appendix E

Presentation/Teaching Guidelines for Drum Circle Facilitators

Objectives: Present and integrate *The Elements of Rhythm Volume I* into drum circle facilitation studies.

Goals: Student will be able to explain the binary theory of rhythm pattern development and demonstrate basic pattern groups in an informal drum circle environment.

Overview: Presentation of binary theory, construction of binary combination tables, re-writing of binary patterns using conventional notation, reproduction of notation in respective music measure formats, performance of patterns in music measure formats.

Integration: The informal nature of drum circles allows facilitators to demonstrate and then discuss the source of all the basic patterns, a discovery that would normally occur randomly through improvisation.

Most participants are likely attending drum circles to simply enjoy the playing experience. Offering an introduction to the origin of rhythm patterns opens doors for deeper appreciation of many styles of drumming. This also allows the presentation to be used as a springboard for helping participants begin a more formal study of rhythm if they so choose.

Structure: Introduction to the system fundamentals can be presented in a 1- hour class, using the recommended sequence of events:

- Present measures and basic beat division, using / as beat and * as division of beat parts
- Introduce new terms: event points, event point levels, event point patterns, and absolute sound shapes
- Assign 0's and 1's to event points as symbols for silence and sound
- Calculate the number of event point possibilities per event point level using the 2^n formula
- Introduce the binary combination tables
- Pair up the 0's and 1's in the binary combination tables
- Re-write the patterns using conventional notation
- Present the re-written patterns in their respective music measure formats

Discussion: Explain concepts of relative nature of notation and counting syllables, and absolute sound shapes; present various music scenarios for the patterns.

Notes

www.TheElementsofRhythm.com

For information about *The Elements of Rhythm* series and related music seminars, please visit our website, where we invite you to learn more about continuing your temporal explorations with *The Elements of Rhythm Volume II, Relative Notation and Counting Syllables*.

The fundamental rhythm patterns we've just seen are presented in a series of multi-staff music formats to teach readers how to play complex notation by first mastering the simpler versions.

A complete list of counting syllables for all examples are provided, along with unique counting exercises, offering diverse approaches to help better understand the relative nature of notation.

Excerpt from
The Elements of Rhythm
Volume II

Relative Notation and
Counting Syllables

The Elements of Rhythm

Volume II

Relative Notation and Counting Syllables

David R. Aldridge

About the Author

David R. Aldridge is a drummer, composer, author and educator/clinician, based in Los Angeles, California. David has written for *DRUM!, Modern Drummer, Keyboard, Jazziz* and *DownBeat.*

For current music information, visit either **www.myspace.com/DavidAldridgeDrums** or **www.DavidAldridge.net**

For blog articles, visit **DavidAldridge.wordpress.com**

www.ingramcontent.com/pod-product-compliance
Lightning Source LLC
Chambersburg PA
CBHW080543230426
43663CB00015B/2698